Virginia in the War Years,
1938–1945

Virginia in the War Years, 1938–1945

Military Bases, the U-Boat War and Daily Life

Joseph P. Freitus

McFarland & Company, Inc., Publishers
Jefferson, North Carolina

LIBRARY OF CONGRESS CATALOGUING-IN-PUBLICATION DATA

Freitus, Joe.
Virginia in the war years, 1938–1945 : military bases, the U-boat war and daily life / Joseph P. Freitus.
p. cm.
Includes bibliographical references and index.

ISBN 978-0-7864-7966-5 (softcover : acid free paper) ∞
ISBN 978-1-4766-1542-4 (ebook)

1. World War, 1939–1945—Virginia. 2. Virginia—History, Military—20th century. I. Title.
D769.85.V8F74 2014   940.53'755—dc23   2014025393

BRITISH LIBRARY CATALOGUING DATA ARE AVAILABLE

© 2014 Joseph P. Freitus. All rights reserved

No part of this book may be reproduced or transmitted in any form or by any means, electronic or mechanical, including photocopying or recording, or by any information storage and retrieval system, without permission in writing from the publisher.

Front cover: digitally restored war propaganda poster © John Parrot / Stocktrek Images, Inc.

Printed in the United States of America

McFarland & Company, Inc., Publishers
Box 611, Jefferson, North Carolina 28640
www.mcfarlandpub.com

To the men of Bedford, Virginia,
Company A, 116th Infantry Division,
who made the ultimate sacrifice on 6 June 1944:

Abott, Jr., Leslie C.
Carter, Wallace R.
Clifton, John R.
Draper, Jr., Frank P.
Fellers, Taylor P. (Capt.)
Gillaspie, Nick N.
Hollback, Bedford T.
Hollback, Raymond S.
Lee, Clifton G.
Parker, Earl L.
Powers, Jack G.
Rosazza, Weldon A.
Reynolds, John F.
Schenk, John B.
Stevens, Ray O.
White, Elmere P.
Yopp, Grant C.

Table of Contents

Acknowledgments — viii

One. The Approach of War — 1
Two. The Naval Bases — 11
Three. The Army Bases — 38
Four. The Coast Guard — 67
Five. The Submarine War — 75
Six. The Home Front — 86
Seven. Women at War — 112
Eight. African Americans — 133
Nine. The Civil Air Patrol — 144
Ten. The POWs — 149
Eleven. The '44 Hurricane — 162
Twelve. War Stories — 166

Appendix One. Military Museums in Virginia — 181
Appendix Two. Virginia's Military Installations, 1938–1945 — 184
Appendix Three. Historical Resources — 187
Chapter Notes — 191
Bibliography — 194
Index — 197

Acknowledgments

I have spent ten years researching, asking questions, interviewing a large number of wonderful, cooperative individuals and gathering suitable historical data related to the Commonwealth of Virginia during World War II.

Writers are always indebted to those individuals who provide the basic research information that eventually becomes the book. I cannot thank Gordon Calhoun enough, a gifted historian at the Hampton Roads Naval Museum, Norfolk, Virginia. He provided valuable research material including a wide range of photographs.

Britta Granrud, Curator for the Women in Military Service for America (WIMSA), kept me moving in the right direction with regards to information about military women and provided a wonderful collection of photographs.

My thanks to Luther Hanson, Historian of the U.S. Army Quartermaster Museum, for his time, expertise and photographs.

Special thanks for material and guidance from the Naval History and Heritage Command, Washington, D.C., and the U.S. Army Center of Military History, Ft. McNair, Washington, D.C.

A special mention to those unnamed veterans who patiently read, corrected and commented on the in-progress manuscript.

Lastly, thank you, Anne.

CHAPTER ONE

The Approach of War

"It was the best of times, it was the worst of times, it was the age of wisdom, it was the age of foolishness, it was the epoch of belief, it was the epoch of incredulity, it was the season of Light, it was the season of Darkness, it was the spring of hope, it was the winter of despair, we had everything before us, we had nothing before us, we were all going directly to heaven, we were all going direct the other way—in short, the period was so far like the present period, that some of its noisiest authorities insisted on its being received, for good or evil, in the superlative degree of comparison only."
—First paragraph from *A Tale of Two Cities*, Charles Dickens, 1859

The Great Depression (1929–1940), also known as the Dirty Thirties, was an historic period of time wherein citizens survived a plethora of disastrous social and economic circumstances. Depending on who you were, where you lived and your social well-being, you most likely felt powerless, frustrated, confused, bewildered, angry, and resigned; above all, lacked confidence in the federal government. The times were real and those who survived would go on to discover a different meaning to life.

Borrowing a quote from Studs Terkel's book *Hard Times*, a young woman, upon being told of the Great Depression by her grandparents, says, "It seemed like a fairytale to me, something of a bedtime story." How different the reality was.

The Great Depression began in 1929 with the stock market crash and ended in 1940. It became the most serious economic collapse in American history. Throughout the next several years, millions of Americans lost their jobs as the manufacturing sector began to shut its doors, farms and homes were foreclosed upon, and banks collapsed. More and more families found themselves living in poverty. Soup kitchens and bread lines became a common sight. Folks who ran out of money moved in with relatives or neighbors in order to survive. Shantytowns sprang up near railroad lines as Americans moved about seeking employment. "It was the best of times, it was the worst of times...."

Virginians were eager to close out the year 1938 on a note of optimism despite a 1937 recession. Employment nationwide, during the Depression, had reached a high of ten million unemployed—25 percent of the workforce. By 1938, there was a faint glimmer of hope that the dark days of the devastating depression were beginning to disappear. The diverse economic situation was slowly but steadily improving ... though during this time prices were high with less income. Unemployment in Virginia was hovering around 19 percent.

The economic impact of the Great Depression appeared to be slightly less in Virginia than in other parts of the country, partly because Virginia had struck a balance between a consumer-related industry, a strong farming sector, and the support of federal money in the Norfolk naval areas. But while the Commonwealth had less than the national above-normal unemployment, it still suffered from the lingering effects of poverty.

The agricultural sector was diverse; it included corn, tobacco, wheat, barley and many so-called table crops, such as tomatoes, cabbage and lettuce. The presence of so many self-supporting farmers lessened the impact of the Depression. Despite these positive situations, the Commonwealth suffered the usual soup kitchens in the crowded urban areas and a growing number of shantytowns.[1]

Mary Kitchner of Danville, in a letter, writes:

> *The times were indeed hard on everyone. My father and mother worked a small five acre farm, and dad was employed in a nearby textile mill, five miles away. When the Depression hit, dad was suddenly without a job. We learned to live off the farm and the land. Times were hard!*
>
> *The minimum wage was 25 cents an hour, gasoline was 10 cents a gallon, a loaf of white bread went for 9 cents. The usual table fare was homemade bread (sometimes with butter), pea soup (minus the ham bone), milk, oatmeal, cornbread and eggs. We kept lots of chickens and sold the eggs to neighbors or traded for other goods. We children learned to harvest what there was available from the wild; blueberries, blackberries, strawberries, elderberries, wild plums, mulberries, even thorn-apples. Everything went to make jams, jellies and preserves which we could sell to a local market for a few pennies or exchange with neighbors.*
>
> *There was little or no money for even the basic necessities, never mind a luxury or two. My sister and I helped mother make dresses and underwear from printed chicken-feed sacks. Mother saved the sacks until she had two or more bags of the same pattern. White flour sacks, although smaller, had a softer weave and were generally used to make underwear such as bloomers and petticoats. The funny thing was, no one laughed at us on Sunday church as many were wearing the same Depression style.*
>
> *Because the railroad was close by we had sad looking men, the hobos who rode the rails stop at the back door and offer work for a meal. Of course there was no work, with two healthy girls on the small farm, but soft hearted mother always found some stew and a piece of homemade bread for them. Despite their rough and ready appearance we never felt in any danger. Mother would always say, after someone left, 'There but for the grace of God go I.'*
>
> *We always felt bad for the blacks as they were living at a poverty level to begin with. Our [black] neighbors' wages were already at the bottom of the wage scale to begin with. They were usually the last hired and the first fired, which meant they were the first to go hungry. I remember many of them never had shoes or socks, which was hard in the winter months.*
>
> *All my friends remember the Depression as a grim time of life, but there are many remembrances I cherish. As a family we were very close and happy as we struggled together. Despite out hardship and lack of money, we knew we were better off than most folks. It taught a lot of us the hard lesson of economic life, cherish the good days and plan ahead for the bad.*[2]

Some still remember seeing starving African American children, in Suffolk, Virginia, who were unable to attend school because they were too weak, who went without clothes, or shoes, or basic medical care. The majority of the nation's African American population lived in the rural areas and generally worked white-owned farms. For them, the Great Depression mattered little, for poverty was a way of life. Subsistence farming locked them into a marginal life of poverty, with little hope of change. Survivors were convinced the chaos of the Depression would never end.

One. The Approach of War

Socially, African Americans suffered the full effects of the Great Depression. Wages were already at the lowest and they faced severe discrimination in finding employment. Since they were generally the "last hired and the first fired," it became more difficult for an African American to provide food for their families to survive.[3]

What was happening in Suffolk, Virginia, was commonplace throughout America. The unemployed male, the breadwinner of the family, found himself begging for food to feed his starving family. Many men spent the day moving from soup lines to bread lines, patiently waiting their turn to obtain a little food for their children. Many counties depended on the Red Cross flour donations, as well as food donations from local church groups. Long lines of men, waiting for a handout of food, were just as common in the communities of Virginia as they were throughout the rest of the United States.

Churches and various service organizations established soup and bread lines. Sometimes bread was served with the soup, along with old cheese and a little dried fruit. The Salvation Army, well known to serve bread with their soup, paid particular attention to the needs of children. Children learned to take their "food pail," stand in line to obtain enough soup to feed their family, and then move to another long line to obtain a little bread. The soup generally was thin and greasy; it lacked vegetables and usually even lacked meat. Bean soup was the most common served, as it was the most inexpensive to make.

Humiliating as most folks found the experience of waiting in line in soup kitchens, everyone in need would quickly get in line and quietly await his turn. Many of these families managed to survive on a single meal per day.

The Third Baptist Church in Portsmouth, Virginia, managed to obtain the leftover or unused food from the mess halls at the U.S. Navy Base Portsmouth and feed a hundred people a day. Other churches located near the newly constructed military bases replicated the process, saving many lives. Well aware of the situation, in some instances the quartermaster of the base would make adjustments in the food requisition to keep a steady supply of basic food items flowing to the church groups.

Some of the small farmers in the Hampton area would allow residents to harvest a few pounds of fruit from their small orchards, especially if there were children involved. Those who could afford to would offer children a meal or two from their homes and would make food donations to their local churches' soup kitchens.

The Hampton Roads Salvation Army obtained discarded military clothing and gave it to the poor to clothe their children. Often these adult articles would be taken apart and re-cut to fit the growing young adults. Shoes became a particular problem for children and many churches went about gathering cast-off shoes, no matter how badly worn, attempted to re-condition them, then offered them to needy families.

Unable to provide the basic necessities for their children, the size of the typical family dropped dramatically, including farm families. The so-called Depression family became two parents and two children, with many newlyweds deciding not to have children at all. Many unemployed became so depressed that they committed suicide, while others turned to excessive drinking. Many marriages could not stand the constant financial stress and failed altogether.

Despite the hard times, vices were still in existence. Moonshiners kept up a steady production of "white lightning"—otherwise called moonshine, alcohol made from fermented yeast—and always managed to find buyers. Industrial tobacco production shifted away from civilian sales to meet increasing military demands. In spite of this change, self-reliant individuals obtained a little tobacco seed, cultivated it, and then rolled their own cigarettes.

During 1937, the nation struggled through a recession, setting back any small economic gains that had accrued. New Deal programs did not solve the problems of the Great Depression; they required a change in world events.[4]

Ominous international signs pointed to change throughout the world that would have an impact on the lives of every Virginian. Occupied with the everyday struggle of life, most Americans ignored events that pointed toward a second world war about to explode on the world stage. With grave domestic problems to deal with, Congress tended to ignore the greater world scene, especially the saber-rattling antics of Adolf Hitler in Germany.

As the Depression wore on, year after year, the American public demanded Congress take care of the country's problems and not become embroiled in any international politics. The Neutrality Acts of 1935, 1936 and 1937 reflected these sentiments, further isolating the United States from the rest of the world. With Congressional legislators declaring their neutrality, the average American little dreamed that one day thousands

German Army entering Poland, 1939 (U.S. Army Signal Corps).

One. The Approach of War

of their young people would be fighting and dying in far-off lands with strange-sounding names.

Most historians report that World War II began at exactly 0431 hours, 1 September 1939, when three sleek German dive bombers (JU-87s) burst from the overcast sky and destroyed two major railroad bridges spanning the Vistula River near the city of Duschau, Poland, northwest of Warsaw.

However, there are those historians who point to the invasion of Manchuria by the Japanese on 19 September 1931 as the beginning of the war. Others point to the Japanese invasion of China in July 1937.

President Franklin D. Roosevelt and Congress were aware of the Japanese incursion into Manchuria and mainland China. As a means of controlling the further advancement of the Japanese, economic sanctions were put in place. It was assumed that the reduction of scrap metal, oil and other necessary natural resources, which Japan lacked, would curtail any further expansionist plans.

Be that as it may, two agonizing days after Germany bombed Poland, her allies—Great Britain and France—declared war on Germany. Within thirty days, the German and Russian armies, by treaty, overran all Polish resistance. During the struggle, Great Britain and France attempted to rescue Poland from the onslaught of the German war machine, whereas the United States continued to adhere to its policy of strict neutrality.

A sizeable segment of the population held to the belief, despite the raging conflict in Europe, that the United States should remain neutral. This was reinforced by the radio and newspapers. This was a war that involved longtime antagonists in Europe and in the Far East; it was not one the U.S. wanted to be a part of if it could be avoided. Famous voices such as Charles A. Lindbergh, Father Charles E. Coughlin, Republican Senator Gerald P. Nye of North Dakota and author Kathleen Norris in the mid–1930s warned that Americans should not become involved in a European war, while others, such as William A. White of the Committee to Defend America, cautioned that it would be impossible for the United States to remain neutral. The Committee to Defend America foresaw the most devastating conflict ever witnessed by humanity, and that its maddening fury would involve the United States. "Prepare for the inevitable," was their watchword.

A noninterventionist group called the America First Committee (AFC) was created in September of 1940 as a means of organizing the American public against the war. Consisting of 800,000 plus members, it quickly became the largest antiwar organization in the United States. Charles Lindbergh, a well-known leading member of the America First Committee, opposed entry into a war with Germany, as he had personally seen German technological developments in the military and understood America was not prepared to fight such a war. The Irish Americans were not necessarily opposed to the war, but they would not approve of aid to Britain. Not only did the organization protest entering the war, it also opposed aid to England and France.

The overwhelming opinion of the United States was in favor of staying out of the war at all costs. Isolationism was entrenched among the Republicans and in the small towns of rural America. William Jennings Bryant and Robert LaFolette argued relentlessly and successfully against any involvement with Europe and "its war." Several noisy antiwar rallies were held in Richmond.[5]

In addition to the AFC, many organizations sprung up on both sides of the issue. One organization in particular, the German American Bund, neither promoted nor favored a war. Leader Fritz Julius Kuhn claimed the organization's purpose was to promote trade with Germany, preserve and promote the German culture in the United States, and adopt those aspects of National Socialism that would help the economic recovery. The Bund was organized along the same lines as the Nazi Party in Germany, and its membership was reported to be 50 to 60 thousand with 100 units located in 47 states. Membership was mostly made up of German-American citizens. Among the German Lutheran farmers of north-central Virginia there was considerable sentiment for the Bund.

Mass rallies of thousands of members were held in many large cities, such as in Madison Square Garden, New York, much to the irritation of other citizens. Flying the American flag along with the Nazi emblems so proudly displayed at meetings angered many. A Bund parade with thousands of members was held on East 86th Street, New York City, on October 30, 1939, and was reported in newspapers throughout the nation.

There were clashes between the members of the Bund and angry citizens who opposed their organization. Many of the "peace organizations" held rallies to oppose the acceptance of the Bund.[6] The Federal Justice Department through the Federal Bureau of Investigation kept a watchful eye on all of the organizations and their activities.[7]

When Germany invaded Poland in 1939, participation in the activities of the Bund and most protest organizations quickly dwindled. When the war began for the United States, strong patriotism evolved among the German-American population. Thousands responded to the call to arms.

Isolationism relates to the historical reluctance of the United States to become involved in any alliance, especially with Europe. Avoiding entanglements and treaties with the nations of Europe began with the very founding of the United States, when our forefathers enacted the Neutrality Act of 1794 to keep us out of the war between France and England. In his presidential address, George Washington reinforced the growing traditional feelings of isolationism: "Hence, therefore it must be unwise in us to implicate ourselves, by artificial ties, in the ordinary vicissitudes of her politics, or the ordinary combinations and collisions of her friendship or enmities."

Those opposed to any involvement in war often quoted these famous lines to reinforce a perspective that had already become, for many, a way of life. During the 1930s, most Americans remained firm in not wanting the country to join any alliance in Europe.

Prevalence of the neutrality mentality initially slowed development of all branches of the Armed Forces, especially the small Army Air Corps. Federal government and military agencies, beginning in 1938, devised ways of paying lip service to the restrictions of the Congressional Neutrality Act, while still preparing the country for war. In

One. The Approach of War

addition to increasing the size of the Armed Forces and its necessary armaments, Congress passed the Civilian Pilot Training (CPT) programs (1938), providing free aviation training to qualified college students. It was evident the war would require a large air force, and that would mean they'd need pilots.

Antiwar sentiment throughout Virginia and the United States suddenly changed in the spring of 1940 with the collapse of France. The antiwar movement was devastated now that England was left to fight the Nazi domination of Europe alone.

With the nations of Europe at war, the industrial complex in the United States quickly geared up to meet their demands for armaments. Everything from bullets, bombs, trucks, tanks, and aircraft to small arms and foodstuffs were produced and shipped to England, and eventually to Russia under the guise of the new lend-lease program. "We'll make it and ship it; you can pay for it later," was the basic concept.[8]

Few Virginia industries, including the agribusiness, went untouched. Before the war began, hog and cotton growers were already supplying an ever-increasing tonnage to aid war-torn England. Cotton, corn, wheat, tobacco and other agricultural products were suddenly in great demand.

Women workers at Newport News Shipyard (National Archives).

With the increased demand for war-related materiel, the need for skilled workers, engineers, administrators and many other related occupations quickly rose. Americans were back at work. But soon farm workers, such as sharecroppers and tenant farmers, fled the grueling hard life of farm labor for the better-paying defense work. Hobos could be seen getting off trains at the rail yards at Newport News. Hobos, unlike "bums" who did not wish to work, came seeking employment in the myriad opportunities available at the shipyards and new military bases.

African Americans and other minorities did not find the same degree of employment and success as white workers. Segregation persisted even in war-related industries, yet even this offered an economic alternative to the crushing poverty of the Depression pre-war Virginia.

Hampton Roads became a beehive of activity as the Newport News Shipyard expanded and struggled to keep up with the orders from England for cargo ships to replace those lost to German U-boats. England, near the breaking point, found itself unable to import the necessary raw materials to manufacture its military needs, such as steel cargo ships. After negotiations, that role was quickly assumed by the Newport News Shipyard and other East Coast yards.

The demands of the Navy "hijacked" Hampton Roads, especially Norfolk, with its war materiel and housing demands. The U.S. Navy was busy at the Naval Shipyard in Portsmouth building the new fast carriers and other combat and support vessels desperately needed to fight a two-ocean war. Hundreds of Virginians and others from outside the Commonwealth flocked to Hampton Roads seeking employment with the rapidly expanding U.S. Navy.

The expansion of the U.S. Navy was matched by the U.S. Army as it selected its own sites in Virginia, constructing many training camp facilities and Air Corps landing fields. These military additions provided thousands of jobs for Virginians. One of the largest Army receiving camps, Camp Patrick Henry, was also located at Hampton Roads. It served as a holding facility for troops awaiting shipment to the war in Africa, then Europe via the Newport News Port of Embarkation.

The rapid build-up of the military produced a sharp increase in the population of Virginia. The 1940 federal census accounted for 2,677,773 inhabitants, but did not include the increasing members of the Armed Forces. The population of Norfolk, not counting the presence of the Navy, was 144,332. It is estimated that by 1943, with the enormous influx of industrial workers, the population of Norfolk was approximately 305,121. The population nearly tripled in just two years.[9] Given the numbers trained at each of the various army bases were 50,000 to 70,000, the population of the Commonwealth of Virginia was estimated to have doubled from 1940 to 1943.

Cargo ships headed for England found the wide, sheltered, natural deep water of Hampton Roads an excellent assembly point for convoys. The large U.S. Army training camps built in Virginia were designed with the Hampton Roads Port of Embarkation in mind. Each camp location was serviced with a rail system that took troops directly from the camp to the port. If the war in Europe finally pulled the United States into the conflict, Hampton Roads was the ideal port to gather and embark troops in large numbers.

One. The Approach of War

Women being trained to operate a cutting machine (National Archives).

It began to appear the poverty of the Depression years would soon end as the ever-increasing orders from overseas continued to pour in. Churchill vehemently pleaded, "Give us the tools and we will finish the job." Nine months before the United States entered the war, a lend-lease program appropriately numbered HR-1776 was established to aid England, China, France, the Soviet Union and other American allies.

From March 1941 through 1946, the United States loaned its Allies $50 billion in food and war supplies. Hitler and Mussolini saw this as an act of war and began attacking U.S. vessels making the North Atlantic crossing to England and Russia.

The good times had finally arrived in the U.S.... or so most people thought. People were making money and the United States still maintained its prized neutrality. The United States was fast becoming the arsenal for the free world. The Hampton Roads shipyards were working around the clock to meet the demands for more cargo ships to carry more and more of the war supplies. Virginians were happy to be back at work.[10]

This euphoria would change on Sunday morning, 7 December 1941, when Japan attacked Pearl Harbor, changing Virginia and the United States forever. The news came as a shock to the federal government—and the public as well—for the attack came completely without warning. Six Japanese carriers managed to make their way to a point 200 miles north of Oahu in the Hawaiian Islands and launch 350 aircraft against the naval installation at Pearl Harbor without the U.S. knowing about it until it was too late. About 170 aircraft, caught on the ground, were destroyed and 8 battleships were either sunk or badly damaged. A total of 2,402 service men and women were casualties that fateful day.

Word of the surprise attack on Pearl Harbor brought to a close the isolationist sentiment in Virginia, changing the Commonwealth's public attitude and economic outlook.

On 11 December 1941, Germany and its ally, Italy, declared war on the United States. The United States could no longer remain isolated from the world at war. It was the second time within twenty-five years that Americans would find themselves involved in a world war. Participation in World War II would cost Virginia 6,007 of its sons and daughters, who would pay the ultimate sacrifice serving their country.

Chapter Two

The Naval Bases

Although the Hampton Roads area has a long history of being settled by the English dating from 1607 with the founding and settling of Virginia, it wasn't until merchant and ship owner Andrew Sprowle built a shipyard on November 1, 1767, on the western shore of the Elizabeth River that it became important to the Royal Navy. At the beginning of the American Revolutionary War, Sprowle, a British loyalist, fearing for his life and that of his family, fled Virginia. The Commonwealth of Virginia seized and operated the Gosport Shipyard, as it was called then. The Royal Navy promptly attacked and burned the facility.

In 1794, the federal government leased the property and commenced to build warships for the new American Navy. On June 15, 1801, the Navy was permitted to purchase the Gosport Shipyard. The yard quickly became the largest U.S. Navy facility during its early days. A self-contained yard, it was populated with a sail/rigging loft, a masting building, assorted workshops, a cooperage, several forges, six large and small rope walks, storehouses for its naval supplies, slipways, and the important timber storage and seasoning sheds. One of the famous American Navy ships was the 1854 USS *Constellation*, a sloop of war built from the original *Constellation* at the Gosport Yards.

Hampton Roads witnessed what is considered by many historians to be one of the greatest ship-to-ship battles, the slugfest between the Union ship, the USS *Monitor*, and the Confederate ship, the CSS *Virginia*, during the Civil War.

It wasn't until the United States entered World War I in 1917 that the Secretary of the Navy would allow nearby land to be purchased for the establishment of the Naval Operating Base, Norfolk, creating a permanent Navy presence there. The 5th Naval District and Headquarters was then established, along with a Naval Recruit Training Center, housing for 7,500 men, the Naval Air Station, a naval hospital, a submarine station and the first Navy aircraft to fly off the deck of a ship, the USS *Birmingham*.

Beginning in 1938, the Navy had one major aviation establishment—NAS Norfolk. All this was about to rapidly change. The U.S. Navy quickly began construction of NAS Norfolk East Field, which let them offer training and house a variety of seaplanes. Additionally, twelve outlying and emergency airfields were constructed to handle the increase of naval aircraft traffic.

With the increase in aircraft carriers being constructed and maintained at the Norfolk Operating Base, facilities were required to house and train the fleet carriers' growing complement of fighter and dive-bomber aircraft. Locating and building more sites became a priority and Virginia offered near year-round flying conditions.

Altogether, the Navy constructed or converted twelve airfields. Several, in addition to training fleet pilots, were utilized as airbases for coastal patrol aircraft. Smaller, well-maintained airfields were needed to provide pilots with emergency landing strips. Honing their skills while the carriers were being overhauled in port, pilots needed "touch and go" airfields as well. Tracking the increasing numbers of planes in flight within the area required a central air control system which was established at the NAS Norfolk.

The Navy's system for designating airfields was:

NAS: Navy Air Station
NAAS: Navy Auxiliary Air Station
NAF: Navy Air Field
NAAF: Navy Auxiliary Airfield
OLF: Outlying Fields

With the advent of the German U-boats sinking cargo ships and oil tankers just off the Virginia and North Carolina coasts, the Navy hurriedly constructed airfields that could handle and maintain a variety of search aircraft instead of just fighter aircraft.

The public's long and historic connection to the U.S. Navy is that of Naval Operating Base in Norfolk, Virginia. Many individuals who did not serve in the Navy do not realize the scope and the presence of the U.S. Navy during World War II throughout the Commonwealth of Virginia. In all, 4,204,662 men and women served in the United States Navy during World War II.

Waging war in several theaters, mainly Europe and the Pacific, Norfolk Naval Base was unlike other naval operating bases, for it played a role in providing carriers and aircraft wherever needed. It is fondly remembered by most individuals who liked to watch the ships, personnel and supplies departing Chesapeake Bay and heading for the war in Africa and then Europe. Carrier units quietly departed Norfolk and headed south to the Panama Canal, stopping at Pearl Harbor before joining the war in the Pacific. Several of the carriers so proudly built at Hampton Roads, such as the *Wasp*, *Hornet* and *Saratoga*, became Navy legends. Few of the Norfolk-built carriers fought in the European theater of war, instead forming the center of task forces that drove the Japanese back to their homeland.

The following information has been provided by the Naval History and Heritage Command, Washington, D.C.

Alexandria

On 12 November 1918, the United States Navy began construction on the building that would be known as the U.S. Navy Torpedo Station at 105 Union Street, Alexandria, Virginia. Located on the west bank of the Potomac River, it was responsible for the manufacture, research and maintenance of naval torpedoes during the five-year span of World War I. After the end of the war, with financial restrictions and a rapid reduction in the Armed Forces, it quickly became a Naval munitions storage facility.

With the onset of World War II and the sudden demand for submarine torpedoes and the newer aerial torpedoes, production quickly intensified. To make up for a lack of space, ten additional buildings were constructed for the design and manufacture of torpedoes. Construction workers flocked to the site, seeking wartime employment. Nearby residents opened their homes to the influx of workers seeking housing. Some saw providing a place to live as their patriotic duty, others as a means of making additional money.

To supply the needed housing for the increase of civilian families, construction of federal housing began on 10 January 1940 and was completed five months later. The project provided housing for 300 families. Completion of the new buildings brought a second wave of workers needed to construct and test the torpedoes, placing an added burden on housing.

When problems with the MK-14 submarine torpedoes unexpectedly surfaced, the research facilities were tasked to solve the problem. Premature detonations, duds and running too deep to target were some of the problems that plagued torpedoes for the first two years of the war, frustrating submariners. Successful modifications were eventually made and production resumed.

The facility was located on the banks of the Potomac River, which made it available to river barge traffic to Hampton Roads and other areas at Norfolk. A local rail line provided access to raw materials and transport of torpedoes to other naval stations and depots throughout the United States.

Production soared during the war; the shipyard produced 9,920 MK 14 submarine torpedoes, 9,839 MK aerial torpedoes, as well as many practice torpedoes.

After World War II, the facility no longer produced torpedoes and was once again utilized as a storage facility, this time for the Smithsonian as record storage. Today the facility is the property of the City of Alexandria and is known as the Torpedo Factory Art Center, one of the Commonwealth's many fine museums.

Arlington

The Naval Radio Station (T), Arlington, Virginia, was the first component of the later command, NAVCOMMSTA, in Washington, D.C. NAVRADSTA (T) Arlington, Virginia, was officially commissioned on 13 February 1913. Contracts for a single tower, 600 feet in height, plus two additional towers 450 feet in height, and several buildings were awarded in June 1911. The towers consisted of self-supporting steel similar to the structure of the Eiffel Tower. The station buildings contained radio apparatus, laboratories, storerooms, office spaces and living quarters for the communication operators.

The land was transferred from the War Department to the Department of the Navy by an act of Congress in 1912. The station was constructed on land that was part of the Fort Myer Military Reservation after it was decided to keep the radio station nearby in Washington, D.C.

Arlington was the first Navy communications facility for which the words "Naval Radio Station" was used, instead of the usual "Naval Wireless Station." This was not long after Marconi made the first Cross-Atlantic communication between Europe and the United States. The first wireless communication between North America and Europe occurred 12 December 1901. The first United States Naval transatlantic voice communication was made in 1913, between the Arlington Naval Radio Station and the Eiffel Tower. For many years the nation set its clocks by the Arlington time signal, which originated at the Naval Observatory, also located in Arlington. Residents would listen for the daily weather reports and plan their day accordingly.

The tall towers were dismantled in 1941, as a menace to increased military air traffic approaching the Washington National Airport. The modern radio station continued clandestinely monitoring vital radio traffic between international embassies, as well as other important signals between world navies at sea. Monitoring the busy radio waves allowed the United States Navy to gain access to wartime codes and begin deciphering them.

On 15 August 1953, NAVCOMMSTA, Washington, D.C., was established, consisting of a communication center located at NAVRADSTA in Cheltenham, Annapolis, and Arlington. On 1 July 1956, NAVRADSTA, Arlington, Virginia, was removed from active service and deactivated after more than 43 years of full-time operation.

Bristol

In addition to the office of the Naval Cost Inspector, the National Fireworks Incorporated manufacturing facility was located at Bristol, Virginia, along with a shell-loading plant. In 1941, just before the war began, National Fireworks constructed a production facility in Bristol to manufacture and load 20 mm, high-explosive antiaircraft shells for naval use. Located in the far southwestern corner of Virginia, it was not too far from the Radford-Pulaski area, where the Hercules Gunpowder Company manufactured a variety of explosive, smokeless gunpowders.

In addition to loading and assembling shells, the plant also handled the fixing of fuses, especially when the proximity fuse was added to antiaircraft shells. Since this was a rural area, with many of its skilled labor in the Armed Forces, or employed at the Radford-Pulaski complex, there was a lack of skilled labor. Women—female workers now known as "Rosie the Riveters"—came to the rescue in large numbers to keep the assembly lines running. Many local African Americans found steady employment for the first time since the beginning of the Depression.

Bristol Aircraft Corporation of Virginia and Bristol Aircraft Products Ltd. of Canada combined to form Universal Molded Products Corporation and located their manufacturing facility in Bristol. Makers of a popular, small, light civilian aircraft prior to the war, they manufactured and assembled tail sections of a variety of military fighter aircraft. These empennage, as the assemblies were called, were shipped by rail to major aircraft manufacturers across the United States. It was a strange sight to see lines of railroad flatcars stacked with tail assemblies leaving Bristol, destined for the major fighter aircraft companies.

Cape Charles City

Cape Charles City, located on the southern end of the Virginia eastern shore, faces into the Chesapeake Bay and Virginia Beach. Before the war, a ferry line had been established between Newport News, Norfolk, and Cape Charles City. A natural harbor, it was selected by the United States Navy as a degaussing range station for the fleet.

Both during their construction, and as they move at sea, steel ships access the Earth's magnetic fields, known as induced magnetism, producing a magnetic signature. The British Royal Navy discovered German magnetic mines on the bottom of the sea would be activated by the magnetic signature of a passing ship. A process of degaussing removed or reduced that signature, rendering the mines ineffective. It was discovered that, by wrapping a highly electrically charged steel cable either alongside the hull of the ship or from the portside, under the hull to the starboard side, the ship's magnetic signature could be disrupted, or changed.

However, after many sea miles, the charge or signature would return, due to the friction between the steel hull and the sea water. When that happened, periodically the ship would have to be degaussed. The station was positioned near the ferry landing and railroad tracks because of the deep water channel.

In addition to the Cape Charles Degaussing Station, other degaussing facilities were located at Willoughby Spit, York River, Sewell's Point and Lambert's Point, Virginia.

The U.S. Coast Guard and the U.S. Army, located at Cape Charles, maintained several patrol craft to monitor the minefields and ships entering the Chesapeake Bay. Several of the patrol boats acted as rescue craft when a number of ships were sunk either by German U-boats or by harbor mines near the entrance to the Chesapeake Bay.

Charlottesville

The U.S. Navy established a School of Military Government and a Navy V-12 unit on the campus of the University of Virginia in Charlottesville, Virginia. The Navy traditionally required its officers to be college graduates. The V-12 College Training Program was instituted to supplement the force of commissioned officers during World War II. Between July 1943 and June 1946 more than 125,000 men were enrolled in the V-12 program in 131 different colleges and universities throughout the United States.

From the University of Virginia, candidates went on to a reserve midshipmen's school for a 4-month basics course. Marine Corps candidates went to boot camp, then on to a 12-week Officer Candidates School (OCS) at Quantico, Virginia, then to the fleet.

Chincoteague

Chincoteague Island is located in Accomack County on the Atlantic side of the Virginia eastern shore. Requiring an auxiliary airfield, NAS Norfolk established NAAS Chincoteague as an outlying facility prior to World War II. The Naval Auxiliary Air Station located there had been a single grass strip utilized by small civilian aircraft flown and maintained by local civilian pilots. With the approach to war in 1941, the Navy inspected the site and determined it would be a good airfield for emergency purposes. It was located on the present site of Wallops Island.

Fleet Air Wing 5, a Naval training unit for coastal patrol, was set up to handle a variety of aircraft, from single engine TBMs and Grumman Avengers to four-engine B-24 Liberators. Many patrol units were trained at the air station in over-water navigation, or experienced hours of flying time before being shipped to the fleet or other areas. Many patrol units, such as VU-7 Patrol Squadron, VP-83, VP-112 and VT-17, trained at the facility. While flying training missions out over the Atlantic, they would often observe German submarines, locate sinking ships, and participate in the rescue of crewmen.

A Naval Ordnance Test Station was established to test the new wing-mounted air-to-ground rockets. The wide-open spaces of the Atlantic suited the research needs, providing a variety of floating targets. Different Navy Air units spent time at the station learning to use the new technology of rockets.

Due to the nature of the research and activities, base security was increased, adding a detachment of U.S. Marines. Buildings for the Naval Aerial Maintenance Detachment were constructed, along with several barracks for housing and administration. Two additional runways were added, as well as hanger facilities to accommodate all the activity. The Naval Auxiliary Air Station was a very busy place, night and day.

Creeds

Naval Auxiliary Air Station Creeds was located just a few miles south of Oceana NAS. It was constructed in 1942 as an auxiliary air base for NAS Norfolk. It was used primarily as a dive-bombing training air base. Several reports suggest the CCCs constructed the airfield in the late 1930s. During 1940, the airport was designated an OLF (Out Lying Field) to Oceana and used as a support training facility. It was officially commissioned in 1943 as a Naval Auxiliary Air Field (NAAF), Creeds, Virginia. Its purpose was to provide training for dive bomber pilots and crew, fleet operations and maintenance of fleet air squadrons.

The site had a single 2500-foot concrete runway, two wooden hangars, a control tower, 1300 base personnel, and barracks, all located on 227 acres of land. Eventually, two more runways were added. Two huge, circular practice bombing targets were also established just east of the field.

Squadrons of fleet Wildcat fighters and Grumman Avenger torpedo-bombers intensively trained for service on CVEs (escort carriers). A special runway the length of a CVE (smaller version of the larger aircraft carriers) was constructed to give pilots the "feel" of the shortened carrier deck distance.

Bomber squadrons, at first flying Dauntless dive-bombers (SBDs), filled the surrounding air. Eventually, they transitioned to the newer Curtiss SBC Helldivers. Bomb Squadrons VF-1, VC-52, VB-8, VF-13 and VB-15 were typical training squadrons. Upon completion of their training, the squadrons transitioned to the nearby carriers at Norfolk, such as the Hornet CV-12.

Bombing Squadron VB-15 was commissioned on 1 September 1943 under the direction of LT. CDR Irwin L. Dew. After training, they were loaded on the USS *Hornet* CV-12 and departed for the Pacific Theater of Operations.

NAAS Creeds was decommissioned 15 October 1945, reverting to civilian control.

Dahlgren

Dahlgren is a small town located on the Potomac River, 35 miles south of Washington, D.C. In 1912, the town, situated in King George County, was named for Rear Admiral John A. Dahlgren. As an expansion of the U.S. Navy's Indian Head Weapons Proving Grounds in Maryland, the Dahlgren Center was utilized as a test station for naval weapons. One of its primary functions was the testing of naval smokeless gunpowder, especially the reliability of bagged gunpowder utilized in large caliber ship and coastal guns. Improper storage often rendered bag gunpowder ineffective and therefore unreliable.

In the early 1930s, one runway served the air needs of the facility. A single large aerial target was added for the testing of aircraft-mounted machine guns. Research and development of reliable aviation ordnance became an integral part of the mission. The 18-mile firing range along the shore of the Potomac River and Machodoc Creek provided a suitable distance and location to test large caliber naval guns. A Naval aerial gunner's mate school, a bombsight training school, and an aviation ordnance school were established within the facility. In addition to Navy personnel, Army coastal artillery groups trained at Dahlgren.

Military engineering projects of historical importance were developed at Dahlgren, such as the famed Norden bombsight, used by the heavy bombers of the Air Force in Europe and units in the Pacific. Few individuals know the role that the Dahlgren Proving Ground played in the development and testing of the Norden bombsight.

Following several years of design failure and modifications, testing of a production model was finally assigned to the Naval Proving Ground. Testing ended in August 1931 when the Bureau of Ordnance accepted the Mark XI bombsight, which went into production just in time for the war.

Famous scientists worked there, such as Dr. Edward Teller and Dr. Albert Einstein, as part of the secret Manhattan Project. The so-called Elsie Project at Dahlgren played a major role in the development of the atomic bomb. The Dahlgren facility was charged with the development of gun (cannon) type atomic weapons. It quickly became the primary site for design, development, test and evaluation of these weapons.

With the end of the war, programs at Dahlgren were greatly reduced, only to be reactivated with the advent of the Korean War. Development and testing of aerial missiles became the facility's primary mission as the Navy sought to upgrade its seagoing armaments.

The present-day Naval Surface Warfare Center Dahlgren Division comprises two organizations: NSWC Dahlgren Laboratory (NSWCDL) and the Naval Surface Warfare Center Dam Neck (NSWCDN) at Virginia Beach, Virginia.

Dam Neck

Dam Neck was originally a Coast Guard life-saving station on Virginia Beach, Virginia, until the U.S. Navy purchased the site in early 1941. Located on 1700 acres of wetland, sand dunes and spectacular beaches, the Dam Neck site was established as a weapons training facility for shipboard aircraft crews.

Problems with a variety of naval antiaircraft weapons were tested and solved. When the Navy decided on making the 20mm and 40mm the standard for shipboard antiaircraft weapons, they were quickly incorporated as the weapons of choice for the gunner's mate training program at Dam Neck.

The early antiaircraft training facility housed a large seaside firing line, an observer's tower, a large magazine for ammunition storage, an office administration building and a suitable maintenance building. Along with the antiaircraft training schools, a fleet rifle range was established for the recruit training facility located at Norfolk, Virginia.

Army Air Force women pilots (WAAFS) flew out of the area and towed sleeve targets for the naval gunners to practice on. The planes would tow the target parallel to the beach, out over the sea. There is no record of the trainees shooting down a tow plane.

The U.S. Coast Guard maintained several beach lookout stations along the Dam Neck coast, keeping an eye for prowling German U-boats, survivors of torpedoed ships and sabotage agents.

After the war, the station became the U.S. Navy Surface Warfare Center, Dam Neck (NSWCDN), Virginia.

Dodge Boat Works

Located on the old Camp Stewart site, the Dodge Boat Works had shut down its facilities during the Depression due to lack of marine sales. Dodge made quality wooden high-speed motorboats, for which there was little or no demand during the hard times of the '30s. With the world at war, the U.S. Navy suddenly had an urgent demand for small craft of all sizes and types. With contracts offered, the facility was able to open in 1941.

The strong Naval and Army aircraft presence in Chesapeake Bay and coastal waters of the Atlantic required durable wooden high-speed 42-foot air-sea rescue boats. Twenty-seven of these boats were constructed, along with 25 smaller harbor mooring tugs and the all-important smaller landing craft. The Dodge works built 74 of the lightweight plywood 36-foot amphibious assault craft, LCVPRs (Landing Craft Vehicle Personnel Ramp).

Dover

Naval Auxiliary Landing Field (NALF) in Norfolk, Virginia, was located west of the city and located at the intersection of Route 17 and Ballahack Road, in Suffolk County, near the Great Dismal Swamp. A single landing strip facility, it was generally utilized for the nearby Lake Drummond Bombing Range. Four Quonset huts were located at the strip and used as light maintenance and storage facilities. Naval aircraft assigned for a day mission would arrive and await their turn at the bombing range.

Modified nun buoys were arranged in a pattern in the lake and the planes would either machine-gun them or use bombs. Dive bombers from the in-port carriers spent time training by bombing a target area of the lake. Most of the aircraft arrived from Fentress or Oceana for aerial target practice. Live ammunition is still found in the bottom of the lake.

Fentress

Naval Auxiliary Landing Field (NALF) in Fentress, Virginia, is near Chesapeake. Located approximately 7 miles southwest of NAS Oceana, it was commissioned in 1941. Comprising 2,500 acres of open land, it has one 8,000-foot hard surface runway. The facility was designed to simulate the size and shape of an aircraft carrier, thereby allowing pilots to perform "touch and go" landings. It was and is utilized by naval aviators to familiarize Navy pilots with the difficulties of carrier landings, during daylight and nighttime conditions, without actually using a carrier. When a carrier arrived at Norfolk for repairs, the aircraft were flown off before entering port and housed at one of the auxiliary air facilities. Maintaining flight skills requires a pilot to fly as often as possible, hence NALF Fentress. Carrier pilots had the opportunity to practice their needed "touch and go" landings, honing their newly acquired skills.

A fighter training school was established as well as an aviation maintenance school. Dive bombers, from the carriers undergoing maintenance and repair, would hone their skills by utilizing one of the dive bombing targets, such as the one located at nearby Creeds.

Away from the actual landing field, a school for shipboard firefighters was constructed. Large open pits with high berms were filled with waste or fuel oil and burned to simulate shipboard fire. Eventually, replica sections of ship compartments were added for realism. Daily towering columns of thick black smoke filled the air, often covering the landing field. It was not long before the Virginia Beach police station was overwhelmed with telephone calls reporting aircraft crashes. The Navy moved quickly to inform the civilian public as to the reason for the daily cloud of dense oily black smoke.

NALF Fentress today is a busy enlarged facility handling fleet jet fighters, performing 140,000 "touch and go" operations annually, and is designated as U.S. Naval Air Station (NAS) Fentress.

Franklin

Naval Auxiliary Air Station (NAAS) of Franklin, Virginia, was located about 40 miles west of Norfolk and 9 miles north of the North Carolina border. The town of Franklin contained a small municipal airport located 2 miles from the center of town that was taken over by the U.S. Navy in 1943 as an auxiliary airfield for Chambers Field at Norfolk. Nearby NAAS Monogram's field was unusable during the rainy season, making it difficult to land aircraft. The Navy solved the problem by leasing the Franklin Municipal Airport.

Required housing and maintenance facilities structures were constructed, and the facility was commissioned in May of 1943 as NAAS Franklin, Virginia. The new site became an acceptance and delivery site for newly manufactured naval aircraft to be delivered to awaiting aircraft carriers and training fields nearby. The ADS's mission at Franklin was the acceptance of new aircraft flown directly from the factories and modifying them for combat use. Since these were Navy aircraft, they arrived without the necessary aircraft carrier landing-hook. An arresting gear testing device, simulating a carrier deck, was in place to check airworthiness. Carrier pilots often utilized the arrangement to hone their landing skills. Radios, machine guns and other bits of necessary combat gear were installed, then tested. A machine gun range tested the newly installed guns and zeroed them in.

Franklin also became a site for storage of spare aircraft for fleet use. Aircraft were transferred from incoming carriers to NAAS Franklin for general maintenance and repairs as well as updating avionics and weapons.

During the course of the war, NAAS Franklin handled over 11,865 Navy and Marine Corps combat aircraft. At one time or another, every type of aircraft the U.S. Navy used in World War II passed through NAAS Franklin.

In 1945, the U.S. Navy added an additional runway of 4200 feet. In addition to being an ADS facility, it also served as an emergency landing field. It was not uncommon for the facility to receive several requests each day for permission from pilots to make an emergency landing.

With the end of the war, the station was placed into a caretaker status in 1946.

With a reduction in force and is no longer being needed as a military facility, NAAS Franklin was gratefully returned to the town of Franklin, where it presently serves as a commercial air facility.

Hampton Roads

Historically and locally known as the Tidewater of Virginia, due to the considerable low-lying surrounding landscape, the confluence of several large rivers (the James, Elizabeth and York), and the many deep water harbors, Hampton Roads comprises a large and historical area. Early in May 1607, three English ships—*Susan Constant, Godspeed* and *Discovery*—arrived in the Hampton Roads and paused before exploring the James River. Captain Christopher Newport found the waters of the Roads pleasing and a fair anchorage. Many ships from many countries would find safe haven and refuge in the waters of Hampton Roads, especially during World War II.

Long the headquarters for the Fifth Naval District, Norfolk has served as the home base of the United States Navy Sixth Fleet, in addition to home port for many fleet ships. The area was rapidly developed during the war to comprise several Naval and Army air facilities and schools.

The naval air center command, naval medical storehouse and ship's store ashore were established during the war. Hampton, Virginia, was the site of several naval training schools at the Hampton Institute: electrical, diesel, carpenter's mates, yeoman, storekeepers and basic engineering.

A large naval medical storehouse was situated in Hampton. The naval facility supplied the constant changing fleet of ships, Marine detachments in the area, Naval Coastal Artillery Units, all NOLS, the Merchant Marine Armed Guard and the Coast Guard.

In addition to a coast Artillery School, located at Fort Monroe, a submarine and destroyer mine depot (SDMD, Ft. Monroe) and the U.S. Army submarine mine school were added. The U.S. Army was tasked with the difficult operation to lay and maintain anti-submarine mine fields to protect the Chesapeake Bay and the Hampton Roads area from the threat of German U-boats.

The U.S. Navy established a recruit receiving depot at Newport News. A night lookout training unit was located at the receiving station. The Naval Office of Construction for Hampton Roads was located within the Newport News Shipbuilding and Dry Dock Company. The supervisor of shipbuilding and the naval inspector of ordnance, port director and the public works depot were all located there. The Horace N. Dodge Boat Company nearby produced a large variety of small boats and landing craft. In addition to shipbuilding, the Newport News Shipbuilding and Dry Dock Company repaired and updated ships damaged during combat tours.

Hampton Roads was a safe haven for ships arriving to form up a convoy headed for England or Europe. Civilian ships also took on important lend-lease cargo at one of the many facilities in Newport News and Hampton. Escort combat vessels would accompany them into the Chesapeake Bay, thence to the Atlantic to England. It was a busy place.

Lee Hall

The U.S. Army Hospital at Fort Eustis was turned over to the U.S. Navy Medical Services in 1942 and served the greater Hampton Roads area, especially the Yorktown naval weapons facility. It was known as the Fort Eustis Naval Hospital and was staffed with naval personnel. During 1943–1945, the overflow of wounded from Europe were received here for treatment or transfer to another hospital. Upon completion of the war, the hospital reverted back to the U.S. Army.

Little Creek

The Naval Amphibious Base of Little Creek, Virginia, is one of four operating bases in the Atlantic Fleet. Today the facility is well known as the Fleet Combat Training Center.

With the war raging in Europe, naval planners understood the need to land large, division-size Army units on enemy beaches. New methods and techniques of landing troops ashore had to be quickly developed. A facility had to be located and developed to train men to be proficient in landing craft and amphibious assault.

A natural deep water harbor, Little Creek had been selected by the Navy and Coast Guard as a facility for coastal patrol training. Shortly thereafter, harbor facilities were constructed to handle Coast Guard patrol craft. Realizing the uniqueness of the site, on the Chesapeake Bay and with access to the Atlantic beaches, four bases were constructed on what were literally swamps, low farmlands and tidal marshes.

Little Creek was a "bare necessity" base, with few buildings and fewer roads, and was generally lacking in utilities. There were plenty of "Army tents" and considerable swampland. Four basic camps were located at the site: Camp Bradford, Camp Shelton, the Naval Frontier Base and the Amphibious Training Base. Camp Bradford became the training base for the Navy construction battalions, the Seabees. During 1943, the camp became a training base for LST crews (Landing Ship Tanks) and other large landing craft.

Camp Shelton trained the naval armed guard crews for merchant ships as gun crews. As additional protection against the German U-boat raiders, the Navy decided to provide trained gunners and place them on armed merchant ships. With the end of the war, the camp served as a separation center.

In addition to the four main training camps, the facility housed a degaussing station, a mine warfare training center, CIC training center, and the main inshore patrol base.

The Amphibious Training Base at Little Creek became the epicenter for all amphibious training. Ships crews for LSMs (Landing Ship Medium), LCIs (Landing Craft Infantry), LCMs (Landing Craft Mechanized), and LCVPRs (Landing Craft Vehicle Personnel Ramp) utilized the facility as their main base of operations.

A large comparable base was established on Solomon's Island, Maryland. Here the practical seamanship necessary for crew operation and practice landings were conducted. Forty thousand Army troops trained to go ashore on a variety of beaches in the Chesapeake Bay.

The first naval combat demolition unit taken from the Seabee facility at Camp Peary trained at the Amphibious Base under the leadership of Navy Lieutenant Fred Wise. Upon completion of training, they would go on to participate in the Allied invasion of Sicily, as the first underwater demolitions team of World War II.

The Army troops that trained at Little Creek and Solomon's Island participated in the invasions of North Africa, Sicily, Italy (Anzio and Salerno), Normandy and southern France. Over 200,000 Naval personnel and 160,000 Army and Marine Corps trained at the Amphibious Training Base in Little Creek, Virginia. After the war, the base was designated a permanent facility in 1946 and remains in use today.

Lexington

A Special Services School was established at the Virginia Military Institute in Lexington, Virginia. Using the Institute's facilities and instructors, VMI participated in the War Department U.S. Army Special Training Program (ASTP) from 1943 to 1946. This special program provided training in special engineering areas to qualified Navy enlisted men. Over 2100 ASTP members trained and studied at VMI. Many of these trainees were U.S. Marines.

Lynchburg

Located at the extreme western end of Virginia in Lynchburg, the Preston-Glenn Municipal Airport played a vital role in the Navy air war. Naval Auxiliary Air Station (NAAS) Lynchburg was selected as the home base for the Naval Air Ferry Command, Squadron VRF-4. Commissioned on 15 November 1944, the squadron was dedicated to acceptance and ferrying direct flights of airplanes from factory airfields to NAAS Lynchburg.

Large numbers of fighters, bombers and seaplanes were being turned out and needed to be ferried to where they could be adapted for combat, such as NAAS Franklin. Battle-worn planes were flown back for major repairs. These ferry pilots were required to fly any aircraft in the Navy's inventory, and they did with only minor mishaps. The scope of the mission can best be illustrated by the fact that ferry squadron pilots of VRF-1 alone flew 15,000,000 miles of actual ferry trips.

Each ferry base had its own maintenance and supply organization. Keeping the aircraft in the so-called pipeline demanded a constant update of aircraft maintenance. Pilots of VRF-4 handled more seaplanes than any of the other squadrons, and these aircraft required more specialized handling skills, as well as maintenance.

Many of the original ferry pilots came from long backgrounds in aviation, commercial airlines, crop-dusters, commercial cargo hauling, aerial circus, stunt pilots, CAA and barnstormers. A considerable number came to the ferry command with 20 or more years of flying experience. Many of the ferry pilots would later be women pilots of the WASPS.

The U.S. Army, in need of an airfield to supply ferry planes, moved in with the Navy and utilized NAAS Lynchburg. With access to Virginia, the U.S. Army was able to deliver needed aircraft for coastal patrol and anti-submarine warfare to places such as Langley and the Army Airfield at Norfolk.

Newport News

The Newport News Ship Yard and Dry Dock Company, located on the James River side of the city of Newport News, was inhabited by several U.S. Navy missions. The office in charge of construction and the Navy cost inspector occupied full-time offices, overseeing the vital defense construction of naval vessels.

A Navy dispensary was included to care for the large number of naval personnel functioning there. A Navy receiving station for recruits was located on the outskirts of the city, where military housing was put in place to handle the large number of inductees and navy personnel who worked at the nearby docks of the port of embarkation.

The port director's office was also located at the embarkation site. A night lookout training facility and training unit was sited at the receiving station. The office of the naval inspector of ordnance was also located at the port of embarkation.

The Newport News Shipbuilding and Dry Dock Corp.

Founded as the Chesapeake Dry Dock and Construction Co., in 1886 the company's name was changed to the Newport News Shipbuilding and Dry Dock Corp. During World War I, the yard built 25 destroyers and the last battleship until World War II. Between the two wars the yard constructed ships for the United States Merchant Marine, such as ocean liners and various large cargo ships.

During 1940, in the Battle of the Atlantic, the British Merchant Navy was losing ships faster than they could be replaced. The Newport News Yard was one of many constructing 60 large oceangoing merchant ships for England. Under the lend-lease bill, 306 additional large cargo ships were placed on order. The emergency shipbuilding program of January 3, 1941, called for the construction of 200 merchant ships similar to those being built for the British.

While other yards across the United States were busy expanding to meet the

Two. The Naval Bases

increased demand for the larger merchant ships, the Newport News Ship Yard was concentrating on rapid completion of U.S. Navy contracts.

The shipyard was one of the nation's oldest and largest shipbuilding facilities, especially organized to build the largest ships, battleships and aircraft carriers. The yard had pioneered the technology that made prefabrication of large ship hulls possible, such as the carriers. The change from riveted steel hulls to welded hulls allowed for the shorter production times. Production coordination with suppliers, subcontractors, technological innovations and in-house departments reduced the amount of time required to produce a single large ship.

With the advent of World War II, the Navy, foreseeing a trans–Pacific, long-distance war, ordered seven aircraft carriers in addition to those being constructed at the time. Fifteen famous fighting carriers were built during the war: the USS *Saratoga* CV-3, USS *Ranger* CV-4, USS *Yorktown* CV-5, USS *Enterprise* CV-6, USS *Hornet* CV-8, USS *Essex* CV-9, USS *Yorktown* CV-10, USS *Intrepid* CV-11, USS *Franklin* CV-13, USS *Ticonderoga* CV-14, USS *Randolph* CV-15, USS *Boxer* CV-21, USS *Leyte* CV-32, USS *Midway* CVB-41 and the USS *Coral Sea* CVB 43.

The battleship USS *Georgia* was built in 1908 as part of a Navy expansion program. The USS *Indiana* BB58 was constructed at the yard while the USS *Alabama* BB60 and the USS *Kentucky* BB66 were being built at the Norfolk Navy Yard. Eventually the yard constructed the battleships USS *Maryland* and USS *Mississippi*.

Eight cruisers and many smaller craft plus 10 auxiliary ships (APAs) known as C2 and C3, as well as 10 of the so-called Liberty cargo ships and 3 tanker ships, were also constructed. Seven destroyer escorts were quickly added to the fleet to protect the cargo convoys. At its peak of wartime production in 1943, some 31,000 workers were employed.

The first LSTs (Landing Ship Tank) began construction mid–1941. By the end of 1942, twenty-three LSTS were commissioned. Many of these early LSTS participated in the invasion of Sicily, Anzio, Salerno and Normandy. Additionally, 12 LSDs (Landing Ship Docks) were constructed for amphibious landings. These unique ships can be seen today at the docks in Little Creek, Virginia.

The Newport News Ship Yard and Dry Dock Corp. established a reputation with the Navy and a presence along the James River and Newport News.

Norfolk

Naval Station Norfolk has a long history and tradition beginning with the founding of the first permanent English settlement at Jamestowne in 1607. Ships quickly found that the area known as the Hampton Roads remained ice-free during the cold months of winter. During the Revolutionary War the British seized the area and remained in control throughout the war.

With the advent of World War I, the Navy purchased 474 acres of land and began construction of a permanent base: piers, warehouses, fuel and oil storage depots, recruit training facilities, a submarine base, and foreseeing the future of naval aviation, a nearby airfield. The NOB Norfolk became 5th Naval District Headquarters.

NAS Norfolk historically began its training of naval aviators at Curtiss Field, located at Newport News. Its mission was to train aviators for anti-submarine warfare and coastal patrol. NAS Norfolk, also known as Chambers Field, is located at the east end of the Navy Operating Base. It was originally a sod landing field built up from the nearby marsh lands and spoils from the dredging of the naval base. It was expanded in the 1930s. Construction increased the area to 5 or 6 times its original size. The need was to handle an anticipated increased carrier force to be located at NOB Norfolk.

World War II changed the appearance of the Naval Air Station with the expansion of all facilities such as hangars, two more adjacent airfields, supply systems and storage, magazines, docking areas, machine shops, barracks and several fleet schools related to aviation. By 1943, the base had increased in size and capability with the addition of several outlying auxiliary air fields. By 1943, one-hundred and seventy-five separate naval entities existed in the Norfolk area.

The crisis in Europe prompted the United States to train Allied pilots from England, France and Russia. Pilots were trained on aircraft that were to be used on anti-submarine patrols and sent to the Allies. British pilots were trained on American fighter aircraft. Few local civilians realized the British pilots were in the air about Norfolk as the aircraft markings were the American star and not the British roundel.

American naval pilots may have trained at various training fields throughout the United States, but all received extensive carrier training at Naval Air Station Norfolk.

In addition to the Naval Operating Base, there was the Naval Air Station, Amphibious Training Base, Joint Operations Center and the Base Material Office. A large naval hospital with a medical supply facility along with a family clinic was also established.

A receiving station for recruits and a training station handled large numbers of volunteers, mostly from the East Coast. Fleet schools were established: aviation gunnery, aviation armament, radar, fleet service, torpedoes, communications (radio), destroyer escort schools, physical training instructors, beach party, fire control, fire fighters, fighter directors, damage control, anti-submarine warfare, barrage balloon, celestial navigation, welders, a machinists mate school, a laundry service school, refrigeration, combat air crews training and fleet electrician schools.

With a growing base fulfilling more and more needs of the expanding fleet, an increase in support facilities was required. The naval supply depot was enlarged to include ship's store ashore, a degaussing station, a base service unit, marine barracks, accounting and distribution offices, Navy barracks, fuel annex (Craney Island), Atlantic Fleet Weather Station, training aids section and a U.S. Naval discipline barracks. A total of 45,526 military personnel were stationed at the Norfolk Naval Base by 1941, with more being added as the war increased.

THE ACCIDENT

The most devastating accident to occur at Hampton Roads happened on Sunday, 17 September 1943 at 11 a.m. An ordnance vehicle towing four bomb trailers overloaded

Two. The Naval Bases

with aerial depth charges was moving between the taxiway of the air station and nearby docks. Unknown to the driver, one of the depth charges came loose from its chain-down and became wedged between the first and second trailers. Dragged along under the trailer, the bomb soon began to smoke from the friction.

A Marine sentry discovered the smoking depth charge and stopped the driver. A nearby fireman hurried to the scene with a fire extinguisher and attempted to cool the bomb. He was too late, for just as he began spraying the bomb it ignited, killing him instantly. The remaining depth charges ignited, resulting in a huge crater.

The blast shattered nearby buildings. It broke windows and blew in doors, in some instances up to six miles away. The explosion was heard throughout the Hampton Roads area, up to 20 miles away. The blast concussion was felt in the cities of Hampton and Newport News. A total of 18 buildings and 33 aircraft were destroyed, along with 426 injured and 40 dead. All 18 nearby buildings were so badly damaged they had to be replaced.

A Navy Board of Inquiry, after a thorough investigation, made many changes to the safety procedures of the handling of ordnance.

Craney Island Fuel Annex

A man-made peninsula was located across from Norfolk Naval Base next to Portsmouth, Virginia. During the War of 1812, the entire defense of the area relied on a small mud-flat island called Craney Island. Construction involved bringing tons of landfill material from the nearby areas to raise the landmass slightly above the highest tide. Once the fort was completed, it was quickly equipped with seven large guns and was tasked with guarding the narrow channel of the Elizabeth River.

In addition to the large guns, it was occupied by 580 regular army troops, as well as 150 sailors and marines. Attacked by a British landing party in 1812, the defenders, backed by their accurate gunfire and that of the USS *Constellation* standing to, managed to drive off the invaders.

Often covered with water during heavy storms, the small island was enlarged in 1918 by dredging the nearby shoals, thus transforming it from a low-lying island to a 2,500 acre peninsula. A lighthouse replaced a lightship in 1859. The Navy installed in-ground and above-ground storage tanks and converted the site into Craney Island Fuel Terminal.

Today, allied with other terminals at Yorktown and Naval Station Norfolk, Virginia, it stands as the U.S. Navy's largest fuel depot. It served the fleet at Norfolk during both World Wars. Additionally, the man-made peninsula serves as a bird sanctuary.

U.S. Naval Air Station, Norfolk

Located next to the Norfolk Operating Base, in 1917 the Navy added an air station for the training of a fledgling air arm. With the addition of the aircraft carrier activity increasing each year, by 1939 the station had an air arm of some 300 various aircraft, repair and maintenance facilities and had grown to encompass 1200 acres.

Just before World War II, naval aircraft flew anti-submarine patrol, on the alert for German U-boats prowling the offshore area. Four carrier groups stationed at Norfolk required more space and flying time. With the increase of activity, more land was acquired, and a seaplane facility as well as ten auxiliary fields were added. These outlying fields were generally used for submarine patrol, pilot training, flying time, dive-bomber training, aerial gunnery and general aircraft maintenance.

USNAAS Dover, Virginia, located west of Norfolk, was utilized as an emergency landing field and a bombing and target range for naval aircraft based in the Norfolk area.

USNAAS Fentress was located just outside the small town of Fentress, Virginia Beach. Using an existing civilian single airstrip, the Navy utilized the facility as an emergency landing site, pilot training and aircraft dispersal from other fields. Late in the war it was designated NAS Fentress (Naval Air Station).

USNAAS Oceana was built west of Virginia Beach as an outlying airfield for NAS Norfolk. It was primarily used for air defense of Norfolk and anti-submarine operations in the Chesapeake–Hampton Roads area. Carrier air groups utilized the field as an operational base. A variety of carrier aircraft were stationed at the field while the carrier underwent overhaul and maintenance. It became a common sight to see carrier planes such as SB2C dive bombers, F6F Hellcat fighters, TBF and TBM Grumman Avengers and Corsair fighters flying in and out of the airfield. It underwent many changes during the war, but was finally designated NAS Oceana. With the advent of the Korean War, it became the Navy's Master Jet Airfield. NAS Oceana operates today handling carrier group aircraft.

USNAAS Monogram served as an auxiliary airfield to NAS Norfolk. It also served as an aircraft service repair and dispersal field.

USNAAS Pungo was established 7 miles south of Virginia Beach, not far from USNAAS Fentress, and served as an emergency landing field and dispersal.

USNAAS Creeds, located on Virginia Beach, served to house Navy dive-bomber squadrons. Two large circular dive-bombing targets provided a training facility for carrier pilots. A large aviation maintenance unit was stationed there handling aircraft and target bomb ordnance.

USNAAS Chincoteague, now known as the Wallops Island Naval Station, was added to locate Fleet Wing 5, a training unit for Coastal Air Patrol. Fighter planes and B-24 Liberators flew and trained daily there. An over-water navigation teaching unit was stationed at the facility, as these aircraft flew far out to sea in search of German U-boats. During the war, an ordnance rocket testing station was constructed. These particular rockets were generally wing-mounted and used for air-ground fighting.

USNAAS Franklin was a temporary stopover for aircraft just off the assembly line. They were made carrier-ready with landing hooks. The facility was also an emergency landing site for NAS Norfolk.

USNAAS Weeksville was located in North Carolina, south of Elizabeth City, near the Pasquatank River. Constructed in 1941 on 757 acres, the site housed anti-submarine blimps. Two large blimp hangars housed six airships each. A PBY flying boat ramp was located near the Pasquatank River. Weeksville served as an outlying field for NAS Norfolk.

USNAAS Breezy Point was constructed in mid–1940 to serve as a seaplane operating base. The facility was built on reclaimed marshland at the mouth of Mason Creek. Small and large seaplanes from the Grumman Goose to PBYs and the large Martins could be seen flying in and out every day.

NAS East Field in Norfolk was located between Chambers Field and Breezy Point Air Station. Utilized to handle and maintain the larger Martin seaplanes, it was also used as a training station for anti-submarine warfare.

USNAAS Elizabeth City, Edenton, Mateo and Harvey Point, North Carolina, were added to the air facilities needed to support the growing aviation needs of NAS Norfolk.

USNOLF Whitehurst, Norfolk, was located southwest of the intersection of Route 170 and Shore Road in Norfolk, Virginia. It was 125 acres of open grassland and was utilized as an outlying field and for emergency landings. It was once planned to be an OLF for LTA (lighter-than air craft) out of Cape May, New Jersey, in 1940, but that never happened.

Portsmouth

Established in 1767 by one Andrew Sprowle, the Gosport Shipyard was located on the western shore of the Elizabeth River, under British rule. Sprowle had one of the most successful shipbuilding facilities on the East Coast of North America. He gathered many of the best shipwrights, ship carpenters, caulkers and sail makers available. At the beginning of the Revolutionary War, all his properties were confiscated by the Colony of Virginia.

The Royal Navy promptly seized the shipyard and burned it to the ground. Renamed the Norfolk Naval Shipyard, it is the oldest shipyard in North America and it is the largest on the East Coast.

The first dry dock in North America was constructed there, known as Dry Dock #1. It remained active up to the beginning of World War I when the yard repaired ships of the Navy's Atlantic Fleet. It was here the Collier USS *Jupiter* was converted to the Navy's first aircraft carrier, named the USS *Langley*. It was the birth of the air arm of the U.S. Navy.

When World War II began, orders for new ships of all types poured in and a major expansion took place. The operations quickly became around-the-clock, seven days a week. Some of the most famous warships of World War II were produced at Portsmouth. The yard's employment peaked at 43,000 workers and it was still undermanned.

The rapid addition of so many workers increased the need for additional wartime public housing. In response, utilizing the Federal Public Housing Authority Act of 1942, 5,000 units were quickly constructed. Land was cleared and water mains put in place along with electrical systems and prefabricated units that were assembled in less than a year. In keeping with the times, 4,250 units were allotted to whites and 750 units to African Americans.

Three of the large new fast-attack Essex Class carriers (CVA), ten destroyer escorts, twenty of the new LSTS (Landing Craft Tank), fifty LCMs (Landing Craft Medium) and many other types of landing craft were developed and launched from the yard. Many of these landing craft would participate in the landings of Sicily and Normandy.

Naval Repair Facility

Maintaining elements of the Atlantic Fleet is a full-time job and the Portsmouth Repair Facility processed several hundred of various types of ships during and after the war. Known as the Gosport Ship Building Facility, the name was changed to Portsmouth Naval Ship Yard. During the war, 43,000 skilled workers were employed making fleet submarines. A total of 70 submarines were constructed between 1941 and 1945. Utilizing updated construction and procedures, the yard was able to produce 31 of the badly needed submarines in 1944. A record was established for submarine construction when the yard launched 4 submarines in one day.

Ongoing submarine research combined with a highly skilled workforce produced the first all-steel submarine. Fleet submarines, although constructed here, spent most of their time in the Pacific battle areas.

When the war ended, the facility shifted to the maintenance and repair of fleet ships but kept its program of submarine maintenance.

Today many of the Navy's ships can be seen undergoing annual or special maintenance routines. The facility is one of the few yards that can dry dock the new nuclear-powered carriers for overhaul and maintenance.

Welding Shipyards

A small steel shipyard located in the Portsmouth area produced hulls of welded steel plate primarily used for bulk carriers. One or more of their ships were sunk by German U-boats early in the war. Bulk carriers are merchant ships designed to carry cargoes such as coal, food grains, ore, cement limestone and clay. They did not have contracts to build larger ships for the Navy.

With the war raging in Europe and the German U-boats sinking an ever-increasing number of cargo ships, the warring nations were faced with a critical shortage of cargo ships. The result was that in mid-1941, the need of assembly-line construction of a standardized ship called the "Liberty Ship" was put into effect. During the war, some 2,571 Liberty Ships were built by various ship yards throughout the United States.

The Newport Ship Yard constructed 10 auxiliary navy combat ships (APA) and 10 Liberty Ships. The welded steel plate and prefabricated sections of these ships were fabricated by the Welding Shipyard of Portsmouth. When the Liberty Ship was redesigned and became the faster Victory Ship, Welding Shipyard continued to produce prefabricated sections for the new ships.

Two. The Naval Bases

Quantico

The Marine Corps Base Quantico, in Prince William County, was and still is a major U.S. Marine Corps training facility. Located at Triangle, Virginia, the site occupies 100 square miles of wooded and open terrain. Old-timers fondly refer to the basic school as the "West Point" of the Marine Corps.

Marine Corps Barracks Quantico was established during World War I in 1917 as a training center for Marine officers and enlisted men. By 1920, the Marine Corps schools were established.

All officers who attend the Marine Corps University receive their basic training at the basic school. When the Marine Corps indicates all officers, Marine aviators are included. During World War II, the Marines devised a system of close-air support in combat. To understand the complexities of ground combat, every Marine aviator undergoes the same training a combat infantry officer receives.

Enlisted technicians from many disciplines received instruction in basic mechan-

Brown Field at Quantico (National Museum of the Marine Corps).

ics, communications, weapons and music. Anticipating a war in the Pacific with Japan, in mid–1925 a plan took shape to utilize and develop amphibious war techniques, which envisioned an island-hopping campaign against Japan.

Upon completion of the study, areas of need were identified and examined at Quantico. Singled-out was the need to supply specially designed landing craft to rapidly deliver large numbers of combat Marines onto the landing beach in a short period of time.

Out of the study resulted the development of the famed "Higgins Landing Boats," the Landing Craft Vehicle Personnel (LCVP) and the LT-V Alligator (Landing Tracked Vehicle). Throughout World War II, the Quantico Marine Base was the primary amphibious development and training center. Amphibious warfare training took place at Little Creek, Virginia. Large-scale unit training took place in the Caribbean on several remote island beaches.

In addition to the basic school for officers, the Headquarters, First Marine Brigade, a provisional OCS and the fleet Marine force were located at the Marine barracks. The

The U.S. Naval Hospital at Quantico (National Museum of the Marine Corps).

command and staff school and Marine Corps ordnance schools were soon added, along with a naval hospital and a post dispensary.

Aviation training became a priority as the Marine Corps developed a ground-to-air control system (MAGTF) for combat units. All flying officers are required to take the Marine basic school courses. U.S. Marine Corps Air Facility Quantico was constructed in 1942 as a primary training site. Prior to World War II, special Marine raider units were given parachute training.

Today the air facility is the site of the Marine Helicopter 1 HMX-1. The helicopter squadron provides rapid and secure transportation for the President of the United States, a mission it continues to carry out to this day.

Units Located at Quantico:

Marine Corps Embassy Security Group
Marine Corps Combat Development Command
Marine Corps War-fighting Laboratory
Marine Corps Recruiting Command
Manpower and Reserve Affairs Division
Marine Corps Systems Command
Marine Corps Training and Education Command
  A) The Basic School
  B) Officers Candidate School (OCS)
  C) The Marine Corps University
  D) Marine Air-Ground Task Force (MAGTF) Staff Training Program
Marine Corps Network Operations Security Command

Richmond

The capitol of Virginia, Richmond was utilized by the U.S. Army and the U.S. Navy, often in joint missions. Twenty-three U.S. Naval sites were located in Richmond. The naval diesel school and welder's school were established in 1943. The Navy V-12 unit was located at the University of Richmond, while the V-12 medical program was located at the Medical College of Virginia School of Medicine, and the V-12 unit was operated out of the School of Dentistry. The U.S. Navy and the U.S. Army processed hundreds of personnel through the various facilities.

A large central recruiting facility processed thousands of new recruits for both the Army and the Navy. The Richmond Army Service Forces Depot, located at Richmond, handled a considerable amount of Navy war materiel. The large municipal airport was used by the U.S. Army Air Force.

The U.S. Navy also used the air facility as a repair and conversion branch of NOB Norfolk. Navy fighter aircraft were converted to carrier-based fighter with the attachment of a tail-hook for carrier landings. These planes were then delivered to NAS Norfolk (Chambers Field) and loaded onto carriers after more testing.

Roanoke

The Navy established several branch offices of the Cost Inspector: Office of Naval Contracts, Naval Advisor to the War Production Board, and the Advisor to Naval Contract Distribution Branch at Roanoke. Later in the war, an Armed Forces induction center and a Navy recruiting station were added.

The Roanoke Municipal Airport was converted and renamed NAS Woodrum, Virginia. A pilot training facility, the airport also contained an aviation repair unit, as the Navy maintained some heavy bombers. Navy ferry pilots flew planes in from the various companies located throughout the United States. From here the planes were flown to other facilities located in Eastern Virginia, such as NAAS Franklin, for assembly completion.

Nearby Buford Airport was designated a Navy OLF for Woodrum and its overflow of aircraft. It contained a 3200-foot grass runway and two wooden hangars.

Saint Julien's Creek

The Naval Ammunition Depot located at Saint Julien's Creek and the Elizabeth River in Chesapeake, Virginia, began operations in 1849 as a naval ordnance and storage site. From 1890 until 1970, the facility supplied ammunition to the fleet, in addition to

Aerial view of St. Juliens Fleet Ammunition Depot in Chesapeake (Hampton Roads Naval Museum).

assembling, loading, issuing, and receiving naval gun ammunition and surveying old, unusable ammunition. Various types of fleet and shore ammunition, no longer suitable or safe to use, was stored in large protective bunker facilities. In 1969, the facility was consolidated as an annex to the Naval Weapons Station in Yorktown, Virginia.

In addition to the Fleet Administration Offices located at the Norfolk Navy Ship Yard, there is a large hospital with an attached hospital corps school. The Navy V-12 Training School was established at the Navy Barracks. An optical training school, a pre-naval mine warfare school, and a naval Loran training school were all located on the yard's grounds. To ensure security, a large detachment of U.S. Marines was billeted at the base. Utilizing the "replace men to fight" program, two full companies of Waves were stationed there. These Waves served in a number of administrative and labor positions such as clerks, truck drivers and as munitions handlers.

Shelton

Beginning in October 1941, with the increase in German U-boat activity in the North Atlantic, the U.S. Navy organized the Merchant Marine Armed Guard to provide gun crews for duty aboard merchant ships as it had done during World War I. The increase in U-boat sinking of merchant marine ships required arming them with a deck gun. A site needed to be selected to train and select U.S. Navy sailors. There were three basic training schools for the Armed Guard. One was located at first at Little Creek, Virginia, but later moved to Shelton, Virginia.

The first U.S. Navy Armed Guard were assembled at Little Creek, Virginia, given three weeks training, and ordered to sail in November of 1941. At the same time, Congress repealed the Neutrality Act, allowing guns to be placed aboard merchant ships.

Men of the Armed Guard served as gunners, signalmen and radio operators on merchant ships, tankers, troop ships and general cargo ships. Their mission was to aid in defending the ship against attack by enemy aircraft, submarines and surface ships.

A total of 144,970 men and officers served in the U.S. Navy Armed Guard and sailed 6,236 merchant ships during World War II. Armed Guard casualties numbered 1,810 killed or missing. The Armed Guard crew consisted of 28 men to a ship. One junior officer, 24 gunners and 3 radio or communications personnel completed the crew.

Located near the Shelton facility was an antiaircraft firing range where live-fire-target exercises were conducted. This range was located at Dam Neck, Virginia, and the Navy provided all aspects of the training.

Waverly

Located between Newport News and Petersburg, Waverly was a small civilian airport utilized by the Navy during World War II. Because of its location, the Army used it as an emergency landing strip for aircraft flying out of Richmond.

The strip consisted of two grass runways, one at 1670 feet and the other at 1500 feet, suitable for landing fighter aircraft. Four small wooden hangars serviced the aircraft and maintenance crews.

The military did not maintain but a few bombing and target ranges, causing pilots to linger in those target areas. Waverly was used to hold planes waiting to utilize the overworked Lake Drummond Target Range at Dover, Virginia.

Williamsburg

The colonial city of Williamsburg is located near Fort Eustis and is the site of the College of William and Mary. The Naval Training School for Chaplains was located at the college. Navy Chaplains were trained and prepared for Naval service, Navy traditions and life aboard ship. Experience was gathered at nearby Navy Operating Base, Norfolk.

A field office of the Naval Intelligence, Fifth Naval District was also located at the college campus.

Beginning in 1943, the Army Specialized Training Program, for enlisted military technicians, was offered at 227 colleges throughout the United States. The ASTP, as it was better known, provided college-specialized, intensive training in such areas as 34 different foreign languages, science, basic medicine, dentistry, and a number of engineering specialties. Students were expected to complete these accelerated programs in 18 months and then were commissioned as officers.

Unit 3321 was located on campus at William and Mary College. Along with the daily military training, recruits took course work in engineering, chemistry, physics, math and foreign languages. They were housed in the Tyler and Brown Halls as well as the Blow Gymnasium on the campus of William and Mary. It was a common sight to see recruits marching from one class to the next, eating in the dining hall and training in available open fields around the campus.

Yorktown

Dating back to early colonial times, Yorktown is located on the York River.

Prior to World War I, the DuPont Company purchased 4,000 acres of land directly on the York River and constructed a dynamite production plant. Before actual production began, the U.S. Navy acquired the site. The Bureau of Naval Ordnance established a mine storage and handling depot. As many as 10,000 individuals worked at the facility.

After World War I, the facility was utilized as an ammunition storage depot servicing Navy ships on the Hampton Roads.

With the approach of war in Europe, the depot underwent considerable improvement. Along with a mine assembly plant, a TNT reclamation facility was established.

The naval fuel annex was greatly enlarged, a naval supply depot was added to the Cheatham Annex, and the naval barracks were increased.

A naval training school for ammunition handling, a commissary store and another increase in barracks due to the increase in personnel and size of the base were added. The Naval Weapons Station, as it is known today, has grown from 12 tenant commands to 25.

Camp Peary

At the onset of World War II, training for the Navy's construction battalions, the Seabees, was carried out at Camp Allen and Camp Bradford Little Creek in Norfolk, Virginia. Lacking space, in 1942 a naval construction training center and advanced base depot were located and constructed adjacent to the present-day Naval Weapons Station in Yorktown. This change in location helped relieve the growing congestion at Little Creek.

In 1942, the U.S. Navy took over a large parcel of land, some 9,275 acres, on the north side of the Yorktown Naval Weapons Station. The Chesapeake and Ohio Railroad constructed a spur track from Newport News to a site near Williamsburg. Today the location is known as Magruder Station near the unincorporated African American town of Magruder. With the expansion of the site, residents of the communities of Magruder and Bigler's Mill were forced to relocate to the settlement of Grove.

Although Camp Peary's address would have been Williamsburg, the actual location was in York County at the Yorktown Weapons Station. Twelve associated commands were established, including preliminary and advanced training for Seabee training, the Navy administrative command, naval recruit training and distribution center, a retraining command, electricians' school, compressed gases school, advanced base training unit and a construction battalion training command (Seabees). A Naval Academy preparatory school, a special recruit and ROTC programs were also added.

Camp Peary contained one of the few POW camps operated by the Navy. Some 950 German POWs were housed and worked at the camp, with many doing menial jobs. The stockade, which contained captured German U-boat crews, was handy for interrogation by Naval Intelligence. The capture of these crews was never announced to the public, thus allowing the German military to believe their personnel were lost at sea and presumed dead. The information gained through captured code books, vessel maintenance books and interrogation of crew members proved invaluable in the war.

With the end of the war, Camp Peary eventually became the property of the newly formed Civilian Intelligence Agency (CIA) and is generally known as "the Farm." As far as the U.S. government is concerned, the site does not exist. Many of the original buildings and roads are still utilized and a 5,000-foot runway strip has been added. Beginning in 1951, the original Seabee base was closed to the public, including the runway, which is now used only as an emergency field. The historic hunting lodge of Lord Dunmore, the last royal governor of Virginia, is located on the closed grounds.[1]

Chapter Three

The Army Bases

With the adoption of the National Defense Act of 1920, the United States Army consisted of 12,000 commissioned officers and 125,000 enlisted men. It remained at that level, more or less, until 1936. During that time period, Congress spent less money on the Army and its air branch, the Air Corps. The U.S. Navy was considered the primary line of defense, though the U.S. Army still ranked seventeenth among the nation's standing armies.

The massive production of weapons for World War I provided a stockpile of obsolete equipment that continued to be used even at the beginning of World War II. The U.S. Army was well aware its battle equipment was rapidly becoming obsolete, including its tanks. U.S. Marines were still utilizing World War I equipment fighting in the Pacific Theater.

While the U.S. Navy struggled to maintain a fighting level of ships for its two ocean fleets, the Army concentrated on reinforcing coastal and harbor forts. The large heavy-caliber 16-inch coastal guns were maintained along with support and training units as the mainland's primary defense against a possible invasion.

The U.S. Army and Navy did not remain idle before the war, but maintained a high level of war planning. With the threat of war, the military began a building program to increase the training of draftees flooding the Armed Services. New facilities were needed and were being hurriedly constructed across the United States.

Virginia, with its large areas of forested lands, was the ideal location to construct large, sprawling Army bases. The port of embarkation was located at Hampton Roads and was serviced with excellent rail service. The U.S. Army decided to locate large unit training facilities outside of Hampton Roads, but connected to these rail lines.

Army camps were the same no matter where in the United States they were constructed. The United States Quartermaster Corps 700 series camp plan called for open, angular, wood-construction buildings no higher than two stories, with tar-paper roofing. Each encampment was designed to be utilized for the duration of the war, therefore temporarily. There was room for 63 iron double bunks on each floor, a central coal-burning cast-iron stove, toilets, lavatories and shower facilities. Mess halls were constructed to feed the thousands of recruits, utilizing the same wooden structure used to house the men. Even the POW camps were eventually constructed in the same manner.

Using wood as the basic construction material allowed for ease and speed of erection. The unit could be fabricated on the ground and easily erected. Many experienced civilian construction crews could erect more than one a day. Each camp, large or small, contained the basic amenities: medical clinics, chapels, theaters, mess halls, post office, recreation centers (USO) and the necessary brig. "See one, see them all," a soldier is reported as grumbling.

Each wooden unit was heated with a large coal-burning stove centered in the middle of the building. During the cold of winter, these stoves did not produce the required amount of warmth to heat the uninsulated wooden barracks. Washing with cold water was the standard of the day, as there was no hot water available.

Until quarters, barracks, service shops, schools and dispensaries were constructed and in place, life for base crews was basic and rugged. They were housed in winterized tents and slept on canvas cots with no mattresses. Many recruits spent their entire training period living in a tent.

Each camp was designed for the training and processing of large units of division strength, numbering 15,000 men. It was not unusual to have 2 or more divisions training at the same army training base. The central camp was located near a large tract of open or wooded land, allowing for large-scale maneuvers. A section of the camp was utilized for recruit training of volunteers and draftees. Upon completion of recruit training, they were integrated into the division. The division went through training for a year: 17 weeks of basic and advanced training, 13 weeks of unit training, 14 weeks of large-scale exercises and 8 weeks of final exercises.

In addition to divisional training, each of the bases provided schools and training for service units, combat medical training, a variety of engineering units and specialty combat units. During World War II, approximately 16,000,000 personnel served in the military, with 8,300,000 serving in the U.S. Army. Ninety-one divisions were mobilized during the war.

Several of the new Army bases were developed with a small utility airfield containing a paved 2,000 foot runway. Generally these airfields were capable of handling small aircraft and the workhorse of Army aviation, the DC-3 cargo plane.

The United States Army Air Forces constructed numerous airfields throughout Virginia primarily for pilot and aircrew training. The majority of these airfields were placed under the command of the First Air Force or the U.S. Army Air Forces Training Command (AAFTC). Several of these facilities were taken over from civilian ownership for the duration of the war and in many instances enlarged to suit the growing need.

Many of the army groups that invaded Morocco, Sicily, Italy and faraway New Guinea trained in Virginia and passed through the port of embarkation at Hampton Roads. Typical was the Dixie Division, National Guard Troopers from Alabama, Louisiana, Mississippi and Florida. The 31st Infantry Division was organized and trained at Camp Blanding, Florida, then moved to Camp Bowie, Texas. From Camp Bowie the division was ordered to Camp Pickett, Virginia, where they received large-unit training in the woods surrounding the camp. When the large unit training was complete, the division received amphibious training at Camp Bradford, Maryland.

Once amphibious training was accomplished, the division returned to Camp Pickett, resupplied, organized its combat equipment, and moved by train to the port of embarkation, Hampton Roads, Newport News, Virginia. On 12 March 1944 the 31st with all its equipment loaded aboard ships embarked from Hampton Roads, and after a very long trip aboard rolling troop ships, arrived at Oro Bay, New Guinea, on 24 April 1944.

These large, sprawling army bases were quickly modified to house the rapidly increasing numbers of prisoners of war from the North African campaign, then from France and Germany itself. Constructing separate prisoner of war camps was costly and required considerable numbers of trained guards. The decision was quickly made to incorporate the POWs adjacent to already existing camps.

The same basic outlay and building construction of the army bases was utilized in POW camps. The only difference was the rows of barbed wire, guards and searchlights.

With the threat of World War II, the Army was given responsibility for the defense of the coastal United States. Confident that neither Japan nor Germany could mount an invasion of either coast, the military did little to prepare for such an eventuality. When Japanese submarines shelled a West Coast community and a single shell scored a direct hit, defenses, in addition to anti-submarine measures, were hastily developed. Field artillery battalion and combat teams were hurriedly stripped from various National Guard units and sent to strategic coastal locations. Heavy and light field artillery pieces were utilized to guard harbors and military beaches.

In Virginia as elsewhere, Civil War harbor forts were rehabilitated and used as emergency placements, until larger, more permanent facilities could be assembled. In Virginia, Fort Monroe, Fort Story and Fort Wool once again saw service, as well as emplacements along the coast of Virginia Beach and the Eastern Shore.

(The following information has been graciously provided by the U.S. Army Center of Military History, Collins Hall, Fort McNair, Washington, D.C.)

Alexandria

Alexandria is located on the opposite side of the Potomac River from the nation's capital in Washington, D.C. Considered a part of Washington, D.C., it was home to the nation's politicians and many military offices. Located approximately 10 miles south of Alexandria was Fort Belvoir. Originally known as Camp Humphries, it was utilized as a training camp for the Corps of Army Engineers replacements during World War I. In 1935, the name was changed to Fort Belvoir, and it was designated as the home of the Corps of Army Engineers.

The war in Europe produced a sudden demand for qualified military engineer officers, so an Engineer Officer Candidates School (EOCS) was established in July of 1941. From 1941 to 1946, the EOCS commissioned 22,000 new second lieutenants for combat engineer units.

The massive increase of recruits prompted a second building boom. Housing was quickly constructed utilizing the typical Quartermaster Corps' wooden barrack to house some 24,000 enlisted men candidates. Temporary wood frame buildings were utilized for everything from housing to storage and quickly encompassed available space.

The first WAAC (Women's Army Auxiliary Corps) unit arrived at Ft. Belvoir in March of 1943. The 50th HQ Company served as clerks, telephone operators, typists, vehicle drivers and mechanics. African American WAACs also trained at Ft. Belvoir, performing the same duties, but were segregated from the rest of base personnel.

Military war dog units were also trained and housed for sentry duty at the base.

FORT HUNT

Construction of Ft. Hunt in 1880 complimented Ft. Washington, which was located across the Potomac River. The fort was constructed on land originally owned by George Washington. With the advent of the Depression, it was converted to a CCC Camp to serve the Washington, D.C., area. Taken over during World War II, it was renamed Ft. Hunt.

A top secret intelligence operation called "P.O. Box 1142" was established there. A large section of the fort was set aside and enclosed in barbed wire, and housing was quickly erected. Despite the obvious separation from the rest of the camp, few outsiders knew what was happening at the site. The unit was used to interrogate high-ranking, skilled German POWs in an attempt to gather information about the technical advances of the German military. Of special interest was the information from POWs who could shed light on the advances in the German U-boats, microwave, radar, radio-direction and rocket weapons.

Four thousand special prisoners of war were brought to Ft. Hunt in buses with the windows darkened. They were held for interrogation for several days before they informed the American Red Cross, who in turn was compelled to inform the International Red Cross that they had arrived. These POWs generally consisted of high-ranking officers and various enlisted men with special training in electronic and weapon areas.

When the war ended, many German scientists were brought from Germany under "Operation Paperclip" and detained here through 1946. Germany's brilliant rocket scientists, mathematicians and engineers were of particular importance, such as Dr. Werner von Braun. Many of these "POWs" became the basis for the United States' fledgling rocket program.

The civilian intelligence office, known as the Office of Strategic Services (OSS), was created in 1942 and placed under the direction of General William Donovan. The OSS maintained training sites located at two national parks: Catoctin Mountain Park (West Virginia) and Prince William Forest Park (Virginia). A special unit was maintained at the super-secret "P.O. Box 1142," Ft. Hunt, to assist in the interrogation of the German POWs.

The Washington Quartermaster Depot, formerly known as the Washington General Depot, was built in 1819 to service the Washington, D.C., area. Located on Duke

Street, Alexandria, it provided storage and materiel in the Civil War for the Union Army, and once again served the Army during World War I.

In 1941, the facility was turned over to the U.S. Army Quartermaster Corps and its name changed to the Washington Quartermaster Depot. The depot provided a wide variety of services, such as PX and commissary services, a recruiting induction center, storage, engineering, logistics, and furniture services for officers and Congressmen. The facility wasn't closed until the early 1990s.

Beacon Field

Beacon Field was located near Alexandria. It was a small civilian airfield taken over when World War II began. After many improvements were made, it was utilized as a civilian pilot training base. During the early months of 1942, Beacon Field was even used for training women ferry pilots as part of the WASP program. The Navy eventually assumed control of the field and used it as a primary training base for Naval Aviation cadets.

Known as the EEBEE Army, the airfield was a gunnery training tow-target site. Two hard surfaced runways and a single hangar served the unit and provided mechanical maintenance for the tow planes. Until standard wooden barracks could be constructed, the air crews and maintenance personnel lived out of tents. Transportation aircraft utilized Beacon Field to service the needs of Ft. Hunt.

Arlington

Fort Myer, originally called Ft. Whipple, was constructed in 1863 by Union engineers to defend Washington, D.C. The site is located adjacent to the Arlington National Cemetery. It was here the famed Wright Brothers staged exhibition flights of their Wright Flyer. A crowd gathered to watch the flights on 18 September 1908 and unwillingly became witnesses to the first aviation fatality when Lt. Thomas Selfridge was killed in a demonstration flight.

Fort Myer served as headquarters to service personnel. It was here that General George C. Marshall, Chief of Staff, made his headquarters. The Honor Guard for the Arlington National Cemetery is housed on the grounds, as well as the 1st and 4th Battalions of the 3rd Infantry Division. The famed U.S. Army band that performs in the Washington, D.C., area is stationed on this base. Located high on a bluff overlooking the Potomac River, the fort serves as housing for some of the Armed Services' top-ranking generals.

The Pentagon

The world's largest office building is the Pentagon, in Arlington, Virginia, occupying 6,500,000 square feet. It is the headquarters of the United States Department of Defense. Approximately 30,000 military and civilian personnel work there. The facility generally has 23,000 military and 3,000 civilian support personnel occupying it on any given day. Officially known as the Headquarters of the National Defense Department, it is commonly known as the Pentagon due to the shape of the building.

The original War Department (Defense Department) during and after World War I occupied the Gregory Building in Washington, D.C. The department grew so fast that it occupied fifteen or more different buildings, spread out in the metropolitan area of Washington, D.C. The situation was unmanageable, especially with the approach of World War II. In order to combine these different departments, it was decided to construct a large, single building. Land located at edge of Ft. Myer was selected for this purpose. The building was designed by architect George Bergstrom, in the form of a giant, interconnected pentagon, with five floors above ground and two below.

Colonel (later General) Leslie Groves was selected to direct the project. Starting in September 1941, crews worked around the clock, seven days a week, to complete the project, utilizing more than 13,000 laborers. A large new town called Fairlington, Virginia, was constructed to house the workers. The Pentagon was dedicated January 1943, just in time for the War Department to move in.

After the war, the War Department underwent a name change and became known as the Department of Defense. Despite the new name, most citizens still refer to the facility as the Pentagon.

Quartermaster Depot

The original depot was constructed in 1819 and for many years was referred to as the Washington General Depot. General Army equipment needed to protect the Washington Capitol area was stored here to be used on a daily basis and in emergency situations. The higher-ranking officers were allowed to store their household furnishing as they awaited their next duty station.

With the advent of war, the depot was seen as being inadequate as a storage facility and the decision was made to replace it. But instead, the facility was expanded in early 1941 and assigned to the U.S. Army Quartermaster Corps.

During the war, the depot provided a large number of military services for Congressmen and officers stationed in Washington, D.C.

Bedford

Twenty-three telegrams were received in the small Virginia town of Bedford on June 6, 1944, repeating the same bitter message: "The Secretary of War desires to express his deep regrets...."

Four thousand men died on D–Day on the Normandy beaches, along with 10,000 other casualties. There were many cities and small towns that lost many of their young men that memorable day, but few suffered a greatly as Bedford.

The 29th Infantry Division, a former National Guard unit, comprised guardsmen from Virginia, Pennsylvania and Maryland. Thirty-five men from Bedford served in the 116th Infantry Regiment. The 116th Regiment encamped at Ft. Pickett, Blackstone, Virginia, and were on their way back from war games held in North Carolina. Departing Ft. Pickett, the regiment returned to its home base at Ft. Meade, Maryland, before departing for England and the eventual landing at Omaha Beach.

Riding the small wooden landing craft, many were killed before they even reached the beach. Murderous enemy machine-gun fire killed many of the men as they tried to exit the craft. Others, weighted down with 60-pound packs, ammunition and other gear, drowned in the offshore swells. In less than 10 minutes after the landing craft dropped their ramps, only a handful of the 230 men of Company A survived.

The grateful citizens and others from the nation raised funds to erect a memorial to honor the young men of Bedford who gave their lives on Omaha Beach.

Blacksburg

The Army airfield at Virginia Polytechnic Institute (Virginia Tech) was known as the Blacksburg Army Airfield. The original civilian landing strip, located in southwest Virginia at Roanoke, Montgomery County, was utilized as part of a flight instruction program offered by the institute. The U.S. Army in 1943 took possession and reconstructed a single grass-gravel landing strip, erected several wooden tar-paper barracks and other support buildings, and introduced an Army Specialized Air Training Program. A total of 3,387 soldiers and sailors were stationed at the base. Along with the program the Army maintained a pilot training program. The U.S. Navy maintained a pre-flight unit and trained naval aviators. The entire operation was coordinated with the staff at Virginia Tech.

Blackstone

In December of 1941, 45,867 acres were taken in the counties of Dinwiddie, Lunenburg, Nottoway and Brunswick. Clearance of the woodlands and construction commenced immediately. Camp Pickett, a former CCC (Civilian Conservation Corps) camp, is located 2 miles southeast of Blackstone, Virginia. Constructed was completed in 1942.

Named for General George E. Pickett, CSA, the camp was a large facility used to train a division-size number of recruits. Camp Pickett was designed to accommodate 75,000 to 80,000 men at one time. The 79th Infantry Division trained at Pickett, as well as the 3rd infantry Division, the 28th, 31st, 45th, 77th, 78th and the famed 3rd Armored Division.

By the end of 1942, more than 1500 wooden buildings were in place, two rail spurs were added, as well as 1,000 enlisted wooden barracks, 12 chapels, 70 officers' quarters, a large hospital complex, firehouses, warehouses and assorted administration buildings.

Two more rail spurs were constructed in 1942 and 1943, increasing the logistical efficiency and rapid deployment of troops.

Shortly after the 79th Infantry Division arrived for training, the 357th Engineering Service Regiment was organized. These African American volunteers lived in a segregated world, completely separate from the white soldiers. They lived in their own barracks and had their own mess halls, chapels, movie theaters, clubs and clinics. These so-called "service units" were destined to be utilized as base maintenance personnel and not combat troops. Many of these service units spent their time digging ditches for water pipes and drainage as well as on "make-work" projects.

The base was also utilized to train a large variety of smaller units, such as engineer battalions, artillery and smaller mechanized units. A WAC training unit was established to handle incoming WAC recruits. Medical schools trained combat hospital men as well as WACS to serve in stateside hospitals. A radio school was added in late 1942.

In addition, rail service to Newport News port of embarkation was greatly improved. A 5,269-foot hard-surface runway was completed in late 1942 to handle Army Air Force cargo planes and smaller light aircraft. Twin engine DC-3s (C-47) transport planes were easily accommodated. A single maintenance hangar, maintenance and air crew facilities were constructed there, as well as a control tower. The Army Air Force utilized the airfield as an emergency facility for nearby Richmond-based aircraft. Many a new pilot landed his disabled aircraft at that field.

The large base hospital was enlarged to accommodate 1900 wounded from the European battlefields. Increasing numbers of wounded arrived by plane or ship at Hampton Roads and were shipped by rail to Pickett's General Hospital.

June 1942, the U.S. Army medical training facility was transferred from Camp Lee to Camp Pickett. Fourteen medical training battalions were organized, trained and graduated. Thirteen-week courses in medical tech, dental tech and combat medical hospital corpsmen were offered at the camp. Camp Pickett quickly became one of the U.S. Army's largest medical replacement training centers.

In addition to training large numbers of troops, the post housed a large prisoner of war camp. It generally held 2700–3000 POWs. Mostly German soldiers, they were used as laborers on the base in areas such as the mess hall and laundry, and for general base maintenance and hospital duties. A large number served as loggers in outlying forest camps to harvest trees needed for the war effort.

Camp Pickett was closed in 1947. With the advent of the Korean War in 1950, the facility was reactivated as a training camp to handle reservists. Renamed Fort Pickett, the base with its accompanying air field remained active throughout the Cold War.

Bowling Green

Named for General A.P. Hill, CSA, Fort A.P. Hill was established as an Army infantry training facility in June of 1941. The idea was to establish a training base that would provide army divisions that could function in either the European or Pacific theater of war.

No information is available to suggest why Caroline County, Virginia, was selected as a site to sustain the use of heavy field weapons and the maneuvering of armored vehicles. Apparently the size of the sparsely populated area and the amount of available land played an important role. In any case, upon investigation of the Bowling Green area, it was decided that the armed services would build the fort in Caroline County. Army 2nd Corps and three recently activated National Guard divisions occupied the facility before it was actually completed. Throughout the remaining years of the war, Fort A.P. Hill would train large-sized corps and several attached divisional units.

In addition to the main base, a large airfield was constructed at nearby Port Royal, Virginia. The facility served the flight needs of two engine cargo planes and some flight training aircraft. A service air crew was also housed there. In addition to the Port Royal airstrip, A.P. Hill AAF Base #1, Moss Neck AAF Base #3 and Mica AAF Base #4 served as auxiliary emergency fields, mostly for Army fighter aircraft.

Fort A.P. Hill, along with Camp Pickett, served as training and staging areas for the division-size units and support units for General George Patton's task Force A in the invasion of Morocco. All units departed from the Hampton Roads port of embarkation, Newport News, Virginia.

In addition to providing training for large-size field units, Camp Lee maintained a U.S. Army nurse training program, graduating 1,252 women. Many of these graduates were shipped to hospitals in England, where they cared for the wounded from the invasion of Normandy.

The year 1944 saw the construction of a large POW camp. Italian POWs were housed there and worked as service troops in such areas as the base medical clinics, hospitals, laundries, mess halls and general camp maintenance.

With the Allies pushing the Nazis back to Germany, the fort shifted its large-scale training program to that of unit replacements. An Officer Candidate School was opened as a means of providing officer replacements.

Fort A.P. Hill remained an active base throughout the years after the war. During the Korean War and the Vietnam War it provided units for replacement of combat units, as it still does today.

Camp Ashby

Camp Ashby was located in Princess Anne County, Virginia. The camp was situated in Virginia Beach, South Hampton Roads. Housing approximately 6,000 German soldiers, many were of the famed Rommel's Afrika Corps. Captured in the early years of World War Two, the soldiers were shipped to the United States for detention.

The camp was erected quickly in mid–1942 on land leased from the Commonwealth of Virginia. The Tidewater Victory Memorial Hospital, located at the site, became the camp's headquarters. A series of low-slung, wooden barracks were erected on the 22-acre, wooded and open field site. Row upon row of barbed wire fencing was used to make certain no POW escaped to town. A few buildings remain today to mark the site.

Camp Pendleton

Camp Pendleton, located in Virginia Beach, was constructed in 1912 on the beach of Rudee Inlet. It served as a small-arms firing range for the Virginia National Guard. The site (not to be confused with the U.S. Marine base in Pendleton, California) is named for Brig. General William Pendleton, CSA, who served as General Robert E. Lee's Chief of Artillery during the Civil War.

During World War I, the base was federalized, then used by the Navy as a coastal artillery training site. The gunners could fire at floating targets in the nearby open Atlantic Ocean. With the end of the war, the National Guard resumed control of the base.

With the threat of World War II, the U.S. Army once again assumed control and used the facility as a coastal artillery battery and artillery training base. The 224th Coastal Artillery Regiment, a Virginia National Guard unit, occupied the camp then. Various coastal units received training there before being shipped to other locations, especially those armed with railway guns and 155mm weapons.

Today the facility is used for amphibious training by the Navy and Marines.

Cape Charles

Cape Charles is located on the Virginia eastern shore, facing the Chesapeake Bay. Virginia's historic eastern shore is a long finger of land that separates the Chesapeake Bay from the Atlantic Ocean. Located along the Atlantic side are 14 undeveloped barrier islands and a multitude of mud flats. There was little fear that the enemy would attack through these islands as the waters were too irregular, shallow and treacherous. Up to and during the war, the area remained uncharted by the U.S. Geodetic Survey. What little information was available had been gathered by years of hunting and fishing by the locals.

War planners who examined the situation considered the mouth of the bay a vulnerable place for an attack by enemy forces. The Chesapeake Bay covers a large area of approximately 64,299 miles and drains 1500 rivers and streams from six contiguous states. Some 200 miles in length, the Bay flows south into the Atlantic Ocean, between Fisherman Island and the northern coast of Virginia Beach.

The entrance to the Chesapeake Bay was deemed to be the most vulnerable to an enemy invasion and required immediate protection. It was decided to utilize the area about Cape Charles City to locate a new fort. Coastal artillery guns, especially the large naval 16-inch guns, could be positioned to cover the threat from the Atlantic.

With the threat of war, Fort Wilson was constructed in September 1941 as a coastal defense facility. Early in 1942, the name was changed to Fort Custis, named for Captain John Parke Custis, a local Eastern shore hero. Ft. Custis was placed under the direct command of Ft. Monroe for the duration of the war.

Constructed in the mid-to-late 1800s, a railroad ran the length of the Delmarva, which was suitable for transfer of the famed M1919 16-inch naval gun from Maryland to the site now known as Ft. Custis. Rail-mounted 16-inch guns could be sent to the area in case of a threat of an all-out invasion. The U.S. Army Quartermaster Corps examined the entire rail length from Maryland to the tip of the Delmarva and pronounced the rail bed suitable to carry the weight of the immense rail guns. The railroad was a necessity as the famed Chesapeake Bay Bridge had not been built yet.

The mouth or entrance to the Bay is about 16 miles wide and impractical to cross with a traditional anti-submarine steel net. Wary of German U-boats that prowled the offshore area, the U.S. Army put in place a series of intricate mine fields, under control of Ft. Monroe, as well as coastal surface patrol boats manned by the U.S. Army, Navy and Coast Guard. Control and monitoring of the mine field fell to the U.S. Army and specially trained mine warfare crews. Local harbor pilots were responsible for guiding the entering cargo and tanker ships once they passed through the mine field's narrow channel. The mine field was not considered a perfect arrangement, but designing and maintaining a mine field to defend such a large area was difficult.

Before the war, harbor and coastal defenses were the primary concern of the U.S. Army. To prevent enemy ships or submarines from attacking the important naval facilities at Norfolk and Hampton Roads, coastal artillery batteries were installed at Fisherman Island and Fort Story at Virginia Beach. The Army Mine Command, based out of Little Creek, Virginia, was responsible for the control of mine fields.

Fort Custis, among a variety of other shore installations, contained two massive 16-inch naval guns, four 8-inch guns and four 155mm field guns. Reinforced cement bunkers were constructed at Wise Point and Kiptopeke, Virginia, for this purpose. Battery 122, Eben Eveleth Winslow, and Battery 7, which consisted of the two casement 16-inch Navy guns, were also contained there.

Wise Point, Virginia, is located at 1.4 miles south of Kitopeke at the very end of the Delmarva. Today Wise Point is where the end of the Chesapeake Bay Bridge connects the mainland to the eastern shore.

Battery 123 was never completed. Railway artillery (Battery 7) consisted of four 8-inch guns. Battery 9 consisted of four tractor-drawn 155 mm guns on Panama mounts, and was eventually replaced by Battery 228. Battery 228 was built for two shielded 6-inch guns.

Barracks, mess halls, post office, church and other necessary camp facilities were quickly constructed there, along with the gun emplacements. Although these buildings have long since been removed, some of the cement casements are still visible, although many are located on National Wildlife property.

Three coastal watchtowers were built near the Cape Charles Lighthouse, on nearby low-lying Smith Island (named for John Smith of Jamestown fame). Old life-saving stations along the Atlantic beach were manned as lookout and coastal patrol stations by Coast Guard Coastal Patrol Units. Once utilized to save the lives of mariners awash from sinking ships, now they maintained a vigil for any suspicious activity at sea or on the nearby beaches.

With the end of the war, a row of nine concrete ships were sunk in place to form a protective breakwater at what is now Kitopeke State Park. This breakwater was then utilized to form a ferry terminal in 1950. The original ferry terminal had been situated at Cape Charles.

Fisherman Island Military Reservation

Coastal defense guns and troops were deployed on the low-lying tidal island during World War I, from 1917 to 1919. Utilizing the old concrete placements, coastal artillery was installed in the old site during 1942.

The gun emplacements consisted of: Battery 227, two shielded 6-inch guns; Battery Lee, two 3-inch guns on pedestals; Battery 24, two 90mm fixed pedestal mounted guns; and Battery 4, four 5-inch pedestal guns.

Fisherman Island provided an open view of the entrance to the Chesapeake Bay. To keep an eye on submarines lurking in the area and on possible saboteurs, the Coast Guard maintained a lookout station. Today, on a visit to the former coastal defense site, one will find the Fisherman Island National Wildlife Refuge. Little remains of the coastal artillery sites except a few cement emplacement foundations.

Charlottesville

The 8th Evacuation Hospital has a long history, beginning with World War I. The University of Virginia School of Medicine at Charlottesville sponsored a base hospital unit called No. 41. The unit served with great distinction during the "war to end all wars" and was disbanded when the war ended.

Dr. Staige D. Blackford of the University of Virginia Medical School felt the University should once again provide a medical unit to serve the troops in the war. With approval from the Surgeon General's Office, he set about convincing the University, which quickly granted permission. With approval, plans were made to provide a 750-bed hospital staffed with school and local medical personnel. The hospital was organized as the 8th Evacuation Hospital, U.S. Army. The University located all the required personnel to bring the unit into existence. Dr. Staige became Chief of Medicine, Dr. E. Cato Drash became Chief of Surgery, and Miss Ruth Beery assumed the position of Chief of Nursing. The unit, with 417 staff, was officially completed by 1 May 1942, then activated on 1 September 1942.

Once activated, the unit was assigned to the 3rd Evac Hospital Unit; together they trained as a single unit called the 8th Evac Hospital, at Camp Kilmer, Stelton, New Jersey.

Once basic training was complete, the unit was shipped to Pageland, South Carolina, for combat-style training. Upon completion of that training, the unit was transferred to Camp Kilmer, Shelton, New Jersey. After a stay at Camp Kilmer, they boarded a ship and headed for North Africa, where they participated in Operation Torch, the invasion of Africa by the Allies. Arriving at Casablanca, they set up and immediately began handling patients. After Africa, the 8th Evac went on to take part in the brutal war in Italy.

Fishersville

The Woodrow Wilson Army General Hospital was located in a small northwest rural community called Fishersville. The site is located a few miles east of Staunton, on present-day Route 64. Located on a 223-acre site, it had 58 main buildings made of brick, including a few warehouses and a central administration building. Constructed in 1943, it had space for 1565 beds and received wounded from the war in Europe. A C&O rail line provided transportation from Newport News, allowing special hospital trains to unload patients directly from the ships into the rail cars and convey them to the hospital. The facility specialized in general medicine, orthopedic surgery and venereal diseases.

A WAC detachment, specializing in medicine, was stationed there for the duration of the war.

Once the war was over and the need for such a facility was reduced, the federal government handed the hospital over to the Commonwealth of Virginia. Today it is known as the Woodrow Wilson Rehabilitation Center.

Front Royal

In 1908, Congress authorized the U.S. Army to establish the Remount Service. The purpose for this was to provide suitable horses and mules, to train and condition them, then to issue them to the cavalry and Quartermaster units. The first remount depot was established at Fort Reno, Oklahoma. In 1911, a Quartermaster remount depot was also established at Front Royal, Virginia.

The township of Front Royal is situated at the edge of the Blue Ridge Mountains, 76 miles from Washington, D.C. The Quartermaster Depot was situated 3 miles from town.

Although the trucks in the 1930s reduced the need for horses and pack mules, the depot, now greatly reduced, continued with its mission of providing draft animals. With the advent of World War II, the depot quickly expanded to include the purchase, breeding and training of war dogs. Commencing on 13 March 1942, the Quartermaster Corps organized and operated the Army's newly formed K-9 Corps. Soon after establishing the U.S. Army's first K-9 training program at Front Royal, it was quickly expanded to include four more dog training centers.

Shortly after the unexpected attack on Pearl Harbor, the American Kennel Association helped mobilize dog owners throughout the United States to donate their dogs to the Army Quartermaster Corps. Initially 30 breeds were offered, but the training regimen soon reduced the number to just five: German shepherds, Belgian sheepdogs, Dobermans, farm collies (the Lassie image) and giant schnauzers.

The Quartermaster Corps trained soldiers as well as Marines, Coast Guard and Naval personnel. Dogs were trained to work as sentry dogs, scout or patrol dogs, as messengers, and for mine detection.

The U.S. Marine Corps made effective use of combat-trained dogs to detect the location of the enemy in the dark, dense jungles of the Pacific. The presence of the dogs greatly reduced the sudden danger of ambush, as they were able to detect the presence of the enemy 1000 yards away. The largest numbers of K-9 sentry dogs were issued to the U.S. Coast Guard for the long, desolate stretches of beach patrol. Once again, the handler depended on the keen sense of smell to warn him of the presence of a possible enemy hiding in the sand dunes.

The need for trained horses for the cavalry or as draft animals was greatly reduced at the beginning of the war. Horses were not needed to fight a modern mechanized war. An unexpected demand in 1943 for 3,000 horses for beach patrol by the Coast Guard invigorated the purchase and training program. Sailors who were selected or who volunteered for training in handling and riding horses were sent to Front Royal for training. By 1944, with a decreased danger of invasion, the beach patrols were greatly reduced, horses were returned to the Front Royal Remount Station, and the sailors sent to other duties.

In 1944, with the mountainous war in Italy, the U.S. Army suddenly required a considerable number of pack mules to haul supplies to troops in the steep mountains. To negotiate the steep ridges and rugged terrain of the North Apennines Mountains and the Po Valley, the 10th Mountain Division employed thousands of mules. Many of these mules, needed in a hurry, were obtained locally in Italy, while the rest were transported from the U.S.

Merrill's Marauders, fighting in the China-Burma-India Theater, utilized mules trained at Front Royal to pack in supplies through dense jungle and mountainous terrain. Few of the mules survived the brutal jungle warfare.

A main POW camp was established at Front Royal, which contained 400 POWs. Their primary tasks involved caring for the dogs and mules. Many were employed in local agriculture labor at surrounding farms, especially at harvest time.

With the end of the war near, the dog training program was greatly reduced and finally eliminated, only to be reactivated during the Korean War.

Hampton Roads

Hampton Roads, also known as the Tidewater of Virginia, is the name for one of the world's largest natural harbors, which include the James, Elizabeth and York Rivers.

The areas of Norfolk, Newport News, Hampton and Virginia Beach comprise Hampton Roads.

The area, inhabited by several Native American tribes, was first claimed by the Spanish, then the English in 1607. The large, open harbor quickly became a key point for military control of the area, including the nearby Chesapeake Bay.

Beginning with the 1830s, several forts were constructed to protect the region from invasion of European forces. Fort Monroe and Fort Wool guarded the harbor with enormous coastal artillery weapons. The famous Civil War naval engagement between the *Monitor* and the *Merrimac* was fought at Hampton Roads.

The area of Newport News and Hampton, with its railroad terminus and docks, quickly became the ideal port of embarkation. During World War I ships loaded with men and equipment departed for the Great War in Europe from there. The wounded were brought to the port and dispersed to various hospitals in the area.

Once again with the advent of World War II, the port would be utilized to ship badly needed war supplies and eventually warriors to the wars in Africa and Europe.

Known as the POE (Port of Embarkation), it was located on the railroad piers and several adjacent sites. During the war, thousands of troops and millions of tons of war materiel passed through the port facilities. Hundreds of ships constantly loaded and unloaded at the docks.

In October of 1942, Task Force A—General George Patton's invasion force—departed for Morocco in north Africa. The majority of his troops were staged at the surrounding area camps such as Fort Eustis, Ft. Patrick Henry and Camp Hill.

During July of 1943, a second major invasion force known as Task Force B, under General Troy Middleton, formed up and departed Virginia for the invasion of Sicily. Hampton Roads became a constant stream of troop and supply convoys leaving for the European and Middle Eastern effort. Eventually in early 1942, German submarines waited to strike the many convoys.

POE Hampton also became a main port of reception for German and Italian prisoners of war. From 1942 through 1945, more than 135,000 POWs were processed at the port, then shipped to outlying POW camps in the interior of Virginia.

Fort Eustis

Built on the James River as a World War I recruit training center, Fort Eustis was known as Camp Abraham Eustis, a temporary facility. Following the war, it was primarily utilized as a storage area for surplus war ordnance and heavy artillery guns. In 1923, the camp's name was changed to Fort Eustis and it became a permanent military installation staffed by small infantry units. During Prohibition it was utilized to detain bootleggers caught in the North Carolina-Virginia area.

In 1940, with the war raging in Europe, Ft. Eustis was utilized as a Coast Artillery training and replacement center. Balloon-handling artillery observers and spotters were trained there for the Atlantic Coast region. Among the units trained for the war, a regiment of British soldiers were prepared for duty in the Caribbean area.

Located but a few miles from the Hampton Roads port of embarkation, Fort Eustis was utilized as an overflow staging/receiving area for troops bound for the war in Africa and later Europe. When troops began arriving after the war, it once again served the same purpose. The large hospital was taken over by the Navy and turned into a treatment center for both Army and Navy returning wounded.

A large, important POW camp was established to hold 4500 or more German prisoners of war. English-speaking prisoners were collected here and used to translate the many scientific documents captured in Germany, including Dr. Werner von Braun's rocket research.

In May of 1946, Fort Eustis became the headquarters for the consolidated command of the Army's transportation center.

Camp Wallace

Basically a satellite facility to Camp Eustis, Camp Wallace was located several miles up-river, on the James. Established in 1918 as the Upper Firing Range for the Artillery School at Camp Eustis, the site consisted of 30 wooden barracks, several warehouses, and 8 mess halls, all located on 160 acres of rugged bluffs overlooking the James River. During World War II, it was the site of an antiaircraft training program and general ordnance storage, mostly small arms ammunition. Targets were floated on the James River and used for target practice by the trainees. The facility was closed down at the end of the war.

In 1971, the U.S. Army agreed to a land swap and closed Camp Wallace. Today the former site is part of a large development of Busch Gardens, Busch Brewery and the Kings Mill Resort.

Camp Patrick Henry

Camp Patrick Henry, named for the famed Virginia patriot (1736–1799), was constructed in Warwick County, Virginia, where the Newport News/Williamsburg International Airport is located today. But unlike today, the area selected was heavily forested, swampy and little used. Camp Patrick Henry was designed as a staging area for the Hampton Roads port of embarkation in 1942. Occupying 1,700 acres, it remained in service until the end of the war.

Constructed to be a temporary holding facility, the entire camp was constructed utilizing the U.S. Army Quartermaster 700 Series encampment building program. Civilian workers flocked to the Hampton Roads area, overwhelming housing and city facilities. The base was quickly constructed and in full operation by 1 December 1942.

Approximately 1,412,107 men and women were processed through the camp during the war. The camp had a capacity at any one time of 35,000 troops waiting to go to Africa, later to Europe, by ship. The spectrum of troops covered every branch of the military as well as several Allied armies that had trained in the United States. Brazilian, Greek, Chinese, Polish, Turkish, Yugoslav, and many Canadian units were staged there. Many specialty units, especially engineer and Quartermaster units, were also processed at the camp.

Railroad Quartermaster units were trained at nearby Fort Eustis and processed through Camp Patrick Henry. Medical and portable hospital units, trained and formed in Virginia, were assembled at the camp, then processed through the port of embarkation.

Large division-size units typically staged at Camp Patrick Henry. Among them were the famed 45th Infantry Division, the 2nd Cavalry, the segregated 92nd Buffalo Infantry Division, and the 85th, 98th, 31st, 91st and 92nd Infantry Divisions. Gathering a full division and all its war equipment and support units took time; therefore, the unit may be housed upwards to a month before it could be loaded on ships and sent to its final destination. Locals lived with the noise and commotion of the area on a twenty-four-hour, seven-day-a-week basis.

The camp was self-contained. It was divided into 9 service areas, each with its own post office, movie theaters, PX, mess halls, motor pool, Military Police, water and sewage, as well as a direct rail system to other camps in Virginia and POE Newport News, Virginia.

A large encampment of 600 German POWs were held and used as service personnel. Later, Italian service units were housed there to work at various base jobs. The first German prisoner of war to arrive did so from the war in Africa. Soldiers of the greatly touted Rommel's Afrika Korps, captured in 1943, arrived at the fort and were held to be interviewed. Five thousand German POWs were held for the duration of the war.

During the early part of 1943, Camp Patrick Henry served as a reception center for wounded arriving from the African and Sicilian campaigns. The excellent rail system provided one-day access to many fine inland military hospitals. In the later stages of 1945, as the war neared its conclusion, the camp became a demobilization processing facility for soldiers returning from the war in Europe to civilian life. Upon completion of the war, the site was sold in 1949 for civilian development, but the U.S. Army maintained a Nike missile site there until the late 1970s.

Camp Hill

Named for Lt. General Ambrose P. Hill, CSA, Camp Hill was a troop staging camp similar to Camp Patrick Henry. It was located in Newport News between present-day Jefferson Avenue and the James River. Constructed during World War I as a staging area for troops headed for Europe, it was reactivated in mid–1940, just before World War II.

Two hundred traditional wooden barracks could house 10,000 troops there. During World War II, a Military Police training unit was housed at the camp, as well as a stevedore training school. The stevedore trainees received on-the-job-training at the nearby Newport News port of embarkation. Land was set aside and a POW camp was constructed to house nearly 1000 Italian prisoners of war. These POWs were later utilized as stevedores at the Newport News POE.

In addition to regular army units, the camp had areas set aside to stage dogs and mules for overseas shipment to Italy. Several transportation schools were located there as well as the various army bands for the POE Newport News. Bands played a variety of musical selections to entertain the departing troops as they boarded the ships. Several private and public service organizations, such as the Red Cross and the Salvation Army, provided coffee and donuts to the arriving or departing ships.

Fort Monroe

Called the Gibraltar of the Chesapeake Bay, Fort Monroe is located on a sandy peninsula that forms the city of Hampton and juts into Hampton Roads. Geographically, the peninsula is called Old Point Comfort. Historically, a fort has stood at this site since 1609 to protect the Hampton Roads area from invading enemies, such as the Spanish. Fort Algernourne was constructed by the colony at Jamestown as a means of keeping the Spanish from sailing up the James River and bombarding the settlement.

The British in 1813 sailed into Hampton Roads, bombarded the small fort and burned the city of Hampton to the ground. After the War of 1812, Congress decided to construct a system of permanent coastal defenses.

In 1834, a substantial stone facility was completed and named in honor of U.S. President James Monroe, the fifth president of the United States. When the Civil War began, Virginia joined the Confederacy, but Fort Monroe remained in Union control.

During World War I and World War II, Fort Monroe and nearby Ft. Wool, with their concentration of large-caliber 16-inch coastal artillery, stood guard over Hampton Roads. The U.S. Army was tasked with the immediate defense of the Chesapeake Bay area. Working with the local Navy defense units, the U.S. Army was expected to destroy any invasion force sent by Germany. Traditional locations from Fort Monroe to Cape Charles were equipped with the long-range M1919 16-inch naval guns, which were considered adequate to repel any attempted invasion.

The defenses of Fort Monroe comprised Eight batteries:

Battery 124	2–16" coastal guns
Battery De Russey	2–12" disappearing guns
Battery Parrott	2–12" disappearing guns
Battery Church	2–10" disappearing guns
Battery Ruggles	4–12" mortars
Battery Anderson	4–12" mortars
Battery Montgomery	2–6" guns
Battery AMTB #23	2–90mm guns

Assorted smaller antiaircraft guns were placed about the area as needed.

The coastal artillery school was located on the grounds, as well as an antiaircraft training school. With the need for artillery officers, the U.S. Army established an Officer Candidates School (OCS). In addition to the storage of heavy weapon munitions, underwater naval mines were also stored.

A small single-strip airfield was built, Walker Airfield, just north of the fort. It mainly served the needs of small service aircraft. During the war, the base hospital was quickly enlarged and served to handle overflow of incoming wounded from Europe.

Fort Monroe is presently closing, and a portion of it is being transferred to the National Park Service.

FORT WOOL

Constructed on a man-made island known as the Rip Raps in Hampton Roads, Fort Wool lies halfway between the cities of Hampton and Norfolk, Virginia. Built to complement Fort Monroe in 1819, it was not completed when the Civil War began. Designed to provide a cross-fire situation between Ft. Monroe and Ft. Wool during World War II, it was utilized as a coastal defense facility. Two coastal 6-inch guns known as Battery Gates were mounted in cement casements, along with Battery Hindman (two 3-inch guns), Battery Lee (consisting of four 3-inch guns), and an array of antiaircraft weapons there.

Mines and anti-submarine nets were positioned between the two forts to prevent enemy submarines from entering the area. Advances in aviation rendered the guns at Fort Wool obsolete, and thus at the end of the war the facility was given to the Commonwealth of Virginia.

FORT STORY

Constructed in 1914 at Virginia Beach, Fort Story was an integral part of the coastal defense system to protect Chesapeake Bay and Hampton Roads. The small base was named for General John Story. After World War I, the base remained inactive until World War II, when it was integrated into the harbor defense command. Large 16-inch coastal guns were in place as well as lesser caliber and antiaircraft guns.

With a reduction in the possibility of a coastal invasion, the facility transitioned from a heavily garrisoned site to a hospital constructed to accommodate wounded veterans from the war in Europe. During this time, the hospital facilities held 14,000 patients. It was used to alleviate the burden on the local military hospitals in the area.

A prisoner of war camp was also erected and housed 400 German and Italian prisoners of war. When the hospital was constructed, these POWs worked in various hospital-service jobs.

Upon completion of the war, Fort Story was transferred to the Transportation Training Command at Fort Eustis. It was designated a Quartermaster Corps installation and is still utilized for amphibious training units today.

Hot Springs

The luxury resort hotel, The Homestead, is located in western Virginia in the middle of the Allegheny Mountains. It is situated near the largest hot springs in the Commonwealth. With the start of the war, the United States interned enemy diplomats and their families in four different luxury hotels. Diplomats were held in the Bedford Springs Hotel, in Bedford, Pennsylvania; the Grove Park Inn, located in Ashville, North

Three. The Army Bases

Carolina; the Greenbrier Hotel in White Sulfur Springs; West Virginia and the Homestead in Hot Springs, Virginia.

Until an exchange for enemy-held American diplomats and their families could be arranged, they would be housed in protected luxury.

The Japanese diplomats and families, consisting of 363 men, women and children, all residing in Washington, D.C., were housed at the Homestead. Although the Immigration and Naturalization Service guarded and secured the facility, the Japanese literally had the run of the facility. Provided with all the required necessities, these internees prepared their own ethnic foods, produced entertainment and carried out necessary services.

When an exchange was finally agreed on, all Japanese diplomats and their families departed for Japan by early 1942.

Langley

Located in Hampton, Virginia, Langley Air Force Base is one of the oldest Air Force facilities in the US. Named for aviation pioneer Samuel Langley, it was constructed in 1916 and used as a flight-training field for the U.S. Army's newly established Flying Corps. Situated between the city of Hampton and the Black River, the base occupies 3,152 acres of land. The facility was originally meant to provide a proving ground for the air branches of the Armed Forces and training for Army pilots. The looming crisis of World War II shifted its emphasis to the development of high-speed combat aircraft. To achieve this, two new high-speed wind tunnels were constructed, as well as an expansion of the entire facilities.

The site fulfilled two criteria: it needed to be close to open water for over-water training, and it had to have land that was flat and open. The open water of the Chesapeake Bay offered an excellent nearby controlled water training area.

With the advent of World War I, two airplane hangars and a lighter-than-aircraft hangar were quickly constructed. Fighter pilots and balloon observers were both trained under the direction of the U.S. Army Signal Corps.

When the war was over, the National Advisory Committee on Aeronautics was created by an act of Congress to research the fundamentals and safety of flight. NACA, as it was commonly known, was located at Langley and became an important research facility, as it is today.

When the U.S. Army Flying Service was changed to the U.S. Army Air Corps, Langley continued as the command's headquarters. Many important changes in civil and military aircraft designs, flight procedures, instrumentation and safety research resulted from the Langley installation.

With the advent of World War II, the Command Headquarters was transferred to Bolling Field in Washington, D.C. The 2nd U.S. Army Air Force Base Unit and the Eastern Technical Training Command commenced operation and prepared for war.

Preparations for war fighter planes and light bombers were readily made available.

These aircraft made Atlantic coastal patrols that went in search of German warships, especially the hunting submarines.

Aviator recruit reception and flight training were added in 1942. Eventually a radar research and training school was added, along with a large air freight terminal and a large hospital. Many wounded military personnel returned from the war to be treated there.

Along with the U.S. Coast Guard, coastal patrol units were stationed at Langley. Successful aircraft hunter-killer air groups dealt a severe blow to the German submarine menace off the coast of Virginia. Use of the four-engine Liberator bomber and its long-distance flying time became a useful tool in destroying the U-boats. Carrying several depth charges, it was successful in sinking several U-boats during the war.

The base remained in operation after the war and with renewed vigor assisted Air Force fighter and bomber units through the Korean War. Today, along with its usual Air Force missions, it is home base to a fighter wing and is still involved in NASA space research programs.

Lexington

The Virginia Military Institute (VMI) was founded in 1839 as a military school to provide well-educated officers for the U.S. Army, and was commonly known as the "West Point of the South."

During the Second World War, the VMI participated in the government's Army Specialized Training Program (ASTP). The program provided specialized training in engineering to over 2,000 selected enlisted men. In keeping with the goals of the ROTC-based program, VMI graduates entered the Army, the Navy, the Marine Corps or the Air Force.

General George Patton, previous to entering West Point, spent a year at VMI.

Melfa

Located on the eastern shore of Virginia, Melfa was a small town with a single grass landing strip that was used by local civilian pilots. When World War II began, the U.S. Navy examined the site as a possible outlying facility. When Creed was selected, they were no longer interested in the site.

Then the U.S. Army Air Force decided to use the site as an emergency landing strip to Langley Air Field. It was activated as a military air field on 1 November 1943. It had one runway. With so many student-training flights in the area, it became an emergency landing field. Known as the Melfa Flight Strip, it serviced only small trainers and some fighter aircraft. A small group of maintenance personnel was kept at the base to make minor repairs.

The airfield reverted back to its owners at the end of the war and today is known as the Accomack County Airport.

Norfolk

Due to its long history, Norfolk appears to be the domain of the U.S. Navy. However, it is also the location of an Army airfield. Constructed as a civilian airport in 1926, it became Norfolk Municipal Airport with a large 3,500-foot runway.

When the war started, the United States Army Air Corps assumed control of the entire facility. The 390th U.S. Army Air Force Base Unit occupied the site and prepared for war. The commercial runway was quickly extended and two more added to handle the increase in cargo aircraft. The 52nd Fighter Group was stationed there and assigned to be the air defense of the Norfolk area. As the war progressed, other fighter squadrons were added to the mix, the last being the 373rd Fighter Group. The fighters also flew with the U.S. Navy, and participated in the anti-submarine warfare defense program.

With the fear of imminent invasion, the airport was quickly ringed with many batteries of antiaircraft guns. Barracks, mess halls, motor pools, movie theaters, post offices and a large aviation repair facility were constructed to house and care for the base personnel. With the war winding down, wounded from Europe were brought to the base hospital then dispersed to outlying medical facilities.

In October 1947, the airfield returned to civilian control and civilian aviation resumed.

Petersburg

Camp Lee, named for General Robert E. Lee, is located in Prince George County, Petersburg, Virginia. With the war raging in 1917 Europe, the United States selected land near Petersburg and constructed Camp Lee as a recruit training base. Within sixty days of its inception, 14,000 men of the Virginia National Guard set up a tent city and lived there until wooden barracks could be completed. Upon completion of the camp, 60,000 men were trained at the facility. After the Armistice was signed, the use of the camp quickly dwindled and eventually it was placed on the inactive list.

When World War II began in Europe, the War Department decided to re-use Camp Lee as a training base. More land was taken as the site was enlarged. The Quartermaster Replacement Training Center took command in February of 1941. The number of trainees grew to about 35,000 in 1944. About 300,000 troops were trained at the camp during the war. More than 32,000 officers, officer cadets and enlisted men were trained at the new school between 1 July 1940 and 3 December 1945. It was here that the old storekeeper, of limited military training, for the U.S. Army was quickly transformed into a combat soldier as well as a quartermaster. The old Quartermaster Headquarters located at the Schuykill Arsenal, New York, was closed and Camp Hill was to become the new home of this new Quartermaster Corps.

The Medical Replacement Training Center (MRTC) transferred to Camp Pickett, Blackstone, Virginia. The entire facility became the domain of the Quartermaster School, a basic and advanced training center. An Officer Candidates School (OCS) was established, graduating officers for the new Quartermaster Corps. Between mid–1940 and early 1946 the Officer Candidate School enrolled 29,660 students and graduated 24,561.

A training center for the Army WACs (Women's Army Corps) was established in 1943. WACs who graduated from the training program were generally assigned to the Quartermaster School.

The camp had segregated facilities so African American recruits could be trained as part of the U.S. Army's 3rd Quartermaster Corps.

In addition to the several Quartermaster schools located at the camp, division-size units were trained at the facility, and those units spent considerable time in the nearby wooded areas, often living in tents for their entire training period.

A large POW camp contained approximately 800 German troops who served as service troops. When Italy signed a surrender agreement, Italian service troops were assigned to the base but in separate facilities. German and Italian troops worked in the large base hospital, clinics, mess halls, and base maintenance, and during the summer months in temporary camps in the outlying forests. These POWs labored in local agriculture and forestry, harvesting crops for the war effort.

With the end of the war, Camp Lee remained as a center for the U.S. Army Quartermaster Corps. Troops for the Quartermaster Corps were then trained for the war in Korea. Camp Lee was designated a permanent post and was renamed Fort Lee.

Plum Tree Target Range

Located in Poquoson, Virginia, this former 3,501-acre bombing and target range is now designated as the Plum Tree Island National Wildlife Refuge. The area consisted of open land inhabited with salt marsh grasses and shrubs, with intermittent wooded habitats. Approximately 1000 acres are low-lying and known to flood daily.

Established in 1917, Plum Tree Target Range was utilized as a bombing and aerial machine gun target range by the U.S. Army's newly formed U.S. Army Air Corps. Despite the reduction in military forces at the completion of WWI, the site remained in use. With the outbreak of World War II, the U.S. Navy utilized the facility during the war to train its fighter pilots in air-to-ground target practice, especially the use of air-to-ground rockets.

Bombing ranges pose several severe hazards: unexploded ordnance, bombs, bullets and rockets were common to the area. Despite its location near Hampton Roads, the site was heavily used during World War II and never really cleaned up by removing their unexploded ammunition.

Radford Ammunition Plant

Just before France fell to Germany in 27 May 1940, President Roosevelt signed a state of limited emergency which allowed Congress to fund the Ordnance Department's budget. The increase in funding allowed for the building and expansion of ordnance facilities.

The Hercules Powder Company was authorized to construct and operate a smokeless powder and propellant plant to be located five miles outside Radford in Pulaski County, Virginia. The Hercules Company was a chemical and ammunition producer located in Wilmington, Delaware. It was one of the major producers of smokeless gunpowder, especially naval powder. The plant went into production 5 April 1941. At the time there were only two of six government plants capable of manufacturing smokeless gunpowder that met military specifications.

A load and assembly plant for artillery and mortar shells was constructed in nearby Dublin, Virginia. The New River Plant was located 12 miles from the main Radford plant. The railroad constructed the necessary track to facilitate the transfer of powder from the production plant to the New River plant and then to various sites throughout Virginia and the nation.

With the rapid expansion of the military, the need for small-arms gunpowder, especially the .30 caliber powder, fell short of demand. Rapid expansion and increased production struggled to keep up with the demand. Lend-lease not only supplied fuels, food and war materials, it also produced large quantities of small-arms ammunition for England and Russia.

Increased production required an increase in workers. People flocked to the small towns located about the Radford plant only to find a lack of housing. The solution was to construct temporary housing in several different locations. During the war women dominated the production lines.

During 1945 the Radford Army Ammunition Plant was renamed the Radford Arsenal. Both facilities are still manufacturing ammunition powder and solid propellant for a variety of military rockets.

Richmond

Richmond's airport was built in 1927 and named in honor of Richard E. Byrd, the famed Arctic explorer. Commonly known as Byrd Field, the airport was built and owned by the city of Richmond, Virginia. The field is located in nearby Sandston, Henrico County, about 5 miles east of downtown Richmond.

When the U.S. Air Force began expanding in size and locations, it began utilizing local airports—among them, Richmond's Byrd Field. Assuming command of the field, the Air Force established the 428th U.S. Army Air Force Base Unit and stationed the 192nd Fighter Wing as a means of training pilots and crews. It quickly became an addition to the coastal protection network as part of the U.S. Army Air Forces Antisubmarine Command. The Army's Air Forces Training Command of the First Air Force also established a command center at Richmond. The 192nd Wing was the first unit to use the new P-47s fighters, which became common sights in the air around Richmond and surrounding communities.

During June of 1943, the 366th Fighter Group arrived and trained on the P-47s. With basic training complete, the group departed for Thurxton, England. In addition to the 366th, the 365th utilized Byrd Field as a training site. In 1943, the 373rd, 371st, fighter groups and the 32nd Bomb Sqadron (B-17s) trained at the field before leaving for England.

A POW camp was built to house the increase in POWs. Some 300 to 400 German POWs were dispatched from Hampton Roads. They were employed in general base maintenance, mess halls, laundries, clinics and the nearby Defense Supply Center.

DEFENSE SUPPLY CENTER, RICHMOND

Located in southern Chesterfield County, Virginia, also known as Bellwood, the Defense Supply Center is situated on the grounds of old Confederate Fort Darling. In 1885, James Bellwood purchased the site and established a 2400-acre model farm.

In 1941, the Army purchased the farms and began constructing the Richmond General Depot for the Quartermaster Corps. Everything that was required by a combat army was stored in the large warehouses. During the war, the depot received, stored and shipped typical army quartermaster supplies, as well as medical and engineering items. The depot was known to employ over 8,000 employees at its peak. Rail cars were loaded and dispatched to ports along the east coast, especially to Newport News. Everything, including gas masks, mess kits, shoes, helmets, shoe polish, etc., was sent.

The constant arrival and departure of freight cars required the construction of a roundhouse that could handle the turnaround of locomotives hauling 800 cars daily.

In 1943, a 2000-capacity POW camp was built on a nearby 50-acre parcel of land. One thousand, two hundred German POWs were known to live and work there.

During 1995, the installation was named the Defense Supply Center Richmond.

MCGUIRE GENERAL HOSPITAL

McGuire General was a large Army hospital housed in the outskirts of Richmond; it contained 1700 beds. The hospital specialized in surgery, amputations, neurosurgery and neurological brain and spine damage. It quickly became a reception center for returning medical patients in the war. Once the wounded were stabilized, they were generally transferred to another medical facility for constant care.

The rail line from Newport News allowed for the rapid transfer of the wounded directly to McGuire for treatment. McGuire was also famous for its neurological work.

Roanoke

Named for Clifton A. Woodrum, a Congressman from the 6th District of Virginia, the civilian air field was constructed by the U.S. Army in 1917 for the First World War. It is located 5 miles north of Roanoke and was utilized as a training facility for new pilots.

A pair of dirt runways served as a civilian landing strip. These were paved and a single hangar added. Barracks were constructed to house the aviation maintenance crews stationed there. Because many training flights from other nearby landing fields conducted drills in the area, it served as an emergency landing strip.

When the war ended, it reverted back to civilian control until World War II.

Suffolk

Originally known as Pig Point Ordnance Depot, in 1929 the name was changed to Nansemond Ordnance Depot. It is located in Suffolk, Virginia, on the James River at the mouth of the Nansemond River. The former site is located six miles across the river from Newport News and approximately eleven miles west of Norfolk. The site was ideally located to supply arms to waiting cargo ships at Hampton Roads.

Constructed in 1917, the site consisted of some 975 acres and was utilized as an Army ammunition storage and handling depot. Thousands of tons of all types of military ordnance was stored, reconditioned or disposed of in various locations from the Depot. During World War II, the facility was the primary munitions depot for the Newport News port of embarkation.

Tens of thousands of all types of conventional ordnance and chemical warfare munitions were warehoused and handled at the site. Anti-aircraft ordnance, mortar shells, Navy air and sea rockets, harbor mines, bombs of all types and captured enemy chemical munitions were stored or buried there.

The Germans manufactured a large variety of chemical munitions, which when captured were eventually shipped to the site for study and storage.

The United States manufactured a variety of chemical munitions and many of these were stored at the site, although they were never used. Instead, they were stored in large earthen bunkers onsite for many years during and after the war.

During the war the burning and chemical cleaning of ordnance took place with tons of refuse being buried at the site. Unused bulk explosives, small-arms ammunition, rocket propellants and bulk TNT were within the confines of the site

With the end of the war, the depot remained active reconditioning stored munitions. After a thorough study, captured enemy munitions were eventually destroyed there. The site was transferred to the Department of the Navy in 1950 during the Korean War.

In June 1960, the facility was declared excess government property and various parcels were donated to the Commonwealth of Virginia and to various commercial companies in the area. Because of the need for handling, burying and disposing of a large variety of munitions and allied chemicals, the former ordnance facility has been declared an EPA hazard site. Based on a detailed, historical study, which recorded and documented how tens of thousands of conventional and chemical warfare weapons were handled at the site, the U.S. Environmental Protection Agency announced plans to investigate the site formally.

Tappahanock

Located in Essex County, Virginia, the Tappahanock Airport was constructed by the U.S. Army in mid-1943. Known as the Tappahanock Flight Strip, it served as an emergency landing airfield for local training flights and as part of the coastal defense system.

A single landing strip, several maintenance buildings, barracks housing and a control tower were erected first. The hard-surface runway was 4,000 feet long with a total landing distance of 8,000 feet. The facility was located 4 miles outside the township of Tappahannock, near the Tappahanock River. With the end of the war, the site reverted to the town.

Warrington

When the owner of the Vint Hills Farms reported he could listen in on German conversations with his short-wave radio, the U.S. Army Intelligence Service immediately showed interest. Due to its location, the site did have the capability of detecting the German Embassy radio conversations with the homeland.

Vint Hills Farms Station, U.S. Army Intelligence Base, covered 695 acres of spectacular, manicured farmland. It was located in Farquier County, Virginia, ten minutes from present-day I-66 and 30 minutes from Dulles International Airport.

The base was established at Vint Hills Farms in mid-1942. A long wire was strung out a window from the mansion to a large nearby tree. Telegraph and voice messages were immediately intercepted within Nazi Germany. By August, a large barn complex had been converted to a permanent intercept station.

In 1943, according to U.S. Army history, a technician copied decoded radio messages from the ambassador at the Japanese Embassy in Washington, D.C., to his superiors in Tokyo, Japan. The message provided detailed information and evaluations relating to the German Atlantic Wall defenses. Of special interest were the data that pertained to Normandy and Calais, France.

With such success, antennas were quickly constructed covering an area of some 450 acres. Of special interest were the messages being transmitted to and from various embassies in Washington, D.C. Retained by the U.S. Army after World War II, Vint Hills Station became the main base for the Army's Electronic Materiel Readiness Commands.

Nearby Zeiger Field, a civilian airfield, was taken over by the U.S. Army and utilized as an emergency landing strip for Vint Hills Station. Two grass runways, one at 2000 feet and the other at 1800 feet, serviced the small Air Force planes. Three wood and steel construction hangars were put in place for storage of aircraft and service maintenance.

Service records indicate the facility was utilized by WASP as a secondary field to Hoover Field, Washington, D.C., and as aircraft storage. A report has the WASP using the facility as an aerial gunnery tow-target base. The facility remained in use during the Korean War as an emergency landing field for Vint Hills Station, finally closing in 1997.

Washington International Airport

When the overutilized, inadequate Hoover Field in Washington needed to be replaced, a site just south of the present-day Pentagon was selected. Construction began in early 1940 and the facility was complete the following year. Unlike most airports at the time, it was designed to have the most modern traffic air control system, as well as large safe runways, passenger terminals, automobile parking facilities and cargo handling warehousing. During World War II, the Washington National Airport became one of the largest cargo handling facilities on the east coast of the United States.

Equipped to handle large cargo aircraft, Washington National Airport quickly became a busy freight terminal, utilized by the Army Air Force's Transport Command. The airport was also used as an air flight service center by the Army and had accommodations for military personnel awaiting flights overseas to England and Europe. With such extraordinary facilities for its time, it was not surprising to see many Congressmen and other important dignitaries crowding the airport awaiting travel arrangements. Whenever President Roosevelt flew anywhere by plane, it was from Washington National Airport. With the heavy use by the military, the airport was a well guarded and secure base. Along with the Army, the Navy made use of the terminals for its air transport system.

West Point

The U.S. Army Air Force Auxiliary Air Field at West Point was constructed in early 1942. The town of West Point is located at the confluence of the Pamunkey and the Mattaponi Rives, which form the York River. Ideally located between the many new military airfields of Hampton Roads and Richmond, it was generally used as an auxiliary emergency airfield. Many training flights used it as a touch-and-go airstrip.

Placed under the command of the 1st Air Force, it was utilized as a dispersal field for fighter aircraft stationed at Richmond's Byrd Field.

A single long runway was constructed but no maintenance hangar was erected. Army guard units were housed in canvas squad tents. Today the U.S. Army airfield is known as the Middle Peninsula Regional Airport.

The Office of Strategic Services (OSS) located a training camp near the airport. It was one of many such training facilities located throughout the United States. Little is known about the training camp and its training programs, since the information remains classified.

LIEUTENANT GENERAL LEWIS B. PULLER

A colorful and famous native of Virginia, Lewis B. "Chesty" Puller was a Marine warrior who served and fought in Haiti, Nicaragua, China, four World War II campaigns, and Korea. General Puller was the only serving Marine to be awarded five Navy Crosses, a Distinguished Service Cross, an Air Medal, a Purple Heart, a Silver Star, a Bronze Star with V, and several unit citations, including many from foreign countries.

Born 26 June 1898, at West Point, Virginia, Puller attended one year at the Virginia Military Institute before enlisting in the Marine Corps in August 1918. He served his country for 37 years, retiring in 1955. "Chesty" was 73 years old when he died on 11 October 1971. He is buried in West Point, Virginia.[1]

CHAPTER FOUR

The Coast Guard

The United States Coast Guard has a long historical relationship with Hampton Roads. Beginning with the Revenue Cutter Service, founded in 1790, it was stationed at Hampton Roads, Portsmouth, Virginia. When the United States Navy was disbanded in 1790, the Revenue Service was the only armed protection at sea. Along with the Revenue Cutter Service, the United States Lighthouse Service established several lighthouses in the Chesapeake area.

With the advent of World War I, the Revenue Cutter Service was combined with the Lighthouse Service and the Life Saving Agency to form the present day U.S. Coast Guard service. The new organization was placed under the Department of Revenue. When the United States entered World War I, it was transferred to the Department of the Navy. The end of the war found the Coast Guard back under the control of the Department of Revenue. Their headquarters at the time were located at Portsmouth, Virginia.

All through mid–1941, German submarine attacks along the East Coast were sporadic, despite the fact that the Battle of the Atlantic was in full force. Germany's U-boats were sinking British merchant ships crossing the Atlantic by the thousands of tons. The Royal Navy lacked suitable numbers of escort ships to protect the increasing size of convoys. In desperation, President Roosevelt ordered the U.S. Navy to provide ships to protect the convoys. By September, the U.S. Navy, undermanned and lacking coastal patrol vessels, was still unable to provide ships and crews to protect convoys along the Atlantic Coast from Florida to Newfoundland, thence to England. The question of how to protect the vast open coastline troubled those tasked with the mission. The solution would involve the United States Coast Guard.

On 1 November 1941, the U.S. Coast Guard was officially transferred from its parent organization, the Treasury Department, to U.S. Navy command, as required by wartime laws. In all, 172,952 men and women served in the United States Coast Guard during World War II.[1]

It was obvious to many military leaders just how vulnerable were the coastal areas of the United States, especially the busy harbors of New York, Boston and the Chesapeake Bay. With the vast expanse of ocean, it would be difficult for either Germany or Japan to invade the United States, but what about sabotage or submarine attacks? Was it possible to land large numbers of enemy agents who could then easily roam the industrial heartland of the country and wreak havoc? The question of how to defend such a vast irregular coastline troubled those who must come up with a solution. The solution was to task the Coast Guard with its defense. The problem became how to accomplish such a feat without the badly needed coastal patrol craft.

With patriotic fervor sweeping the country, hundreds of yachtsmen flooded existing Coast Guard Auxiliary Flotillas, volunteering their boats and their services. Both men and women enrolled in order to qualify for officer commissions in the active Coast Guard. Commissioned Coast Guard officers served as task force commanders, landing craft flotilla commanders, convoy escort, and combat beach masters, as well as enforcing the traditional duties of the Customs Department, navigation rules, and all federal laws related to the high seas.[2]

Shortly after 7 December 1941, German submarines were dispatched to the Chesapeake Bay area and offshore shipping lanes. By the time the submarines arrived off the Chesapeake capes, the U.S. Army had managed to put in place a protective mine field of 365 mines, effectively blocking the 16-mile-wide entrance to the Bay.

During this time, the U.S. Navy had its hands full as it struggled to supply ships for a two-ocean war. Protecting the valuable merchant ships sailing along the eastern coast of the United States quickly became a priority. In early 1942, Coast Guard aircraft operating out of NAS Norfolk became involved in anti-submarine warfare patrols and convoy duties off the Virginia and North Carolina capes.

By the end of 1942, the Coast Guard had laid anti-submarine minefields, maintained the traditional coastal chain of rescue lifeboats, lookout towers, beach patrols and coastal patrol offshore rescue boats, and in general kept the vast coastline of the United States under constant surveillance.[3]

The Corsair Fleet

Early in 1942, when German U-boats began sinking tankers and cargo ships off the East Coast, the U.S. Navy lacked offshore patrol craft to protect Allied shipping. The previous year, Alfred Stanford, the commodore of the Cruising Club of America, was unsuccessful in convincing the U.S. Navy to utilize private craft to patrol the coast lines. However, on 4 May 1942, Admiral King, Chief of Naval Operations, finally accepted and asked the Coast Guard to take over the operation of the small boat force program. The Coastal Picket Patrol was organized through the U.S. Coast Guard. This organization of small boat force was given to the newly formed Coast Guard Reserve. The task proved too large for the reserve auxiliary, so the Coast Guard assumed responsibility.

With the constant urging of yacht club members around the country and the lack of coastal patrol boats, the Coast Guard began accepting sailing and motorized yachts. They were quickly put to use and organized as coastal patrol units. Large sailboats and luxury motor cruisers were also offered. The procedure was to purchase the craft at the going price of $1. These beautiful boats were immediately painted gray to conform to Navy procedures. After some training, Coast Guard crews manned the boats and were immediately put into service. The accepted boats had to be "capable of going to sea in good weather for a period of 48 hours at cruising speeds."

Four. The Coast Guard

These vessels could be motor yachts, sailing craft or fishing boats. Their duty was to supplement the Coast Guard's patrol craft already operating in the area. Their orders included both observing and reporting of enemy submarines, and attacking them when properly armed. Most of the civilian crews carried a few shotguns and a pistol or two as their only armament.

It was a temporary stopgap measure, but it worked! It was quickly dubbed the "Hooligan Navy" by the Coast Guard regulars. Officially, it was known as the "Corsair Fleet" by the Coast Guard. It was a sight to see these luxury sailing craft, manned by armed Coast Guard sailors, patrolling the deep waters along the coast. These small boats gallantly patrolled the vast coastlines of the United States during the rest of the war, on the lookout for sinking survivors and German U-boats.

Unaware that this was the U.S. Coast Guard, the German U-boats were annoyed by their presence and persistence. In many instances, the U-boat captains warned them to "get out of the way!" They could not accept the Corsair Fleet sailboats as official patrol craft. This "Bucket Brigade," a nickname given to the Corsair Fleet and other available civilian craft utilized along the eastern coast, served as a warning system against German U-boats. Practically anything that could remain afloat was equipped with a working radio to warn of submarine sightings and their positions.

Contrary to popular belief, submarines did not always run submerged, but rather spent most of the time on the surface, seeking their prey. Notification of a sighting was relayed to Coastal Command and one or more patrol bombers were quickly dispatched. At the beginning of the war, there were meager numbers of aircraft to call upon, but as the war progressed, the number increased.

Records state, "Time after time, these Coast Guard auxiliaries took their vulnerable small craft, a few armed with only a rifle or a shotgun, others with boat hooks and flashlights, to haul drowning, burned, oil-covered merchant seamen from the peril of the sea." More than 500 merchant seamen were rescued during the early phase of the Battle of the Atlantic.

With the large numbers of sailing and motorized boats in the Hampton, Newport News, Portsmouth and Deltaville area, owners there hurried to meet the Coast Guard's needs for patrol craft, especially the Chesapeake Bay area and adjacent offshore waters. Boats of 50 to 100 feet were organized as part of the U.S. Navy's Eastern Sea Frontier defense force. To many military personnel it appeared a foolish task—sailboats against the technologically advanced German submarines seemed ridiculous, but history shows how successful it actually was.

The Coast Guard Auxiliary Flotilla 33, Kilnarnock, Virginia, was formed as Unit 4-4 in 1941. Their primary mission was to watch for possible enemy activity in the Chesapeake Bay. There was a constant fear of German U-boats attacking shipping at the mouth of the Bay. Many rumors of U-boat sightings spread among the public, causing fear and anger. Tales of U-boats sailing directly into the Bay and tying up at one of the many piers kept folks on edge. German sailors were reported to be watching movies at one of the nearby theaters, as well as buying ice cream and groceries. No German submariners were ever seen walking downtown, but that is not to say saboteurs were never sent ashore to cause havoc. There are several instances where they actually landed (in New York and Florida) but were apprehended before they could cause any harm.

This wonderful patchwork of boats and men, the "Corsair Navy," became known as the "Donald Duck Navy" when Walt Disney studios designed their cartoon character logo.

With the increase in the Navy patrol craft, the Navy opened a sub-chaser training school in Miami, Florida. The school trained about 10,000 officers, as well as 38,000 enlisted men. By mid–1943, the so-called "Donald Duck Navy" replaced the Chesapeake Bay Corsair Fleet.[4]

Beach Patrol

With the threat of enemy submarines landing saboteurs onto the empty Atlantic beaches, on 25 July 1942 Coast Guard HQ ordered Coast Guard units located within naval districts to organize and maintain a well-armed beach patrol. Each beach patrol unit was to operate as part of a port security system; in Virginia, that command was located at Norfolk.

Foot, boat or motor beach patrols had to cover 3,700 miles of open coastline.

K-9 dog training with members of the U.S. Coast Guard beach patrol (U.S. Coast Guard).

Four. The Coast Guard

Secure beach areas utilized armed patrols only at night, as it was thought that saboteurs would only land in the dark of the moon. So areas of potential saboteur landing sites were monitored around the clock by beach patrols.

The Chesapeake Bay Coast Guard added K-9 dogs to the beach patrol, once trained dogs became available. By September of 1942, horses were added. In Virginia, both dogs and horses were trained at the Front Royal Quartermaster Depot, Virginia. One year after the order was issued, there were approximately 2,000 dogs and 3,200 horses assigned to the U.S. Coast Guard throughout the United States. In the dark of night, these dogs and horses were quiet, unlike motorized beach patrols. The mounted patrols did not patrol the more congested areas, such as New England and New York. Instead, the mounted patrols were utilized to cover the long stretches of isolated beaches like those in Virginia and North Carolina. Very quickly uniformed men made their appearance on the desolate beaches, replacing the many civilian volunteers.

In mid–1942, with a lack of resources, the Coast Guard realized the valuable addition of trained dogs in patrolling the coastal beaches. Their keen sense of smell would enhance the beach patrols and hopefully reduce the number of men required to patrol. A 50-to–70 pound, alert, snarling dog, baring its full set of teeth, could be more intimidating than an armed sailor with a rifle or pistol.

Jack Teagardten, Seaman 1st Class, a native of Norfolk, Virginia, volunteered for the "canine beach patrol" because it sounded exciting. He was accepted and sent to Hilton Head, South Carolina, for dog handling training.

Jack was introduced to a two-year-old, 55-pound German shepherd named Butch. They hit it off immediately and set to train each other.

Returning to Hampton Roads, the two were assigned a stretch of beach near Dam Neck, Virginia. Dog patrols were usually conducted at night and covered a distance of a mile of open beach. Teagardten relates an episode from one night's patrol:

> We had been walking silently when Butch bristled and stood still. I looked about but in the darkness could see little to nothing. Taking a hint from Butch, I moved down to the edge of the water and there found a body, in an oil-covered life jacket, washing back and forth in the tidal area.
>
> Finding the body would be our only excitement for the next two years. Within the year, the canine beach patrols were eliminated and I was ordered to a patrol craft in England, getting ready for the invasion of France. To this day, I think of Butch and our time together, silently walking the Virginia outer beaches, wondering what I would do if I encountered an enemy agent.[5]

When the Life Saving Service was officially established 3 March 1847, a number of "stations" were constructed close to beaches that were known to have many shipwrecks. These stations generally consisted of a small house to provide shelter for a permanent life-saving crew. Often a family lived in the same house. One or more large shacks were constructed to house the lifeboat from the elements. These stations were often positioned at three- to seven-mile intervals and eventually numbered some 150 along the east coast.

With the outbreak of war and the transfer of the Life Saving Service to the U.S.

U.S. Coast Guard beach patrol station (U.S. Coast Guard).

Coast Guard, these stations quickly became Coastal Patrol Stations. In Virginia, such stations were located at Cape Charles, Smith Island, Wash Woods, Sand Shoal Inlet, Chincoteague, Cobb Island, Pope's Island, Little Creek, Little Island, Milford Haven (Mathews), Parramore Island, Virginia Beach, Assateague and five other stations, from Dam Neck south along the coast to Ocracoke Island.

Using these old life-saving stations provided a facility already in place for the beach patrols to operate from either on foot, with K-9 escort, and/or on horseback. When the German U-boats began sinking offshore shipping, these patrols spotted and reported locations of wreckage and survivors. Because of their presence, many survivors were rescued and lives saved.

The damage to the merchant fleet was so intense it was not uncommon to walk the beaches and find remnants of wrecks littering the beaches. Residents, alerted by the sudden flash of light from distant explosions, would gather at the beach and watch the ships burn. More often than not bodies were found tangled in the flotsam and debris washed onto the beaches.

During the first days of the war, the merchant fleet averaged losing two ships each day to the German U-boats. Beginning January 1942 to June nearly 400 ships were sunk between Florida and New York. The coastline became known as the graveyard of the Atlantic.

When the war started, the American public was fearful of secret night landings

U.S. Coast Guard beach observation tower (U.S. Coast Guard).

of enemy agents along the eastern coast. The dedicated, constant presence of the U.S. Coast Guard Coastal Patrol reassured the public that they were protected by vigilant coastal patrols.[6]

Coast Guard officers were sent to U.S. Navy training schools such as diesel engine, electrician's, yeomen, storekeeper, quartermaster and basic engineering. It was convenient, as these schools were all located in the Hampton Roads area. Many attended the U.S. Army submarine warfare school at Fort Story, or manned the harbor entrance control post (at Fort Story), or the weather reporting stations located throughout the Hampton Roads, the inshore patrol at Little Creek and the nearby naval frontier base at Norfolk. The traditional Captain of the Port and the U.S. Coast Guard District Offices were established at NOB Norfolk.

The Women's Reserve Act of 1942 authorized the organization of SPARS (taken from the Coast Guard motto, Semper Paratus, Latin for "Always Ready"). Women who were accepted for Coast Guard service were sent to the Palm Beach Coast Guard Training Camp in Florida. Upon completion of their training, most were sent to schools for further training in a specific skill, such as typing, stenography, or weather observation, or as drivers, aviation mechanics, storekeepers, lookouts or telephone operators.

Male graduates of these schools served on various ships, from navy destroyers to cargo ships sailing in the dangerous waters of the North Atlantic.

In addition to patrolling the beaches and offshore coastal waters, the Coast Guard manned and maintained 30 destroyer escorts used primarily for convoy escort duty in the North Atlantic. This action helped relieve the U.S. Navy of giving up badly needed crew members. Many of the small landing craft, such as the Higgins boat (LCVP) utilized in amphibious landings in the Pacific, North Africa, Italy and the landing at Normandy, were manned by Coast Guard coxswains.

The Coast Guard not only patrolled the beaches and searched for enemy agents, but they admirably rescued many survivors of burning, sinking ships. The Coast Guard proudly assured the American public that American shores were kept free from an enemy bent on destroying freedom.[7]

CHAPTER FIVE

The Submarine War

After the Japanese attack on Pearl Harbor, 7 December 1941, Hitler surprisingly declared war on the United States. All restrictions previously placed on German U-boat activity were immediately removed. Admiral Dönitz drew up plans to have U-boats strike the rich, mostly unprotected shipping lanes along the east coast of the United States, especially the Chesapeake Bay region.

The plan was complicated, requiring the placement offshore of U-boats located at strategic ports such as New York and the Chesapeake Bay, Virginia. The admiral decided to cut the lifeline of goods to England, thus bringing that nation to its knees and forcing it to sue for peace.

Five U-boats—U-123, U-66, U-130, U-125 and U-109—were assigned to sail for the east coast of America, beginning 18 December 1941. This was the beginning of Operation Drumbeat (Paukenschlag).

When a U-boat was traveling on the surface in fair running seas, it could average a speed of ten knots. At that speed, a voyage to their stations off America from France would take three weeks. Orders forbade them from attacking any vessels along the way. In order to succeed, they needed the element of surprise.

These five U-boats were the Type IX. These modern submarines carried a crew of forty-eight men, fifteen torpedoes and an impressive array of surface armaments. Contrary to popular belief, submarines did most damage with their deck guns, accounting for a large number of ships sunk.

With all five boats in position, on 13 January 1942 they set about openly attacking shipping from Cape Cod, Massachusetts, south to Cape Hatteras, North Carolina, and into the Gulf of Mexico. Within a short period of time, ships began exploding along the coast of the United States from the oil-rich Gulf of Mexico to New York City.

By the end of February, 145 ships were known to have been sunk off the east coast without losing a single U-boat. They managed to sink 150 ships during the month of March alone. The successful German captains and their crews were sinking a ship about every eight hours, most within sight of land.[1]

It was not surprising that the United States Navy was unprepared to defend against the onslaught. Everything required for an adequate anti-submarine defense was woefully lacking, from search aircraft, blimps and patrol craft to men. There were no fast fleet destroyers (DD) or destroyer escorts (DE) to render effective anti-submarine warfare defense. The speedy destroyers had been removed and hurriedly assigned to the Pacific in late December of 1940. Small craft such as cutters and Navy patrol craft (PC)

Depth charging German U-boat off Virginia coast (U.S.N.).

of 110 to 165 feet were pressed into service. Small craft such as these were no match for a German submarine sitting on the surface, armed with deadly accurate deck guns.

It was not long before bodies, enormous oil slicks, life jackets, rafts and other flotsam washed ashore. Beachgoers from the Jersey capes south to Florida often watched as U-boats brazenly attacked ships in broad daylight. Despite the war and the attempt to enforce wartime conditions on the public in general, the public tended to ignore these demands and view the disasters as a sideshow to their day at the beach. Many individuals combed the beaches looking for flotsam and jetsam. Among the so-called "pickings" they found containers of fresh tropical fruit, cans of food and often one or more life-jacketed bodies.

Knowing the U-boats were using the shore and harbor lights to silhouette the ships, the military asked inhabitants to douse their lights at night. Lighthouses and lighted harbor buoys clearly marked the channels and entrances to every harbor along the coast. Several U-boats would simply follow a merchant vessel into port, completely undetected. Kapitanleutnant Reinhard Hardegen took the U-123 close enough to New York harbor to view the lights of the harbor.

Five. The Submarine War

In March 1942, Virginia's Governor Colgate Darden requested the elimination of all illuminated signs on piers, street and highway lights, and any visible light along the coast. Blackout curtains were slowly and grudgingly installed in homes, hotels and restaurants. The U.S. Navy ordered a ban on all night lights, including automobile headlights.

Fearing for their tourist business, shore resort towns and cities refused at first, but as the threat grew, so did the fear of enemy agents landing on the beaches, so the businesses complied.

The first statewide blackout occurred on 19 June 1942, but it would be one of few. Sporadic blackouts, as determined by each community, were followed until the frustrated U.S. Navy soon demanded lights along the shorelines be extinguished every night, depriving the U-boats of a target silhouette. Some noted individuals demanded the guiding light of lighthouses be extinguished as the submariners were using them as navigational aids.

Protecting Chesapeake Bay and Hampton Roads were large, coastal 16-inch guns and other large-caliber guns, which were located at Fort Custis on Cape Charles, Fort Story, Fort Monroe, Fort Wool and Camp Pendleton. These were considered ample enough to protect Hampton Roads against enemy ships, but were discovered to be useless against the U-boat.

To repel enemy ships and adventurous enemy submarines from entering the Chesapeake Bay—the "Atlantic Gibraltar," as it was known because of its fortifications—the Army put in place a considerable mine field consisting of 365 contact mines.

Since they were unmarked on the surface, it was feared that ships who did not have updated charts would wander into them and explode. Some did, causing considerable distress for nearby residents.

To deter the enemy submarines, a net was put in place between Fort Monroe and Fort Wool to Willoughby Spit. For fear that a high-speed motor torpedo boat attack might attempt an assault on the Yorktown munitions facility, an anti-torpedo net was placed across the York River. A large minefield was also placed offshore around Thimble Shoals and many antiaircraft guns were added on land.

Despite the 16-mile distance from Cape Henry to Cape Charles, twenty-two groups of mines were also planted in the main ship channel off Cape Henry. Two lines of contact mines were put in place near the lighthouse at Thimble Point. Any ships entering or departing Hampton Roads were escorted by patrol craft, thus making it difficult for submarines to make a surface attack, especially during daylight hours. Despite the tight security measures, there were constant reports by nervous citizens claiming to have sighted German submarines boldly running on the surface just off some beach area in broad daylight.

To ensure success, the German submarine captains adopted the technique of lying on the bottom near a large port, such as Chesapeake Bay, and waiting for the ships to come out or enter at night. Without naval escorts, the cargo and tanker ships were sitting ducks for the U-boats once they cleared the nets.

Gasoline was the natural resource that drove the machinery of war. Thus, U-boat captains sought the slow-moving, heavily laden tankers as they moved from the oil-rich ports of the Gulf of Mexico and South America to the New York and New Jersey refineries. Slow-moving and cumbersome, the tanker was an easy target and dangerously explosive. U-boat captains realized they could sink a tanker with just two instead of the usual four torpedoes required to sink a standard cargo ship.

It was not long before the loss of crude oil took its toll on oil supplies. Within months, gasoline prices went up to ten cents a gallon and rationing was placed into effect, limiting each family to five gallons per week.[2]

On 18 January 1942, U-boat Captain Richard Zapp brought the U-66 into position off the Virginia coast. The tanker *Allan Jackson,* which was carrying fuel oil, was en route from Cartegena, Colombia, to New York. The U-66 fired a single torpedo, ripping a large hole in the starboard side. Before the crew could take evasive action, a second torpedo exploded near the first. On shore, the night's revelers watched in horror, unable to completely comprehend how a German U-boat could be so close to shore and sink a tanker without being detected beforehand. The *Allan Jackson* exploded in a ball of fire and broke in two, spreading flaming oil over the surface of the water. Eleven crewmen managed to escape, to be picked up later by the USS *Roe* (DD-418). The killing had begun. This was the first of 145 ships to be attacked and sunk by the middle of February 1942.

The sea lanes off the East Coast were filled with vessels heading north, off the Virginia coasts, carrying fuel and cargoes needed for the war effort in England. The German U-boat captains would find the pickings rich, indeed.

One of the victims would be the unarmed and unescorted *W.L. Steed,* a Standard Oil tanker hauling 66,000 barrels of crude oil, heading north along the coast toward New York. Encountering rough weather off the Virginia coast, the ship's master, Harold McAvenia, decreased the tanker's forward speed to almost a crawl.

Early one morning, approximately 90 miles off the coast of Ocean City, Maryland, one of the German U-boats attacked. Three torpedoes struck the tanker just forward of the bridge, igniting the cargo of light fuel oil. Prepared for the event, all 38 crewmen were able to abandon ship in lifeboats.

The U-103 surfaced and, utilizing just its single deck gun, commenced to shell the burning tanker, firing about seventeen shells until the ship finally sank. After burning for some time, the tanker finally sank. When rescued, several of the crew were barely alive in the lifeboats. Several men froze to death due to the severe cold. With the sinking of the tanker, "Operation Drumbeat" was in full force.

During the first six months of the war, the German U-boats managed to sink some 397 ships totaling 2 million tons, taking 5,000 lives, with the loss of only 7 U-boats. It appeared the U-boats would destroy the Allied merchant fleet plying the Atlantic waters off the United States coast, thus denying Great Britain valuable war supplies.

When the United States Navy finally decided to adopt the British Royal Navy's convoy system, Chesapeake Bay was utilized as a form-up site. Hampton Roads became inhabited with ships of all types, with nations arriving from Mexico, Venezuela and ports in the Caribbean to be formed into a convoy. German U-boats waited until the convoy cleared the minefields at the mouth of the Chesapeake Bay and either used torpedoes or deck guns to sink several ships, especially the tankers.

Five. The Submarine War

While on the prowl one night, the U-130 caught the *Frances E. Powell,* a 7,800-ton Atlantic Refining tanker near the mouth of the Chesapeake Bay, and torpedoed her. En route from Port Arthur, Texas, to Providence, Rhode Island, she carried a cargo of gasoline, light fuel oil and a crew of 32 men. The torpedo struck just aft of the bridge, breaking the ship's back and causing it to dangerously break up amidship.

Ten survivors managed to make it into lifeboats. The *Powell* burned throughout the night, finally sinking around 7 o'clock in the morning. The CAP (Civil Air Patrol) arrived, spotted the sinking tanker and notified rescue personnel of the survivors. After the Coast Guard Patrol Craft rescued the survivors, it is reported that the German U-boat chased them, but the Coast Guard boat managed to outrun them. The survivors were taken to Assateague Island on the eastern shore of Virginia.[3]

In the early hours of 31 March 1942, the unarmed seagoing tug *Menominee* was towing three barges loaded with coal and lumber, bound for Stanford, Connecticut. She was attacked by the U-754, half a mile east-southeast of Metopkin Inlet, Virginia, near the entrance to the Chesapeake Bay. Unable to utilize torpedoes due to the shallow draft of the barges, the U-boat remained on the surface and fired three rounds from its deck gun at the tugboat. The tug quickly cut its tow ropes and attempted to escape. The submarine fired 2 or 3 rounds into each barge, then gave chase to the fleeing tug. They hit the vessel with four rounds and managed to finally sink it. Survivors were rescued by the Coast Guard motor lifeboat from the Metopkin Lifeboat Station.[4]

The German submarine U-85, running on the surface in shallow water just off the North Carolina coast close by the Bodie Island lighthouse, patiently waited for unsuspecting targets. Just after midnight, 13 April 1942, the refitted World War I destroyer, USS *Roper* (DD147) detected its presence as a weak radar target. Once the *Roper* started to investigate the contact, U-85 quickly headed toward deeper water.

The following is taken from an after-action report provided by the U.S. Navy, filed by the USS *Roper* Destroyer Division 54, Norfolk, Virginia:

> *During the night of 13 April 1942, the USS Roper of DES DIV. 54, out of Norfolk, Virginia, on anti-submarine patrol, made contact with U-85. Near Brodie Island, the Roper made radar contact with an unknown object. The sounding (Sonar) operator shortly picked up rapidly turning propellers. When in range of 700 yards the track of a torpedo passed close aboard the port side. Using #24 search-light a submarine was identified. With the light illuminating the submarine, the Roper utilized its machine guns to cut the sub's crew from manning their deck gun. Using the ship's 3 inch gun, a direct hit was made on the conning tower, near the waterline and the sub began to sink. About forty of her crew appeared on deck, as she sank. Because the U-boats are known to work in pairs, rescue before daylight was too risky.*
>
> *A PBY plane arrived assisting in the search for a second U-boat. Oil slicks and debris were carefully investigated.*
>
> *At 0717 hours the Roper placed two whaleboats in the water to search for survivors and floating bodies. At 0727 an airship approached and was asked to circle the ship and keep a lookout for any U-Boats.*
>
> *In all, twenty bodies were recovered.*

End of report.

U-85 was the first German submarine to be sunk by a U.S. warship during World War

II in American waters. The entire crew went down with the submarine, there being no survivors; 29 dead German sailors were finally recovered from the debris-laden waters by search teams. They were searched for important military items, then buried at the Hampton National Cemetery, Hampton, Virginia, with full military honors. Fifty-two German sailors detained at the Fort Monroe POW facility dug the graves. Each gravesite has a marble headstone engraved with the sailor's name. The dead remain at rest in the same site.

On 7 May 1942, a patrolling aircraft spotted a German submarine running on the surface, just off Cape Hatteras. The patrolling aircraft dropped four aerial depth-charges. Unfortunately, the U-boat quickly submerged and managed to escape.

On 9 May 1942, the U-352, running on the surface, spotted a freighter and fired two torpedoes. Apparently, both failed to explode or hit their target. Unfortunately for the submarine, the ship turned out to be the Coast Guard cutter *Icarus*. It quickly made the turn and fired 5 depth charges on its initial attack run, several of which damaged the submarine's conning tower and the deck gun.

Two more runs dropping depth charges forced the submarine to the surface. The U-boat commander, Kapitanleutnant Helmut Rathke, ordered the crew to scuttle and abandon the sub. Seventeen crew were killed and 33 taken aboard the USCG *Icarus*, thence to Charleston, South Carolina, as prisoners of war.[5]

Newspaper editors throughout Virginia, Maryland and North Carolina raged against the seeming freedom enjoyed offshore by the German submarines. They demanded action other than small craft and the occasional snit-submarine aircraft patrol. The Navy's answer was the slow-moving blimp. The lighter-than-aircraft was the most effective means of detecting submarines in shallow, offshore waters. Once the suspected submarine had been detected, the blimp could remain on station for hours until available anti-submarine ships or aircraft arrived.

When they're underwater, submarines generally travel slower than surface ships, so they would usually approach ships on the surface. Blimps proved to be relatively much faster than submarines, with speeds up to 80 mph. They generally carried a number of deadly depth charges as well as iron bombs, though very few German subs were sunk by blimps during the war along the east coast.

Records indicate only one blimp, K-74, was ever shot down by enemy submarine gunfire. On 18 July 1942, while making a bomb run on the U134 south of Miami, Florida, K-74 was hit by small-arms machine gun and rifle fire and slowly deflated. Seeing its chance to escape, the sub moved off, leaving the deflating blimp to settle on the water.

The United States Navy utilized some 200 lighter-than-aircraft during the war to protect coastal areas and in anti-submarine duties. Blimps patrolling the North Carolina and Virginia coast lines were stationed out of Elizabeth City, North Carolina.[6]

The Saboteurs

Throughout the country, warnings of enemy ears listening in the U.S.—the work of enemy spies—filled the newspapers, magazines and radio news. "Loose lips sinks

Five. The Submarine War

ships. Be alert for Enemy Spies or Report All Suspicious Activity," may have given the illusion spies were everywhere. That wasn't actually the case, but it was made to appear so by the media.

Cameras were quickly banned from any military reservations, wartime industrial plants, and near movements of troops for fear the enemy were taking pictures of our secrets. Workers at the Newport Shipyard were constantly checked for cameras. If one was found it was quickly confiscated and the owner had to appear before a board of inquiry to explain why he had it in his possession. Any individual found lurking near a railroad observing train movements would be arrested and held until the FBI could interview and clear him.

Local authorities responded by providing extra police, Civil Defense air raid wardens, aircraft spotters, more beach patrols and manned highway checkpoints. The actual danger didn't justify the early wartime level of hysteria, but there was a basis for concern. The lack of reliable information was replaced with rumors. Through the Newport News and Hampton Roads areas, German U-boat sightings were common and saboteurs were seen lurking near all military installations. The area police departments received calls daily, especially in the evening hours from citizens claiming to see German saboteurs going into the movie theaters, local bars and grocery stores.

Especially vulnerable were the deserted, wide-open beaches and their miles of sandy dunes. The fear of German submarines delivering small teams of agents at any point on the many deserted beaches stressed the local nearby communities. Several local organizations, such as chapters of the Veterans of Foreign Wars and the American Legion, utilized their membership of former World War I military veterans to form groups that were tasked with patrolling the open beaches at night. Under the control of the local county sheriff's department, men were assigned duties of patrolling on foot upwards to a mile of empty beach armed usually with a shotgun or handgun.

The local civilian beach patrols were quickly tied into the growing Aircraft Warning Service. Norfolk, with its large war room and plot map, was the center for the Commonwealth's Aircraft Warning Service and coordinated all information from the fifteen spotters' posts, which was then relayed to the beach patrols and the various military branches.

Combining the 750-plus Aircraft Warning Service civilian staff and the 2,000-plus beach patrol volunteers, the skies and beaches surrounding the Norfolk area were constantly under observation for enemy agents or aircraft. These civilian beach patrols were quickly replaced when the Coast Guard was tasked with protection of the coastal areas, though it should be said that not one German spy was apprehended making his way ashore.

On 13 June 1942, a few minutes after midnight, the German submarine U-202 surfaced in the shallow waters off the coast of Amagansett, Long Island, New York. Four men dressed in German Marine fatigues, with four crates and a sea bag in a rubber boat, landed on a deserted beach. They were discovered by an alert Coast Guard beach patrol.

A short while later, on 17 June 1942, U-boat 584 surfaced off the coast of Florida, south of Jacksonville. Once again, a rubber boat was lowered carrying four men dressed in swim trunks, along with their gear, who headed for a deserted stretch of beach. On 24 June 1942, seven days after stepping foot on the beach, all were in FBI custody.[7]

With heightened awareness of German submarines lurking in the offshore waters, all former Coastal Life Saving Stations were converted and manned as Coastal Lookout Stations, headquarters for beach patrol units. Especially watchful were the former Life Saving Stations of Parramore Island, the barrier island of the eastern shore, Virginia Beach, Assateague Island, and stations from Dam Neck south along the coast to Seatack, North Carolina.

There was good reason to stay alert and watchful. During 1942, German U-boats regularly and sometimes successfully laid their own mines at the entrance to Chesapeake Bay.

Mining the entrance to the vast Chesapeake Bay became a priority for the German Navy. Early in 1942, several attempts by U-boats were successful, resulting in the sinking of several unsuspecting Allied cargo ships.

These German U-boats utilized seven-and-a-half-foot bottom mines, each of which carried a 1,275-pound explosive charge and was easily launched through the torpedo tubes. Once in place, these magnetic ground and acoustic mines lay on the bottom on the bay, waiting for a victim.

During the night of 11 June 1942, U-701 laid 15 TMBs (Torpedo Mine Bottom) in the narrow 16-mile-wide approach to Chesapeake Bay. The TMBs, unlike the standard round mine with contact prongs, were launched through the torpedo tubes, traveled through the water for a distance, then settled on the bottom and waited.

Late the next day, convoy KN-109, which included several tankers, proceeded north from Key West toward Hampton Roads. Early in the morning, the convoy ran into the German minefield. The tanker *Robert C. Tuttle* struck one of the mines. Minutes later, the tanker *ESSO Augusta* struck another one. The destroyer escort, USS *Bainbridge* (DD246), while searching for a submarine, struck a mine but managed to remain afloat and make it into Norfolk for repairs.

The U-230, with Captain Paul Siegmann, entered the Chesapeake Bay during the night of 27 July 1943, fours mile off Cape Charles, without encountering a single patrol vessel. Running on the surface, the U-boat was able to clearly see the lights of Virginia Beach. Fearing they would be attacked by several of the cargo ships, Captain Siegmann ordered the U-230 out to sea where they lay on the bottom until the next night.

Re-entering the bay on 28 July 1943 at 2145, the U-boat cautiously made its way on the surface into Chesapeake Bay and headed in the direction of Norfolk. At 0200 hours, U-230 slowed to a stop and for the next two hours deposited twenty-four mines on the bottom of Chesapeake Bay. Once the mines were in place, the U-230 calmly returned through the narrow passed of the bay and out to sea, without ever being detected. Despite rumors, hearsay and perhaps legend, this is the furthest any German U-boat penetrated Chesapeake Bay.[8]

Fearing the Atlantic supply line would be cut off due to high losses of merchantmen suffered along the east coast during the first two months of 1942, the British Admi-

Five. The Submarine War

ralty sent twenty-four armed trawlers to help out with the situation. Commercial fishing trawlers were coal burners, weighing on average 900 tons; they were rugged seagoing fishing boats that were utilized by the Royal Navy to hunt submarines and convoy ships at sea. Armed with one or more deck guns, ranging from 3-inch to 5 inches, the trawler was a very effective anti-submarine vessel.

Six armed trawlers were assigned to the Norfolk area to assist in anti-submarine detection and patrol. The first of these six trawlers to be sunk, on 11 April 1942, was the HMT *St. Catham*. After colliding with the freighter *Hebe*, it sank in the Little River in South Carolina.

Next, on 6 May 1942, the French converted trawler, the HMT *Senateur Duhamel*, was rammed by a U.S. destroyer near Moorehead City, North Carolina, and sunk. The U.S. Navy reported the destroyer had assumed the trawler was a U-boat on the surface.

On 10 May 1942, while operating out of Moorehead City, the HMT *Bedfordshire* and the HMT *St. Loman* were ordered out to sea in search of a reported U-boat. Operating together, the two ships were identified by the U-558. The submarine fired two torpedoes at the HMT *St. Loman*, but missed. The hunt was on! The search continued into the dark of night.

Early on the morning of 11 May 1942, U-558 caught the HMT *Bedfordshire* on the surface off Cape Lookout and fired a single torpedo, but it missed. Before the trawler could respond, a second torpedo scored a direct hit. She sank immediately in the Hatteras anchorage, taking 37 crewmen with her.

Later on 14 May 1942, four bodies washed ashore on Ocracoke Island. When additional bodies continued to wash ashore, they were gathered up by local inhabitants. After the sailors had been identified, their remains were buried with full honors in a small plot in the local cemetery of Ocracoke Village. In remembrance of their service, a British flag was flown over the small cemetery plot.

The small plot of land was later deeded to the British government and a British flag flies at all times over the grave site. The United States Coast Guard maintains the gravesite. A second British cemetery is located in Buxton, North Carolina. Two sailors from the British merchant ship *San Delfino* are buried at the site.

While operating off Cape Henry on 15 June 1942, at the entrance to the Chesapeake Bay, the British anti-submarine trawler, the HMT *Kingston Ceylonite* (FY-214), struck a mine laid by U-701 and sank within two minutes, taking 18 of her crew with her.

After minesweeping operations had located and detonated mine after mine, the port was placed back in operation. However, on the afternoon of 17 June 1942, Convoy KS-511 was forming up when the collier (coal ship) *Santore* struck a mine and sank.

The German submarine had successfully planted mines in the vicinity of Buoy 2CB. In the span of 48 deadly hours, this small minefield caused the disruption of all shipping in the Hampton Roads area, as well as sinking three vessels and severely damaging a fourth.

On 12 June 1942, the U-701 was running at periscope depth, heading south, away from the Chesapeake Bay, along the North Carolina coast when she was spotted by a patrol aircraft. A B-17 commanded by 1st Lieutenant Arthur H. Tuttle, U.S. Army Air Corps, 2nd Bomb Group out of Langley Field, Virginia, spotted a periscope wake, made a bomb run, and dropped six 325-pound depth charges. Two of the hits produced an oil slick on the surface. They continued to circle but never saw a submarine surface, so they stayed, observing the site until 1420 hours, when the attack was finally broken off.

On 7 July 1942, while flying at 1500 feet, an A-29, commanded by Lt. Kane, 396th Bomb Squadron, 2nd Bomb Group, out of Langley Field, Virginia, sighted the U-701 running on the surface. An attack from 50 feet altitude was made, and three MK17 depth charges were dropped. The third charge struck just forward of the conning tower just as the submarine was submerging. About 15 minutes after the explosions, large quantities of air bubbles and oil appeared. About 30 men of the U-boat crew came to the surface.

At this time, a U.S. Navy blimp appeared and assisted with the rescue. They were able to locate and rescue just 5 crew members. A life raft, food, water and blankets were dropped at the site. The crew of the blimp reported a detailed search of 15 miles, locating only 5 dead bodies in life jackets, with many empty life jackets and large sharks swimming in the same area.[9]

Despite the alarming German submarine losses, the attacks continued. The following is taken from the Official Report, Naval Intelligence, Third Naval District, New York City, New York:

> On 2 June 1943, Convoy NG-365, composed of 14 ships, was on a course 181 degrees, making 8 knots at 37–43 North Latitude, 73–16 West longitude when the USS Fury, PC 565 (Patrol Craft) made an underwater contact, 1600 yards off the port bow. Realizing this was a German submarine, the Fury commenced an attack, dropping five depth charges.
>
> Turning to another attack, the submarine partially surfaced its conning tower awash. When the range was about 400 yards, the submarine was seen to sink rapidly. A single survivor was rescued, Kapitanleutnant Klaus Bargsten. Like so many rescued German submariners he was hauled aboard, treated with kindness and eventually shipped to the POW reception depot, Hampton Roads, Virginia.

With the establishment of training bases along the Virginia Tidewater and the increasing numbers of U.S. Navy PCs (Patrol Craft) by early 1943, the presence of German U-boats along the east coast became too difficult and costly for German Admiral Karl Doenitz to maintain. Military air patrols in large numbers took charge of the Virginia offshore waters, effectively putting the submarine threat to an end.

The U-505 Incident

Using deciphered German submarine messages, Naval Intelligence knew that U-boats were operating in the Cape Verde area some 300-plus miles off the West African coast. They decided to send a small task force on a search-destroy mission. Task Force 22.3 consisted of the small escort carrier USS *Guadalcanal* (CVE-60) and five destroyer escorts.

Five. The Submarine War

The task force sailed from Norfolk, Virginia, in mid–May and arrived on station to search for German U-boats. At 1100 hours on 4 June 1944, off the coast of Rio de Oro, contact was made off the USS *Chatelain*'s (DE-149) bow. Firing anti-submarine Hedgehogs, she passed over the sub and made a turn to fire depth charges.

Less than ten minutes after the depth charge attack, the damaged U-505 surfaced less than 700 yards away. Two nearby aircraft and other ships immediately commenced firing with smaller weapons.

Oblt. Lange, believing the U-505 was too badly damaged to be saved, ordered his crew to abandon ship. The engines still functioned but with a damaged rudder, the sub barely remained afloat and circled in a clockwise direction.

The USS *Pillsbury* (DE-133) sent an eight-man boarding party to the sub to secure valuable charts and code books, close scuttle valves, and disarm any activated demolition charges.

Unable to bring the sub in tow, the *Guadalcanal* attached a line and proceeded to tow the sinking submarine. Finally, after pumping out all of the water, the salvage crew was able to bring her to full trim.

Three days later, 19 June 1944, the sub was transferred to the seagoing tug *Abnaki* (ATF-960) and towed to Port Royal, Bermuda. This was the first time a U.S. Navy ship had captured an enemy vessel since 1812.[10]

The U-505 was maintained at Bermuda and intensively studied by the U.S. Navy Intelligence. The intelligence treasure included code books, signal books, weather data and a code device called the Enigma machine. The Enigma machine was studied, then turned over to British Naval Intelligence. When the intelligence and Navy engineer personnel were content they had gleaned all they could, the sub was towed to Norfolk, Virginia, and maintained at a dock in the Portsmouth Navy Yard. Plans called for the U-boat to be used as target practice until she sank.

After sitting at the dock and decaying for ten years, in September of 1954, the U-505 was donated to the Museum of Science and Industry in Chicago by the federal government, where she rests today. The making of the movie *Das Boot* required a German U-boat, and the U-505 briefly recaptured her old image and glory of the lone hunter at sea and the miserable life sailors spent on these "underwater coffins."[11]

Chapter Six

The Home Front

When World War II began in Europe in 1939, the industrial might of the United States quickly played a vital role in providing armaments, military equipment and food supplies. A country slowly emerging from a grinding, depressed economy, this employment of vast numbers of people quickly brought the Great Depression to a halt. Government statistics set the unemployment rate for 1939 at 17 percent, whereas the rate fell to 4.7 percent during 1942. The lowest percentage occurred in 1944, when industrial war production was at its highest.

The Depression is often romanticized, but the war that followed was not a romantic time for those who had to live through it. For many it was a time of greater financial opportunity. With the war raging in Europe, China, Manchuria and Japan, most saw it as "their war and not ours." Who wanted to go to war when the opportunity to make money was at hand?

Ten million men were either drafted or enlisted in the Armed Forces, producing a shortage of labor across the country. Many farms closed as well as small businesses and other services. "Closed for the duration" signs were placed in many store windows throughout the country.

In Virginia, the military, which was already a presence, took over the Commonwealth nearly overnight, from Norfolk west to Radford and north to Arlington. A mass exodus from the rural areas brought an overflow of workers seeking employment to all military installations.

Within months, manufacturing companies, large and small, stopped making civilian products and launched into full-scale production of military supplies. Companies that were producing automobiles, bicycles, frying pans, toasters, washing machines, and electric motors suddenly found themselves shifting production to making guns, tanks, bombs or parts for military weapons.

The sudden influx in the Hampton Roads area created severe traffic jams, overcrowding, and a dramatic increase in the crime rate. Also, there was a considerable lack of suitable housing, public schools and transportation were overcrowded, and medical services overtaxed.

Along with the influx of people—which inevitably brought in more bars, tougher red-light districts, and a basic increase in crime—the near-lawless Norfolk area required Commonwealth intervention. Hampton Roads was not alone in managing the increase of outsiders. Anywhere the military decided to construct a facility, urban or rural, the population doubled, producing problems associated with uncontrolled growth.

Six. The Home Front

In response to the sudden rise in crime and the threat of enemy saboteurs, Governor James H. Price of Virginia, realizing the federal government would nationalize the Virginia National Guard, which would leave the Commonwealth without a protective force, established the Virginia Protective Force on 1 January 1941. The all-volunteer Virginia Protective Force was renamed the Virginia State Guard and charged with the maintenance of public order, protection and security of public buildings, warehouses, important bridges, industrial sites and railroad facilities. Armed with surplus Lee-Enfield rifles and clothed in blue-gray uniforms, the force assumed in-state missions that would normally have been tasked to the National Guard.

With the end of World War II and the return of the National Guard units, the Commonwealth deactivated the Virginia State Guard in 1947. There were 16,880 men and women volunteers who served from 1941 to 1947.

Transportation became an increasing problem due to gas rationing. The majority of people drove their autos into the garage, put them up on wooden blocks, removed the tires, filled the engine blocks with motor oil, and left them there for the duration of the war. Those who could organized car pools or took whatever public transportation was available. In Norfolk, it was not uncommon to see trolley cars overloaded as they made their way along the city tracks. Pickup stations were always crowded with more passengers than there was street car seating or space to stand. Trains out of Hampton Roads were always crowded and overbooked with military personnel. Servicemen and women were allowed travel priority, leaving little space for civilians, so most people simply gave up distance travel for the duration of the war.

Not everyone accepted the need for increased labor and the problems related to it. The memorable sign, "Dogs and Sailors Keep Off the Grass," was associated with wartime Norfolk, Virginia. With the influx of workers, beer halls, bars and houses of prostitution sprang up downtown, recalling the memories of the western "boom towns." The problem became so great in Norfolk that the chief of police requested the federal government build a concentration-type camp to hold the hundreds of violators (military and civilian) being arrested on a daily basis. The U.S. Navy and Marines expanded the size of the Norfolk brig several times to keep up with the increase.

Eventually the military, industry and labor force adapted to each other's needs and put forth a stupendous effort directed at winning the war.[1]

Propaganda

The need to organize the populace into a cohesive force drove the federal government to the mass media due to their capability to inform, especially using the radio for propaganda purposes. President Roosevelt created the Office of War Information to control and disseminate a unified propaganda effort. The government utilized radio as a medium to keep the citizens informed of the world situation; basically, it was the war as they wanted the people to see it. The real object was to foment hatred of the enemy. To this end, President Roosevelt established his periodic "fireside chats."

The motion picture industry played a critical role in portraying what the American citizen had to do to share the burden of winning the war. Story lines that portrayed America winning the war were presented to the public in hopes it would convince them of the need for their participation. All proposed films had to go through a pre-approval process ensuring compliance with federal restrictions.

Actors and actresses enlisted and served in the Armed Forces while some were stationed in "Fort Hollywood," California, making propaganda "war movies." Famous war movies of the time included *The Flying Leathernecks*, *Casablanca*, *The Fighting Seabees* and *Why We Fight*.

Many actors individually responded by joining the Armed Forces and serving for the duration. Some served before they became famous and used the GI Bill to attend college, then went into acting. Actors such as Tyrone Power, Tony Bennett, Jimmy Stewart, Henry Fonda, Clark Gable, Ernest Borgnine, Neville Brand, Harry Belafonte and Charles Bronson served during the war. Local actor Lin McCarthy, from Norfolk, served for the duration of the war.

Military training films served to instruct recruits in why they fought; how to identify enemy planes, ships, and tanks; proper military etiquette; and do not forget the famous "VD" films.

The need to persuade became a constant bombardment of information aimed at the public. The simple use of posters—inexpensive, ever-present, colorful and easily reproduced and distributed—made them an ideal propaganda agent. They covered almost every aspect of life, and had simple, catchy slogans. Wartime posters usually appealed to patriotism and linked the military front to the changing home front, though they were also subtly and blatantly racist, anti–Japanese and anti–German. Wherever workers and the public in general gathered there would be the ever present poster to remind everyone of spies and the evils of rumors and to encourage folks to finance the war effort by buying war bonds.[2]

War propaganda played a key role in urging the public to participate in scrap drives as a means of securing much-needed resources. The public eagerly saved and recycled such scrap items as used rubber, iron, steel, aluminum, tin, newspapers, magazines, table fats and even madam's silk stockings (for parachutes). Special offers were made by movie theaters. Films were shown at reduced prices for those who contributed iron, tin or aluminum scrap to the appropriate container outside the theater. It was common for a youngster to get into see a war propaganda movie for the price of 10 cents and an old rubber tire. Seventy-five thousand tons of scrap metal, mainly iron, was collected in this way.

Many an antique auto collector today bemoans the World War II scrap drives, as many often rare and expensive classic cars of the 1930s disappeared into the furnaces of recycled iron and steel. Many community zoning inspectors, on the other hand, were pleased, as this cleaned many "junk cars" from the nuisance litter of backyards. Collection centers were arranged and it was not unusual to see one or more junk autos being towed to the site on any given day. Old water heaters, bathtubs, sinks, boxes of old nails, bedsteads, bed springs, frying pans and whatever could be salvaged ended

Six. The Home Front

Typical scrap metal drive (National Archives).

in the collection to be loaded onto a truck or railroad flatcar. It was not uncommon to see Boy or Girl Scouts dragging a large piece of iron from the nearby woods and cheerfully depositing it at the collection site.

With so many ships being sunk by the German U-boats, a drive was launched to collect ripe milkweed pods (Kapok) to be used in filling life jackets. The problem soon became evident that the drive had been launched at the wrong time of the year and they would have to wait until the fall to collect the ripe pods. One report indicates the collection finally went well and storage quickly became a problem.

Girl Scouts, Boy Scouts, school groups and other organized youth groups, in small towns and cities across the nation, conducted paper drives. It was not uncommon for these youngsters to collect enough newspapers and magazines to fill one or more railroad boxcars in a single day. Women were urged to forego wearing nylon or silk stockings so the material could be utilized to manufacture parachutes, heavy equipment strapping, etc.[3]

Making do with what was available quickly became a way of life for everyone. A vegetable dye with a color similar to tanned skin could be purchased at a local drug store to simulate nylon stockings. Some women even drew a line down the back of the leg to provide a "seam."

The Draft

Support for the draft, as a means of rapidly and fairly raising an army, was generally widespread throughout the U.S. The contentious issue of drafting fathers was generally avoided when possible by each draft board. The military was more interested in drafting or enlisting eighteen years-olds, despite a draft age of 21 to 35 years old.

The 1940 Selective Training and Service Act, the first peacetime draft, provided for an annual induction of 900,000 men into the military. Local draft boards were established, comprising men who were local community leaders. Given quotas by the military, the draft boards sought to examine the available male population and determine who was fit to be drafted for service. As a result of the prolonged Depression, not every male was healthy enough for service. Every male of draft age was compelled to sign up and was given a draft card with his draft classification. Once drafted, the individual served one year, but this was extended in 1941 to longer and longer periods.

Shortly after the attack on Pearl Harbor, the act was quickly revised, lowering the draft age to 18. By the end of the war, 45 million men had registered for the draft. Ten million men were inducted into the Armed Forces, comprising 65 percent of the total available manpower in the U.S. By war's end, 16,112,566 men and women had served in the U.S. Armed Forces from 1941 to 1945.

Three hundred thousand men and women from Virginia served in the Armed Forces from 1941 to 1946. Eleven thousand were killed in action (or for other reasons).

With the need for a large work force, it was necessary to defer certain men who were needed for many skilled jobs. Too many trained engineers and skilled mechanics were drafted and served their country as privates in the Army. Among these were farmers who were needed to raise and harvest the necessary crops to feed the public and the Armed Forces (including our war-battered Allies).

Draft classifications were devised and enacted based on the outlines of the World War I draft.

Draft Classifications:

1A: fit for general military service
1B: fit for limited military service
1C: member of the Armed Forces
1D: students fit for general military service (college)
1E: students fit for limited military service (college)
2A: deferred for critical aviation work
3A: deferred due to dependents
4A: already served in the Armed Forces
4B: deferred by law, i.e., draft and other officials

4C: alien
4D: clergy
4E: conscientious objector
4F: physically, mentally or morally unfit for military service

More than 25,000 conscientious objectors throughout the United States proudly served in the Armed Forces in many noncombat capacities. Despite all the fervor and patriotism, there were those who sincerely objected to serving in the war and outright refused to do so. Six thousand of these objectors were investigated, counted and imprisoned for their refusal to serve in any capacity.[4]

Rationing

When World War II started, the nation's economy quickly shifted to a war-production basis. Military production became the priority. The war directly affected the food supply, gasoline consumption and the making of clothing. Early in 1942, the War Production Board issued guidelines restricting the types of clothing materials and styles that could be used for fall and winter clothing. The board issued a long list of restrictions that clothing stores in the Commonwealth of Virginia dutifully posted in their front windows.

The following are but a few examples:

> No lining containing any virgin or reprocessed wool
> No cuffs on coats or jackets
> No hoods or scarves
> Belts of any kind, cloth or leather, could not be wider than 2 inches
> French cuffs or sleeves were prohibited
> Prohibited for men: no second pair of trousers of matching material
> Felt for hats was restricted
> Woolen underwear was restricted to two pairs

To prevent hoarding of available consumer goods and vital resources, the U.S. Office of Price Administration (OPA) was created by an act of Congress. Prices were immediately frozen on practically everything, beginning with coffee, sugar, rubber tires, gasoline, fuel, heating oil, bicycles, silk cloth, shoes, meat, dairy products and canned goods.

Commuters were forced to abandon their automobiles and bicycles when the agency announced the cessation of civilian rubber tire production. "Due to the war time conditions and the military needs there is no spare rubber to produce tires for the public need." All the natural and synthetic rubber stocks were diverted to the military.

Virginia residents were issued ration books, stamps and tokens. The number of ration stamps and tokens a citizen had controlled how much he could by of such goods as sugar, meat, butter, coffee, silk, nylon, fuel oil for stoves, tires, shoes, and many other items the general public might need. Ensuring equal distribution of daily necessities,

Women in line for sugar rationing, Norfolk, Virginia (National Archives).

every person, married or single, rich or poor, received a ration book, including children. To obtain the necessary ration stamps, one had to appear before the local rationing board and receive a classification.

Each ration stamp allowed a purchase of rationed goods, quantity and time designated, guaranteeing a family its fair share of available goods. Each family member or individual was allowed a certain number of points on a weekly basis with an expiration date. There was a stamp for every item that was listed on the rationing list.

Rationing of gasoline and tires depended on one's job and the distance involved. Those issued an "A" sticker received 4 gallons of gas per week. Those individuals with priority jobs and who traveled a distance received more gasoline than others who traveled short distances; they were issued a "B" sticker and allowed 8 gallons of gas per week. When purchasing a few gallons of gasoline, the driver had to present a ration book as well as a gas card. Few individuals complained, as this was a shared sacrifice.

For many the amount was less than their needs, so the family auto was placed in the garage for the duration of the war, the tires taken off, and the engine block filled

Six. The Home Front

Ration book with stamps (courtesy Anne H. Freitus).

with motor oil to prevent rusting as the car was stored off the ground. All forms of auto racing were banned, as well as the usual family Sunday afternoon sightseeing trips.

Needless to say, there were those who took advantage of the situation and sold rationed goods on the black market. Those caught selling on the black market were prosecuted and spent time in jail. Despite the possibility of being caught, the black market thrived and many individuals made extra money to supplement their wages.

The simple luxury of butter soon disappeared, as it was provided to troops overseas and at various bases. A previously little-used substitute was used instead, called oleomargarine. Instead of using animal fats, this margarine was composed of various vegetable fats and oils. To offset its white, lard appearance, a small packet of vegetable food coloring was provided to make it resemble butter. Someone reasonably good at mixing and blending might attain a real butter color, but not the flavor. With the shortage of butter, the longstanding restrictions brought about by the dairy lobby against the sale of margarine were finally relaxed.[5]

Beer, wine and whisky were not rationed, but government controls did not allow much for public consumption. By mid–1944, similar to the days of prohibition, whisky all but disappeared from stores, and it was not sold for public consumption. Most of the whisky production went into creating industrial alcohol for use by industry and the military. The public reaction was to go into production for itself. The main problem was the availability of raw sugar, which was strictly rationed. Purchasing on the black market allowed the moonshiner to remain in business.

When raw cane sugar was not available, a close relative was substituted—sweet sorghum. Grown by most of the nearby farmers as cattle feed, corn sugar—or sorghum molasses, as it was commonly known—was easily substituted. The use of sorghum made it easier for the moonshiner to maintain production of "white lightning," but difficult for the federal agents to check on his source.

Despite the demand of a wartime nation, the drinking of "spirits" did not diminish; instead, the price of a bottle of brand-name whisky rose sharply. A re-emergence of "bathtub" spirits was practiced by those in need of refreshment. Since Colonial days, families had produced and maintained one or more barrels of "hard cider." With available ingredients, wine and beer were added to the family spirits production. Many of the necessary ingredients were harvested from local wild fruits. Despite federal controls, many law-enforcement agencies simply looked the other way.[6]

At the end of 1943, the Office of War Information declared that 131,600,000 copies of War Ration Book #1 had been issued, along with 126,331,000 copies of War Ration Book #2.

Victory Garden

Fresh fruits and vegetables went to the military areas in Virginia as a priority. The solution was to grow your own by planting a "victory garden." With a small patch of land a family could raise a number of vegetables and fruit to can. Putting food aside by drying, canning and prewar freezing was a way of life. During the early stages of the Depression many families already maintained a garden patch beside their homes, the so-called cottage garden, to supplement their food supply. Enlarging the area yielded more food, which could carry them through the cold winter months. So it was not unusual for families to turn over a suitable size garden and enjoy fresh vegetables when they were difficult to locate at the local grocer. If the family was industrious a large garden was worked and the bounty either canned or dried. Because metal for cans, tin, was a priority metal for the war effort, glass canning was most common. Freezers were available, but most folks were prepared for the old-fashioned way of preserving garden vegetables: hot, sterile canning in glass jars.

The Department of Agriculture reported that during 1943 there were approximately 18 million victory gardens across the country. These did not include the gardens maintained by farm families.

To encourage victory gardens and canning, the local county extension agent as well as many communities in Virginia offered courses and either rented or provided stovetop canners. Home Economics teachers provided, through the school, courses in food preservation by canning as well as drying.

Beverly Gordon of Richmond remembers:

Dad was a commissioned officer in the Army and was awaiting shipment overseas. Everyone thought it best if mother and my two sisters went and lived with Gram and Grandpa.

In order to feed everyone, the first thing Gramps did was to have a man with a small tractor come and plow the fenced backyard. The plot was about 50 by 50 feet. Everyone helped to remove the old grass sod and what few stones there were. There was a well located in the back corner and he hooked a small hand-driven water pump to it to water the plot. Gasoline was rationed.

After raking the soil, we planted everything from tomatoes, several varieties of beans, carrots, beets (which I did not eat), egg plant, cabbage, rows of corn, broccoli, turnips and potatoes, both sweet and white. If my failing memory serves me right, almost half the garden was filled with potatoes.

Not only was it wonderful to have fresh vegetables at each meal, but by helping Gram we learned the skill of drying and canning the abundance, especially the corn and tomatoes. We children scoured everywhere looking for glass jars that Gram could use for canning. Once washed, they were sterilized to ensure the food did not become contaminated. The root vegetables Gramps stored in the cellar in a large pile of sand to keep through the winter.

It was my first lesson in caring for older people. My grandparents always saw to it that the two old ladies next door had fresh vegetables on their table. Despite the hardships of the war, it was a good lesson for us girls.[7]

Where possible, neighbors joined together to plow a large plot of land and/or maintained a community garden. In some instances, cities utilized vacant lots and allowed communities to establish large vegetable victory gardens. Everywhere posters were displayed urging the public to do their share and plant a victory garden.

Schools through the Commonwealth of Virginia adopted vacant plots of land and cheerfully turned them into victory gardens. It became a common sight to see a wide range of vegetables growing beside a school. Several schools developed gardens on the roofs of the buildings. Most of the produce was utilize to subsidize the school luncheon program.

Home Economics classes canned that which was not eaten to be used at a later date. It was always a delight to serve canned fruits during the winter. Often the school adopted a social agency feeding those in need.

The Norfolk Victory Garden Committee determined there to be 32,000 gardens planted in just the Norfolk area. It is estimated that the victory gardens increased the local food supply by 40 to 50 percent.

Canning sessions became a social event. Many of the canning containers were not meant for preserving food; therefore, it was not unusual to see various shapes of glass jars sitting on a cupboard shelf filled with delicious foods.

In addition to canned vegetables, many collected fruit growing wild in nearby woods, such as blueberries, blackberries, strawberries, hackberries, wild plums and crab apples. Many a brave soul learned to make elderberry wine and enjoy its flavorsome taste.

War Bonds

Known as debt securities, War Bonds were a means of financing the increasing debt created by the military. Many of President Roosevelt's advisors favored a system of tax increases and enforced savings plans. Secretary of the Treasury Henry Morgenthau, Jr. preferred a voluntary program that sold national defense bonds, a program implemented during World War I.

Three new series of bonds, Series E, F, and G, were introduced, of which the Series E would be sold to individuals as Defense Bonds. War Bonds actually were a loan by the public to the government to help pay for the staggering expense of the war. The first Series E bond was purchased by President Roosevelt.

The massive sale of War Bonds produced the necessary money to finance the war. The public was urged to purchase a $25 bond for just $18. Selling at 75 percent of their value, the bonds were available in denominations from $25 to $10,000. Forty years later (1982–1985) the $25 bond could still be redeemed for its full value.

Even students in school were encouraged to buy War Bonds, 10 cents at a time. Ten-cent stamps were sold in the schools, banks and post offices. The buyer was issued a booklet in which to place the stamps. When the book was full, the purchaser went to the bank or post office and turned it in for a bond.

The War Finance Committee was in charge of selling the various types of defense bonds. After the attack on Pearl Harbor, the term was changed to War Bond and the need to sell more bonds increased dramatically. The War Advertising Council geared up its promotion of buying War Bonds in the name of national defense and preserving the great American way of life. The advertisements began with radio and newspapers, the most common form of communication at the time. The promotion was unique, as it was sponsored by the private sector and the federal government working together to create the advertisements. The public was constantly told it was the ideal way for those on the home front to help finance and be a part of the war effort. Most workers established an automatic payroll deduction to purchase War Bonds.

Hollywood joined the War Bond bandwagon. Movie stars, using every media possible, urged the public to buy war bonds. War Bond Drives were held throughout the country featuring many movie stars such as Kate Smith, Bob Hope, Bing Crosby, Betty Grable, Dorothy Lamour and many other notables too numerous to note here. Kate Smith, famous for her rendition of "God Bless America," was featured in a single 16-hour radio marathon on CBS. Millions responded by buying $40 million worth of War Bonds.

The Girl Scouts of America conducted many a "War Bond Stamp Drive." Each scout donated a single 10-cent stamp. When collected, the total number of stamps were turned in to purchase bonds. Other youth organizations promoted similar types of bond or stamp drives. The U.S. Postal System offered cardboard containers that had slots for 75 quarters, which equaled an $18.75 bond. These could be taken home, filled and redeemed at a local post office.

Scouting organizations would take these coin folders and go door-to-door seeking contributions. These containers were very popular with defense workers in the Hampton Roads area, who saw it as a good investment. When shipyard workers lined up to receive their paychecks, there were the cardboard containers in plain sight on nearby tables and shelves.

Buy War Bonds poster (transferred from original color poster; National Archives).

One famous and well-known War Bond drive that toured the country featured Norman Rockwell's paintings, the Four Freedoms. The response was overwhelming, raising $132 million in just a single year. Many local and national movie theaters held free movie days with the purchase of a bond or a specified number of 10-cent stamps.

To boost morale, the War Department permitted the U.S. Navy at Norfolk to display a Japanese midget submarine captured at Pearl Harbor. A War Bond drive was organized at the same time in downtown Norfolk. Needless to say, many bonds were sold that day.

It has been said that without the bond drives this country might not have been able to support the war. During the course of the war, 85 million Americans purchased $185.7 billion worth of War Bonds.[8]

War Industry

The United States plodded through the Depression with a large surplus of available manpower, staggering unemployment, soup and bread lines, and a severe manpower shortage by 1943. The military utilized large numbers of the unemployed, but it was the constant lack of essential war materials production that was troublesome, and would remain so for the duration of the war.

There was a fear in Congress that the labor unions would take advantage of the situation, raise havoc and strike during the crucial moments of the war. The largest union, the CIO, made the decision to remain supportive of the war and made every effort to support a wartime pledge not to interrupt wartime production with a major strike. Despite complaints by the membership, the union did not break their pledge.

The Mine Workers Union, under the leadership of John L. Lewis—and not affiliated with any major union—threatened numerous smaller strikes. In 1943, Lewis led his miners in a twelve-day strike that nearly crippled the production of coal. President Roosevelt threatened to send in the U.S. Army to work the mines. To that end, a search was begun to locate servicemen who had worked the coal mines and send them in to keep the coal flowing.

Despite the tension, the labor unions received good marks for not striking and dealing with the deep racial problems within their membership. Despite strikes by white workers in Detroit, who protested hiring and promotion of black workers, and a few strikes in the Alabama shipyards, a mass racially motivated transit strike in Philadelphia and a few strikes in steel plants in Baltimore, Maryland, relative calm prevailed in the Hampton Roads. That is not to say racial tension did not exist; rather, it was dealt with by the various industries and local administrators.

Newport News Shipbuilding and Drydock Company was the nation's largest shipbuilding facility, especially used to build the largest ships, such as battleships and carriers. In the early years of the war, the shipyard suffered from a shortage of skilled and unskilled labor. Many men working in the shipyard were of draft age, and with the

Six. The Home Front

African Americans launching a ship at Newport News Shipyard (National Archives).

progression of the war, more and more workers were required. The goal of producing the vast numbers of fighting ships would always lag behind schedule.

The shipyard placed posters everywhere and made frequent announcements on local radio programs asking for workers. "Do your part to win the war, help us get the ships out to our fighting men!"[9]

John Guthrie was one of many eighteen-year-old men who responded to the call. When he registered for the draft, John was classified as 4-F: with one leg shorter than the other, he was quickly disqualified from serving in the Armed Forces. A neighbor, who was an electrician and a supervisor at the shipyard, persuaded him to go to work in the yard and train as an electrician. He recalls: "I laid miles and miles of interior electrical cables throughout the new LSTs [Landing Ship Tank]. It got so I could do it in my sleep, and I suppose there were times, working at night, I did just that!"

John kept an eye on the news of the war in the North Atlantic, paying close attention to ships built by the yard. "It made me proud to see many of the LSTs we put together involved in the D–Day landings in France."[10]

No matter how many extra hours the gangs put in, they could never keep up with the demand for more and more ships. It was not long before private industry and the federal government sought to encourage women, a vast untapped work force, to join the production lines. The traditional role of the woman was to remain at home and raise the children, but as more and more men left for military service, the need for industrial workers increased, and that view quickly changed.

Women responded to the call for workers and quickly adapted to become highly skilled riveters, welders, crane operators, inspectors, metal fabricators, lathe operators, aircraft assemblers, weapons testers, and any position a man could fill. Rosie the Riveter became a famous poster icon showing a woman trained as a metal riveter working on a ship. The image was to encourage women to join the work force and do a man's work for a man's wages. In many instances, a woman was employed with the idea that it was to free a man to fight.

Most of these women labored under the double burden of working on the job and being parents at the same time. Women working at the several Hampton Roads shipyards were generally married and caring for one or more children at home. Most defense factories, especially the shipyards, worked around the clock, seven days a week. Working a six-day week left little time to manage a home and family in their one day a week off. Leaving the children with a family member, parent, grandparent or neighbor quickly became the standard. Some factories maintained a day care center for working mothers.

Women also drove buses, cabs, and trucks, delivered the mail, cleaned the many troop trains, pumped gas, delivered milk and manned Air Raid Warden positions tracking enemy planes.

Women working in factories at first were expected to maintain their femininity and wear traditional dresses. Safety measures required they wear clothing that did not endanger them in the work place. They soon discovered that slacks and overalls were more practical and comfortable factory wear. Silk, rayon and nylon were no longer available, as the material was needed for the production of parachutes. Women, sensing a degree of freedom from fashion restrictions, quickly and cheerfully adapted to the new dress codes.

Social prohibition frowned on women wearing slacks or men's trousers in public, but this was war. Many factories and corporations eagerly provided denim coveralls and other practical clothing for the job with an eye to increasing job safety. A worker at home due to injury was not always replaced at her job due to a lack of trained replacements.

While doors of opportunity were opened to women in the booming defense plants, not all women were so eagerly sought after. African American women who sought employment at the high-paying shipyards were generally given menial, lower-paying jobs. Many women in Virginia found work at food canneries and military supply bases, or cleaning troop trains. Local Japanese-American women, who were traditionally bound to the home, were denied entrance to industry. Many on the west coast lacked the opportunity, as they were placed along with their families in detention centers for the duration of the war.

The addition of women to the work force still did not yield the number of workers required. Several industrial states changed their mandated child-labor laws to permit

Six. The Home Front

the employment of teenagers. At first only young men were allowed, but then young women were permitted to work as well. Teenagers generally were placed under the apprentice program, which accepted young men and women in industry. The lure of more money than they had ever earned working part-time lured many from school or university. Many schoolteachers deserted the teaching profession to make higher wages of industry. The number of students enrolled in high schools throughout the Commonwealth of Virginia dropped by 15 percent.[11]

In 1943, the federal government demanded the right of minorities to join the labor force, with equal pay. Before the war, the African American population was concentrated in ethnic communities in Virginia and they suffered severe job discrimination. Now African Americans would be allowed to join the war effort, either by serving in one of the branches of the Armed Forces or by joining the labor force.

Despite the need for their skills and labor, discrimination continued. "White Only" and "Negro Only" signs were kept visible and common in the work place. Once the African American participated in the work force, they dispelled many of the social labels the white citizens enforced as a means of keeping them in a restricted society. "They lack the education to learn new skills" was a common pronouncement, as well as, "They're too lazy." The African Americans' contribution, as well as that of other minorities, gave a boost to wartime production.[12]

Through these many forward-looking social changes and an increase in the badly needed work force, wartime production was greatly increased, but a lack of enough workers continued. By mid-1943, thirty-one thousand workers had built a variety of ships at the yard.

With the end of the war, the yard turned to recycling many of the ships and still constructs nuclear-fueled submarines and the large-size fleet carriers today.

Along with the increase of heavy industry in the Hampton Roads area, small machine shops, food processors and other suppliers shared in the bounty of work. The shipyards farmed out much of their smaller jobs in order to concentrate on the major, large aspects of shipbuilding. Several small companies throughout the Commonwealth contracted to manufacture instruments for navigation, boiler room gauges, high-tolerance pieces and special tools.

The U.S. Army Quartermaster buyers negotiated with farmers to grow specific crops to be processed by local food processors. The idea was to present a balanced meal, especially to the many soldiers who were already at some level of malnutrition due to the Depression. In many cases, farmers turned to land that had not been worked for years, increasing their crop yields to meet the surge in demand.

Virginia food processing plants produced dehydrated foods for the military war rations, such as the famed "K-ration," and canned local produce, especially from the eastern shore. Potatoes were highly prized, as they were easily dehydrated and turned into "instant mashed spuds."

The increase of poultry provided the military with various chicken products and eggs. Many of these eggs were processed and packaged as dehydrated eggs, to be utilized by troops in combat areas. "Powdered eggs" quickly became a mainstay in military cooking, as well as potatoes, pumpkins and milk. In addition to dehydrated dairy products, fruit grown in Virginia was processed, dried and canned for rations. Much of the production was delivered to local bases and ships.

Smithfield Foods, Smithfield, Virginia, produced as a variety of either dried, refrigerated, processed or canned foods. Providing ham and ham products for the Hampton Roads area, Army and Navy camp mess halls and ships ensured fresh meat. The typical dry or canned field rations were provided by many meat-packing companies, among them Smithfield. Many soldiers fondly remember the field rations with its tasty small cans of ham chunks, as well as ham and lima beans, meat hash and the notable Spam. Bakers and cooks relied upon the use of lard in their cooking, and of course Smithfield provided many tons of the traditional cooking ingredients.

Although shipbuilding became the leading industry in Virginia, the wartime demand caused other industries to increase their output. Virginia was especially suited to the manufacture of military clothing, with several communities not only producing the fabric but cutting and manufacturing the uniform.

The Dan River Textile Mills, located in Danville, Virginia, had 14,000 workers maintaining 12 weaving mills, producing fabric for uniforms and other military needs. Dan River Mills subcontracted to several small manufacturers in the Hampton Roads area to produce snaps, leather and fabric belts and a variety of metal buttons for combat fatigues. The Williams and Dickie Company produced denim for the familiar kaki fatigue, as well as for flight and work uniforms.

The historic Tredegar Iron Works, located in Richmond, which produced weapons and munitions during the Civil War, geared up to meet the mounting demands of the military. Despite the large work force maintained after the Civil War, the company immediately increased the number of employees and added to its physical plant. The iron works received several E for Efforts Awards during the war.

Du Pont E.I. De Nemours and Company constructed a synthetic fiber plant to produce rayon fiber for tire yarns. With the great demand for truck and aircraft tires, the plant worked around the clock to meet the military demands.

The Newport News Shipbuilding and Drydock Company located a shipbuilding yard on the James and constructed destroyer escort ships. The United States Foil, located at the Virginia Naval Ordnance Plant, produced rolled aluminum rod, foil sheets and aluminum mold casting for aircraft parts.

Central Coca-Cola Bottling Company in Richmond, Virginia, hurriedly geared up to increase production of the favorite soft drink to be distributed to servicemen worldwide. The company's president, Robert Woodruff, pledged, "We will see that every man in uniform gets a bottle of Coca-Cola for 5 cents, wherever he is and whatever it costs." Men and women in uniform drank over 10 million bottles of Coca-Cola between 1941 and 1945.

In Central Northern Virginia, the Snead Company, located in the small town of Orange, shifted their production to manufacturing M-4 type pontoons for the Army; they also supplied complete hospital wards.

The United States Rubber Company located a production plant in Scottsville, on the north side of the James River, and produced rubber tire cord for military tires. The O'Sullivan Rubber Company had a production plant located in Winchester, Virginia, producing rubber parts for combat boots and other military shoes.

The Virginia Smelting Company, West Norfolk, Virginia, speeded up its production of industrial chemicals such as liquid sulfur (for the rubber industry), sulfur dioxide, sodium hydrosulfite, zinc sulfate and other wartime-related products.

At the outbreak of the war, many ore mines located in Virginia quickly expanded to meet the increased demand of metals and chemicals. The Piedmont region of Virginia has been searched and mined for minerals since early Colonial days. Prince William in Spotsylvania, Louis and Buckingham Counties worked several mines producing copper, lead, sulfur and zinc. Sulfur was greatly in demand, as it was a key component of gunpowder.

The Panaminas Mines, located in the small town of Paytes, Virginia, produced a steady supply of valuable raw minerals needed for wartime production such as zinc, lead and copper sulfide concentrates.

John H. Dulay and Son processed fruit and vegetables at its Exmore plant, on the eastern shore of Virginia. In this area, long a produce garden for the Commonwealth of Virginia, local farmers increased farm acreage, especially potatoes, and other root vegetables. These were sold to the Dulay processing plant and shipped to the military as either fresh or processed foods.

The Hercules Company, located in the two towns of Pulaski and Radford, Virginia, dramatically increased production of war-related materials, especially the explosives DNT, TNT, nitroglycerine powder, Pentoline, rocket propellants and the invaluable smokeless gunpowder.

Despite problems such as labor strikes, miners worked to increase the production of anthracite (hard coal) and bituminous (soft coal). Even with an abundance of coal, England requested shipments to keep their wartime industries running. The shortage of miners resulted in a reduced supply of locally mined coal that could not keep up with the demand.

E.I. Dupont nylon and rayon production plants were located in Martinsville, Virginia. They manufactured rain ponchos, vehicle covers, truck canopies, shoelaces and many other military needs.

The Allied Chemical and Dye Corporation built a new plant in Front Royal and produced sulfuric acid.

The Southern Welding and Machine Company, with the U.S. Navy located at Hampton Roads, manufactured arresting gear for Navy aircraft landing on aircraft carriers. The Belle Meade Distilling Company shifted its production from good brandies and other liquors to the wartime need for 120- and 190-proof industrial and medical alcohol.

Cigarettes, the so-called "Soldiers' Smoke," were provided free by companies such as Philip Morris and R.J. Reynolds. Included in each K- or C-ration packet was a small box of four cigarettes. Millions of cigarettes were provided courtesy of the tobacco companies. The result was most servicemen became "hooked" on nicotine and become potential customers after the war.[13]

The Railroads

The first large-scale use of railroads during wartime was during the Civil War, when both the Northern and Southern armies moved massed numbers of troops. During World War I, large numbers of troops were moved throughout the greater United States to training facilities, then to ports for shipping to the war in Europe.

During World War II, almost all military personnel were transported by rail. World War II was to become a war of massive movement, and only the railroads offered the required speed and volume assets. The estimated figure is over 40,000 men and women a day spent time on a troop transport train. Large numbers of military personnel and materiel could be moved across the continental United States in a matter of five days.

Such a massive movement of troops required organization and coordination of several railroads and considerable rolling stock. It is generally considered by many that the federal government stepped in and attempted to federalize the railroads in order to obtain the necessary control required during the war. Agreement by the railroads to organize and gear up for wartime conditions prevented the federal government from doing so.

In Virginia, which had the largest railroad, the Chesapeake and Ohio and the Norfolk and Western ran trains day and night, carrying thousands of recruits throughout Virginia to training centers across the state. In order to carry the increased number of military personnel, the normally "for freight only" rails were utilized to carry troops. Not only did this require a considerable increase in passenger cars, but in additional Pullman cars.

The C&O carried the heavy coastal rail guns to their locations of emplacement, as well as the necessary ammunition, fuses, troops and various supplies. Such trains, highly visible with their large guns, were marked as dangerous and were given special rights of way along the line.

Trains carrying munitions traveled in specially marked boxcars, especially those carrying the highly dangerous Class-A explosives. The transport of these hazardous explosives required special handling; they were assigned soldiers as guards and placed under speed restrictions. These munition trains, such as those shipping from Radford, Virginia, carried bag powder bound for the larger combat ships at Hampton Roads. Ammunition trains were generally hauled by coal-burning locomotives, which endangered the entire shipment of ammunition. It was obvious to everyone when such a train was headed from Radford to Hampton Roads, as it traveled slower and carried armed guards, and the placement of the cars was no closer than five cars from the coal-burning engine.

Moving a full division of 15,000 men and tons of personal and military equipment after training, from a place such as Camp Pickett to Camp Patrick Henry, Newport News port of embarkation required upwards to 20 to 25 trains. These trains were made up of 200 to 225 passenger and Pullman cars, plus many baggage cars. Depending on the distance traveled, several kitchen cars were added to ensure the proper feeding of the troops.

Six. The Home Front

In addition to troop trains, U.S. Army truck convoys also made the trip, hauling the heavy weapons such as artillery, tanks, Quartermaster and hospital units.

Special coaches were either converted from Pullman cars or were constructed specifically for use as moveable hospital units. Unlike the regular passenger coach with doors at either end of the car, hospital coaches had double doors to admit loading and offloading of stretchers. The double doors were positioned in such a way that they were level with the loading platform, easing the burden of the wounded on stretchers.

When wounded from the battles in North Africa began to arrive in increasing numbers at the port of embarkation in Newport News, Quartermaster hospital coaches were there to quickly transport them directly from the ships to awaiting hospitals located throughout Virginia. It was not unusual to see awaiting hospital or troop trains lined from the train depot from Newport News west to Williamsburg.

When suitable numbers of larger cargo aircraft became available to transport the critically wounded, transport by hospital rail cars remained the most important means to handle the greater numbers.

Shipping coal overseas as part of the lend-lease program required large numbers of coal-carrying gondola cars from the coal mines of West Virginia and western Virginia to Newport News. It was not unusual to have a coal train made up of 200 to 300 cars heavily loaded with soft coal. Despite the fact that the English worked a large number of coal mines, they required shipments to sustain their way of life, since many men were off fighting the war and not working the mines.[14]

Wartime Housing

There was a large-scale migration from the rural small towns of Virginia to the heavy industry of Hampton Roads, producing an instant, severe housing shortage. Massive numbers of housing units were suddenly required if workers were to be maintained. Norfolk, as an example, was suddenly flooded with several thousand defense workers and Armed Forces members. The number of married workers vastly increased, making demands on every social organization, especially school systems and public transportation.

Housing at first was scarce to nonexistent. The worst housing situation was near the shipyards. Seeing an opportunity, many residents took in boarders. Families were known to convert one- or two-car garages and large sheds into living quarters, sharing the bathroom facilities of the main house. This adaptation was still unable to meet the overwhelming need.

The solution was to construct some type of emergency, low-rent public housing, something Norfolk had been deliberating for years. In November 1940, the U.S. Navy constructed 1,200 units to house workers at Newport News Shipbuilding and Dry Dock. Constructed as 100 units each to house 12 families, these generally consisted of two-floor, two-bedroom apartments capable of holding small families. The Navy transferred the facility to the Federal Public Housing later in 1941.

Virginia in the War Years, 1938–1945

Workers in Norfolk signing in for housing (National Archives).

On 30 July 1949, the City of Norfolk Council enacted the Norfolk Housing Authority and utilized $2 million appropriated by the United States Housing Authority for slum clearance. With the steady arrival of military personnel and defense workers, Norfolk decided to move forward and place slum clearance on hold. In July 1941 the Housing Authority began construction of a 300-unit housing development located at Compostella Road.

In 1941, utilizing barracks-style housing produced by Orcutt Homes, Newport News constructed 13 buildings containing 148 apartments for shipyard workers. These units were not necessarily meant for families, but rather for single workers. It did not take long for them to be occupied once they were completed.

The first low-rent housing project was Merrimack Park, with 500 units in early 1941. Barracks-style housing, using prefabricated Orcutt Homes, were quickly erected in the East End District. Thirteen buildings, containing 142 first-floor two-bedroom, apartments were constructed.

Broad Creek Village, located on 507 acres near present-day Virginia Beach, contained 2600 temporary wood constructed units. It contained an elementary school, police and fire stations, a large attractive shopping center, recreation facilities and storage buildings.

Early in 1941, the Norfolk Redevelopment and Housing Authority (NRHA) approved the construction of low-income housing, replacing a large, growing slum area. Two hundred and thirty housing units in 25 buildings were built on Princess Anne Road, known as Roberts Park. When defense requirements for available housing increased, Roberts Park was converted to war housing.

Temporary housing for 124 families was constructed in 1943 near Roberts Park. Commonwealth Apartments, at Colley Avenue and 25th Street, housed 344 families. Another temporary housing project for 224 families was located in Titustown.

With the need to offer affordable housing to the increasing number of defense workers, an additional 3,462 dwellings were constructed at Merrimack Park and Oakley Park. One thousand, five hundred and ninety-two temporary dwellings, 540 single dormitory rooms and 300 trailers (mobile homes) were added at Lewis Park.

Single women who filled many of the defense oppositions had difficulty locating housing. The problem was partially solved with boarding houses, or with a single room in a family house where the young women could be supervised. Dormitory rooms were few and far between.

Many of the longtime residents of the Hampton Roads area viewed the new housing as luxurious, because every unit had a bathroom with a toilet and a bathtub. A census completed in 1940 indicated that 35 percent of the residents in the area had no indoor toilet or bath facilities.

Utilizing the new Federal Public Housing Authority Act, the communities located near the shipyards authorized and constructed several large housing developments. Utilizing federal monies, 16,700 dwelling units were constructed: in Norfolk, 6500; in Portsmouth, 5000; and in Newport News, 5200. The majority of these hastily constructed structures were meant to be taken down at the completion of the war. Instead, most housing units remained for fifty years after the war, with many still in place during the 1990s.

Despite the urgent need for defense workers, housing continued to remain segregated. Many African Americans were fortunate to find a room with a local African American family. In many instances, they shared a room, sleeping in a bed when the roommate was at work—the old "hot bunk" arrangement.

With the southern migration of 750,000 African Americans to the northern industrial cities, demands for racial equality accelerated. At first, African Americans were relegated to inferior, menial jobs, both in the military and industry. However, as the war demands increased, more and more African Americans and other minorities moved into skilled jobs and demanded better housing. Despite the war and its demands, public desegregated housing was slow to occur. Whenever new housing was constructed, African Americans continued to be segregated.[15]

Agriculture

Virginia has a long history with agriculture, producing many of the basic staples, such as wheat, corn, vegetables and especially tobacco. When the Lend-Lease Act of

1940 was introduced, in addition to military supplies, one part of the plan was to purchase a number of vital crops at market value and ship them to England. With so many men fighting for the life of their country, England lacked the men to work the farms and therefore provide enough food to feed the populace.

American farm families, according to the United States Department of Agriculture, sent more than 1.8 million young men and women into the Armed Forces. It was a difficult situation as the nation faced an unprecedented demand for an increase of foodstuffs. Even with the lack of workers, a reduction in gasoline supply and a severe lack of parts for farm machinery, the farmer was expected to increase production levels. Each day some eight million servicemen had to be fed, as well as millions of civilians in Great Britain and Russia.

In Virginia, wheat, corn, peanuts, potatoes, meats and poultry products were increased to meet the sudden demand. From 1942 to 1945, the federal government requisitioned increasing amounts of locally grown and processed agricultural products, especially processed meats.

The eastern shore of Virginia, known for its excellent quality seafoods, increased its harvest of fish, shellfish and crabs. Processing plants were enlarged to suit the need for canned and dried fish. Accomack County, home of a large poultry industry, increased it facilities and population of chickens. One of the results was the increase in the output of eggs, which were then processed and dried. In 1942, ten poultry processing plants were located on the Delmarva Peninsula and processed 38 million broilers.

In this area, known as the vegetable garden of the Atlantic States, despite the lack of workers, additional land was cleared and fallow land brought back into use to produce more vegetable crops to be canned, dried or frozen. Potatoes and other root crops were grown on large acres of the fertile sandy soil.

The need for better food preservation prompted the USDA along with the military to increase funds for research. The traditional K-rations (dry) and C-rations (canned) became the focus of the research. To meet the needs of the military, dehydration and freeze-drying facilities were greatly expanded. Under the slogan, "Food Will Win The War and Write The Peace," thousands of tons of prepared foodstuffs were loaded and shipped to England from the Hampton Roads area.

German submarines lurking off the Virginia and North Carolina coasts did not deter the seagoing fishermen from taking their vessels into harm's way. The demand for food spurred the commercial fishing industry to increase its annual haul of a variety of fish stocks. Canneries, with an increasing demand from the military, beseeched the fishermen to bring in more fish.

Chesapeake Bay watermen answered the call for men to serve their country in large numbers, leaving the very young, women and older watermen to bring in the fish. The Bay, with its natural spawning and fishing grounds, provided suitable stocks without having to venture into the dangers of the Atlantic.

The relatively small number of deep-sea fishing fleets still put to sea despite the threat of U-boats. The Coast Guard got the fishing ships to sea by escorting groups of ships through the minefields and nets at the mouth of the Chesapeake to the open sea. Once on their own, the ships dispersed to their favorite seasonal fishing grounds, ignoring the lurking U-boats. Luckily, the submarine captains ignored the fishing boats for fear of giving away their position.

This rapid increase in agriculture solved many food supply problems for the military, but the need for more servicemen, as well as the drain on local and rural manpower for the shipbuilding industry, proved nearly fatal for the Virginia agricultural industry. When the number of German and Italian prisoners of war increased, many were sent to local farms to successfully harvest the much-needed crops.

Part of the agriculture labor solution came from the federal government, which allowed workers from places such as Mexico, Jamaica, Haiti and Central America to enter the United States on special work permits. With Mexico declaring war on Germany on 24 May 1942, President Avila Camacho allowed Mexican laborers to enter the United States and work in agriculture jobs. Thus was born the "Bracero" program, which lasted for several years after the war ended. Virginia agriculture now had an inexpensive supply of migrant workers. Production soared, much to the pleasure of the local military.

By 1943, the federal government purchased 80 percent of all lower grades of beef, 40 percent of all other beef cuts, 30 percent of all butter production, 30 percent of veal, 40 percent of all lamb, and 50 percent of all canned fruits and vegetables. The greater production of chicken eggs was processed through dehydration as powdered eggs for military rations. This in turn resulted in a shortage of these items in the civilian marketplace, driving prices up.

The supply of hemp (marijuana) quickly became in short supply when Japan cut off coarse supplies from Southeast Asia. Hemp was vital in the production of maritime ropes, canvas and durable clothing. During the war, farmers in Virginia and other suitable states were encouraged to increase production. Those farmers who did were excluded from military service. The fiber was also one of the vital resources needed in the lend-lease program, with England and Russia utilizing great quantities of the supply. In Virginia, some 36,000 acres of hemp were cultivated during the war.[16]

The Women's Land Army

Shortly after the beginning of World War II, despite the four million deferments, a large number of farmhands left the farms to join the Armed Forces or went to defense jobs for better money. The labor remaining force was simply not sufficient to plant or harvest the increased demand for crops. If the farmers did not receive badly needed replacement labor, the crops would rot in the fields.

The Emergency Farm Labor Act of 1942 provided extraordinary provisions for increasing farm labor. Occupational bulletins 17, 18, 19, and 20 announced occupations critical in agriculture, food processing, forestry and fishing. Able-bodied men in these special categories would be exempted from the draft.

In addition to allowing foreign workers to till the land, the Department of Agriculture organized the Crops Corps. The objective of the Crops Corps was to locate and sign up every available volunteer—men, women and teenagers—to plant and harvest the crops.

The enactment of the Women's Land Army, based on the English Women's Land Army model, was seen as a quick way of increasing farm labor. On 29 April 1943, Congress authorized the Women's Land Army of America, seeking 60,000 women from town and urban areas. Fifty thousand of these were to be considered as part-time or seasonal labor, while 10,000 were to be full-time workers. These women farm laborers were to supplement the mechanical planting and harvesting of crops.

Women of all ages, from every walk of life, responded to the call and signed on. After all the paperwork was completed, these women took part in a three-week training period to learn the basics of farm work, including how to handle farm equipment, how to use certain tools and farm machinery, and of course general farm safety regulations. They were instructed in how to tend the different types of crops, in harvesting procedures, and in grading and packing, especially of fruit crops. Proper handling of tractors, plows, and cultivators, and the cutting and baling of hay, as well as the proper care and feeding of livestock, were taught by farmers who became a part of the program.

Once the women were indoctrinated, they were sent to individual farms that had signed up for the program, and arrangements were made by each farmer to house and feed the Land Army. The women demanded, and received, a fair wage as well as an 8-hour day. What they would do during that 8-hour day depended on the crop to be harvested.

The women who signed up for the program arrived in time to save many crops in Virginia. The apple, pear and plum crops were harvested just before they would have rotted on the ground. Along with local volunteers, the Women's Land Army harvested assorted vegetable crops, eggs and tobacco. It should be noted that African Americans also signed up for the project and worked well alongside their white counterparts to keep the food pipeline flowing.

Providing tobacco and cigarettes for the troops meant harvesting the large, unfamiliar plants in the field, which was hot work. From learning to plant the crop, to handling a mule, then with a large knife to cut and bundle the leaves to be hauled to the curing sheds, it was backbreaking work, and many a serviceman enjoyed his smokes because of their labors.

With the assistance of the Women's Land Army, suburban and urban volunteers, and the German-Italian POWs, agricultural production increased to such an extent Smithfield Hams hired on many extra laborers to provide processed meat for the local military camps. With the increased demand for textiles, cotton production doubled, then tripled, as did cultivation of the famous Virginia peanut. Not only did servicemen and women enjoy salted peanuts, but peanut butter became a tasty food staple.[17]

Air Raid Wardens

The U.S. government did not believe the Germans or the Japanese had the capability of reaching the continental United States with aerial bombs as Germany did in England, though it still needed to prepare the civilian population for that eventuality. The Office of Civilian Defense (OCD), a paramilitary organization, was instituted by the federal government on 20 May 1941. The state of Virginia, at the direction of the federal government, instituted the Virginia Office of Civil Defense, also known as the famed Air Raid Wardens.

The Office of Civil Defense was responsible for the enforcement of regulations related to an air attack. Air Raid Wardens carried out air raid drills, prepared for both air and gas attacks, and were responsible for enforcing blackouts.

The first area-wide air raid drill was carried out on 25 May 1942. It was considered a failure, but considerable experience was gathered, and a better understanding of the process was developed. The next air raid drill produced much better results.

All volunteers for the Office of Civil Defense, men and women alike, were trained in first aid, fire precautions, rescue and debris clearance, as well as in the location and maintenance of air raid shelters and in assisting the local police where necessary.

The increasing number of citizens produced a problem for the Air Raid Wardens; basically, how to locate sufficient shelters in case of an air attack. Realizing there were many such problems, the military and local industries assisted by designating many areas and buildings as shelters that might not have ordinarily been put into use. Local schools, large structurally sound public buildings, work place facilities and underground structures were examined.

The area's increasing numbers of children prompted the Air Raid Wardens to go into the Hampton Roads schools and conduct information sessions. It was not long before the rest of the public was subjected to air raid drills. These drills were commonplace during the first years of the war. Many citizens remember the safety drills in school.

Wardens were stationed in neighborhoods, in the work place, near schools, and even in shopping areas such as department stores. They wore uniforms similar to military types, displaying the highly visible armband, and could often be seen wearing the white helmet.

The Virginia Office of Civil Defense was disbanded at the end of the war.[18]

CHAPTER SEVEN

Women at War

With the war raging in Europe, Congress considered a bill to allow women to enter the Armed Forces, as they had done during World War I. The politicians dithered in their usual fashion, listened to the vehement protests of the all-male military, and made promises of considering a bill that would permit the military to establish a women's auxiliary of some type, on a limited basis. The bill stalled in Congress, as it obviously did not have the backing of the various branches of the military.

Having women serve their country in uniform during wartime was unacceptable to the greater American public, especially males in early 1940s. The concept held by the public was that the American woman was intellectually incapable of handling jobs that required considerable mechanical skills. Eventually the bill was introduced before Congress, and Congress claimed they were deliberating, but secretly they put off acting on it.

A very stubborn and impatient Congresswoman, Edith Nourse Rogers of Massachusetts, along with First Lady Eleanor Roosevelt's backing, introduced a bill on 28 May 1941 to establish a Women's Army Auxiliary Corps. She realized that the army, fighting a war on two fronts, would soon require a larger military force, and that the role women had played during World War I was not going to be suitable for this war. In World War I, women civilians filled military jobs. These women received no official status, had to provide their own food, quarters, and medical treatment, and had no legal protection. Congresswoman Rogers was determined that if the women were accepted into the military, they would do so with full military status, including equal pay, pension and medical benefits, the same as their male counterparts.

It was late November and Congress still had not acted on the bill. An impatient General of the Army, George C. Marshall, bypassed the dithering Congress and took it upon himself to order the War Department to establish a women's corps. The Japanese surprise attack on Pearl Harbor, 7 December 1941, changed the viewpoint of Congress and the military.[1]

Despite further stalling by Congress, the search was on for a director of the Women's Army Auxiliary Corps. On 14 May 1942, Oveta Culp Hobby, wife of the governor of Texas, was named director and given the rank of major. Now the search began to locate training facilities and create a training program, along with determining a proper uniform for the women and proper equipment. The public debated the appropriateness of allowing young women to be trained on bases with so many eager young men. Many churches, civic organizations, and even famous personalities opposed the

Seven. Women at War

law on moral grounds. The discussion against women being in the military carried on through the duration of the war.

Women saw being in the military as a chance to leave home and perhaps see the world outside their hometown. The usual pattern for a young woman was to graduate from high school, stay at home and wait to be courted by some eligible young man, have children, and take care of her parents. Proudly serving in the military was a way of changing all that, and they did by the thousands. Their service was to be an adventure that would change the way women were viewed by society forever.

WAACS

Her name was Edna Collier Fortier, and she was 24 years old when she joined the U.S. Army. She was working as a civilian record keeper at the newly built Army Richmond General Depot in Richmond, Virginia. It was her job to check on those who checked materials received. Being redundant was part of the system of accounting.

WAACS (became WACS) servicing truck (Women's Memorial Foundation Collection).

She was working the weekend, checking invoices, when it neared 4 o'clock in the afternoon of 7 December 1941. Suddenly a friend ran through the warehouse, shouting, "THE JAPS JUST BOMBED PEARL HARBOR!" They all just stood there, not realizing what had happened. She remembered someone asking, "Where is Pearl Harbor?"

Edna watched men one or two at a time go off and enlist in one of the branches of the service. She wanted to join up, but at the time women were not allowed in the Armed Forces. When the law was passed in May of 1942, allowing women to serve in the Women's Army Auxiliary Corps, she wanted to enlist. "Of course my father did not agree. It was his belief that women belonged in the house raising a family and not in uniform somewhere."

With no husband or family of her own to worry about, she felt she was free to do as she pleased, so she joined the U.S. Army WACs. She gave some thought to the WAVES, but just being in a rowboat made her seasick!

Edna was sent from Richmond to Fort Des Moines, Iowa, an old Army stable, for basic training. She claims she enjoyed every moment of her training. She was one of several selected to attend Medical Hospital Man School, located at Camp Lee, on the outskirts of Petersburg, Virginia.

Upon completion of her training, she was promoted to Private First Class (PFC) and stationed at McGuire General Hospital in Richmond, Virginia, assisting nurses in the wards. "As you can see, I did not go far from home, which pleased my father." She met a very nice Army doctor and married him once the war was over. They raised two wonderful girls together.[2]

Edna Collier Fortier was one of over 140,000 women who served in the U.S. Army as a WAAC. The primary purpose of the WAACs (later changed to WACs) was to free a man to fight. However, they made available to the Army the skills and special training of highly qualified women for the duration of the war.

Initially the Armed Forces resisted the idea of accepting large numbers of women into their ranks. There was little understanding of how they could function in an all-male army. But as the need for more support personnel became more compelling, the idea gained more and more acceptance. Under the slogan *"FREE A MAN TO FIGHT,"* more than 350,000 women would eventually serve in uniform.

Wherever possible, a WAC replaced a soldier doing service work. Their duties included work as clerks, stenographers, and typists, weather forecasting, being vehicle drivers, parachute riggers, automotive mechanics, aviation maintenance workers, air-controllers, radio and radar operators, cooks, bakers, photographers and various skilled medical staff at clinic and hospitals.

WACs served at more than 400 U.S. Army and Army Air Corps installations and were involved in 239 non-combat positions. They were stationed at Army installations such as Fort Pickett, Blackstone Army Air Field, Front Royal, Fort Hunt, Fort Eustis, Army facilities located at Hampton Roads Port of Embarkation, Langley Field, Fort Monroe, Norfolk Army Air Field, Camp Lee, McGuire General Hospital, Fort Belvoir and the Richmond Army Air Field.

It was decided that women entering the Army would be given the same basic training as the men, with some modification. Since women were considered frail and fragile personnel, the requirements were reduced for physical training and work positions.

The following military standards were established:

a. Individual must be a U.S. citizen
b. Must be between 21 and 45
c. No dependents
d. Minimum height of 5 feet
e. Minimum weight of 100 pounds

Women quickly adapted to the daily routine of physical training (PT), barracks and personal inspections, marching in formation, military protocol, discipline and, of course, Army food. In the absence of proper training facilities, many Virginia recruits were trained at places like Ft. Des Moines, Iowa. As the numbers increased, others were shipped to Ft. Oglethorpe, Georgia. At the newly constructed Naval Air Station in Daytona Beach, Florida, two miles west of the city, a large tent city was erected to house 7,000 WACs. It was easy to spot WAC structures by the signs, "Military Reservation—Restricted." There were thousands of WACs there, with thousands arriving and being processed every ten weeks.

Newly arrived recruits were processed, indoctrinated for three days, then sent to Tent City. Once they completed four weeks of basic training, they awaited orders that would send them to a military base somewhere in the United States.

Some of the first WACs were sent to the AWS (Aircraft Warning System). Fear of German planes attacking the larger cities along the coast produced a visual early warning airplane identification system. Upon graduation, WACs were stationed at the U.S. Army bases along the coast of Virginia.

The first officer training class (OCS), consisting of 440 selected women, was established at Fort Des Moines, Iowa, on July of 1942. Forty black women also entered the OCS program. These candidates were placed in a separate platoon and lived apart from the rest of the women. They attended all the same classes and activities as the white OCS candidates, but other than that, they lived apart. Later on in 1943, the Army established another OCS school at Fort Devens, Massachusetts. Basic education required a college degree to qualify for OCS and many did.

WAC graduates were assigned to bases of the U.S. Army Air Corps, the U.S. Army Ground Forces Command, and the U.S. Army Supply Services. Initial jobs included clerk typists, file clerk, stenographers, drivers, messengers and officer's aides. Gradually the Army required more and more of these well-trained soldiers. The Army Air Forces utilized 40 percent of all WAC graduates and employed them as weather observers, parachute riggers, bombsight maintenance, aerial photographers, control tower operators and tabulating operators. It quickly became commonplace in Virginia to see WACs filling positions ordinarily held by men.

One such WAC, Mary M. Salm, Sgt. Radio Operator, expressed how women felt about their role in the military with a poem:

I am a WAC
I am a soldier in skirts
Don't laugh, mister. It is no laughing matter.
I wear the uniform of my country
Because my country is at war.
I'm no super patriot. Millions of
Young men have laid aside pencils,
Typewriter, golf clubs, to shoulder a gun,
To fight, to bleed and to die,
That this great United States of America
May remain free.
I am a WAC
A private, if you please.
I want you to know this
I am proud to the last fiber of my body
That I am privileged to wear the uniform of my country.[3]

Women soldiers were stationed at the Nansemond Ordnance Depot located at Suffolk, Virginia. They routinely performed such dangerous tasks as compiling data on inventories, mixing gunpowder, defusing enemy shells for inspection, loading shells, and organizing dangerous waste materials.

Additionally, an undisclosed number of highly qualified WACs served on the famed atom bomb program called the Manhattan Project; they were clerks, statisticians, compotators, and worked in information storage and interpretation.

The WAAC had met with unqualified success. On 3 July 1943, Congress signed a bill transitioning the Women's Army Auxiliary Corps to the Women's Army Corps. The change provided full military status to the serving women, providing them with privileges, honors, pay and respect.

When the turning tide of war in Europe pushed Germany back from France, WACs were sent in ever-increasing numbers, especially to England. Eighteen thousand WACs served overseas in 21 different countries. The lasting popular image of the WAC has her serving as a driver for some handsome officer or as a clerk-typist. They did these and 237 other important military jobs, and did them well.

Although women were restricted to non-combat roles, one-hundred eighty-one women died in the service and 16 were awarded the Purple Heart. Sixty-six women were captured, taken prisoner by the Japanese Army, and survived the hellish ordeal of the concentration camps for 4 years.

WACs served with honor in North Africa, Sicily, Italy, the Middle East, Europe, the Southwest Pacific, Burma, China, India, and even the cold climes of Alaska. Military commanders who once had stated they would have women serve as soldiers over their dead bodies eventually changed their tune. Observing the women do their jobs with quiet efficiency, they soon asked for an increase in their numbers.

They were soldiers, neat and trim, precise and military in all respects. In her remarks to the first graduating class of WAACs, Colonel Oveta Culp Hobby (Director) reminded the women that they had a "debt to democracy and a date with destiny." Little did these brave women realize they had forever changed the military.[4]

Seven. Women at War

WAVES

In early August of 1942, Mildred McAfee was commissioned a commander in the U.S. Naval Reserve. Her assignment was to direct the newly established program, Women Accepted for Volunteer Emergency Service, later to be known as the WAVES. Prior to this, she had been President of Wellesley College in Boston, Massachusetts. Promoted captain in November of 1943, she went on to command 100,000 women. Captain McAfee remained on active duty until March 1946, when she retired and returned to Wellesley College.

Many naval officers did not believe or accept that women had a place in the U.S. Navy and decided that the women would not survive the rigors of their basic training. Unlike the establishment of the WAAC, creating the Navy's WAVE program was a

WAVE aviation gunnery instructor (Women's Memorial Foundation Collection).

lengthy process. Since these women were going to be a part of the Navy's Reserve, legislation had to be accepted and voted on by Congress. The bill authorizing the WAVES was passed and signed into law by President Roosevelt on 30 July 1942.

Several prominent women educators and legal professionals were selected to guide the creation of the WAVES. The Navy utilized its existing recruiting service to induct interested women volunteers. A suitable uniform was devised, training facilities identified, and an organization put in place to deal with the women.

WAVES were trained in such places as Hunter College in the Bronx, New York; Milledgeville, Georgia; Stillwater, Oklahoma; Radcliffe College and Harvard University, Cambridge, Massachusetts; Smith College at Northampton, Massachusetts; and Bainbridge, Maryland. An intensive 12-week training program entailed eight-hour days of classroom study, marching in close-order formation, physical therapy (PT), maintaining their living quarters, standing guard and practicing military protocol.

Women who were accepted into the program had to meet the following qualifications:

a. between 25 and 30 years of age
b. 20/20 vision
c. normal hearing
d. speaking ability
e. quick reactions to stressful situations

The need for WAVE officers quickly became evident. The appointment of women naval officers generally involved the same standards as for male serving officers, but the educational background of enlisted women was much higher than that of the men. Female recruits, for the most part, were better educated than the typical male recruit. Women tended to have a diploma, whereas fewer men had completed of high school. Physical training requirements for women were slightly different from those of the men. The military understanding that women could not compete with men on a physical basis reduced the number of strenuous activities.

The first WAVE Officer Candidates School (OCS) was established on the campus of Smith College, Northampton, Massachusetts.[5]

Twenty-nine-year-old Janet Marks worked in the main office of a retail store when the Japanese bombed Pearl Harbor. She felt the patriotic need to serve her country and decided to enlist in a branch of the Armed Forces. She understood what her role would be—to replace a man for combat—and decided to join the WAVES.

She reported as directed, and after the usual physical and mental examinations, she was given orders to report at Smith College. She would be part of the first class for WAVE officers. One hundred and twenty women candidates reported for duty aboard the "USS *Northampton*," as the campus was called. They went through actual Navy training with real sailors, who taught them the skills and protocol they would need as officers. In addition to their regular classroom activities, they had to learn close-order drill, and everything a young Navy man would receive when he went through boot camp. They were smart in their appearance and proud of who they were.

So great was the Navy's need for people who could speak Japanese and serve as interpreters that several officer candidates were sent to language school.

Ensign Marks was assigned to the Ninth Naval District as a recruiting officer, which included North and South Dakota and Minnesota. She was to serve as an example to young women desiring to enlist in the Armed Forces. In addition to being trained in the Japanese language, these women were placed with code-breaking units, U.S. Navy Intelligence, radio listening posts and photo interpretation.[6]

The Navy established the WAVES to perform similar duties to those performed by the WACs in the Army. WAVES were not permitted to serve on combat ships, but they soon found themselves replacing men, and being allowed to go to sea. However, not all men were happy with the arrangement, and some protested losing their "stateside" job to a woman.

Each WAVE recruit was given four basic uniforms: the new summer work grays, the traditional summer dress whites, the familiar sailor's working blues, and the dress blues winter uniform. They were required to wear their hair short but feminine at all times, plus skirts and gloves. WAVES working at dirty jobs, such as aviation mechanic, cleaning armaments and overhauling machinery, were allowed to wear a version of the sailor's dungaree uniform. It was not unusual to see WAVES dressed in dungarees doing maintenance on a fighter aircraft engine at NAS Norfolk.

Others trained as aviation radio operators, air navigation, gunnery instructors, link trainers, radio, yeomen, cooks and bakers, hospital corpsmen, machinist mates, aviation repair, engine repair, and parachute riggers, and as instructors in many other areas. Women were finally awarded equal pay and status in 1943, which made the service all the more attractive.

When their training was complete, WAVES were assigned to all naval base operations in Virginia, especially naval air stations. Naval aviators were reported to have felt more secure knowing a WAVE had packed their parachute or a female air controller was guiding them to a landing. WAVES assigned to Navy installations in Virginia were trained and highly skilled in 38 different ratings. Approximately 8,000 officers and more than 75,000 young women served in the U.S. Navy during World War II.[7]

Marines

The Marine Corps was the last service to enlist women. Lt. General Thomas Holcomb announced the formation of the United State Marine Corps Women's Reserve on 13 February 1943. It took the Marine Corps time to understand how they could utilize women in an all-combat force.

Unlike women serving in other branches of the Armed Forces, the women Marines had no catchy acronym, such as WACs or WAVES; instead, the Commandant of the Marine Corps, when asked what to call these enlisted women, said, "We'll call them Marines!"

Women Marine radio operators (Women's Memorial Foundation Collection).

When women were authorized to serve in the Marine Corps in 1943, approximately 23,000 women did so. Ruth Cheney Streeter was appointed director of the U.S. Marine Corps Women's Reserve. She was the first woman to hold the rank of major in the Corps. She would be promoted in 1943 to colonel and be responsible for the care and training of some 23,145 officers and enlisted women.

Seven. Women at War

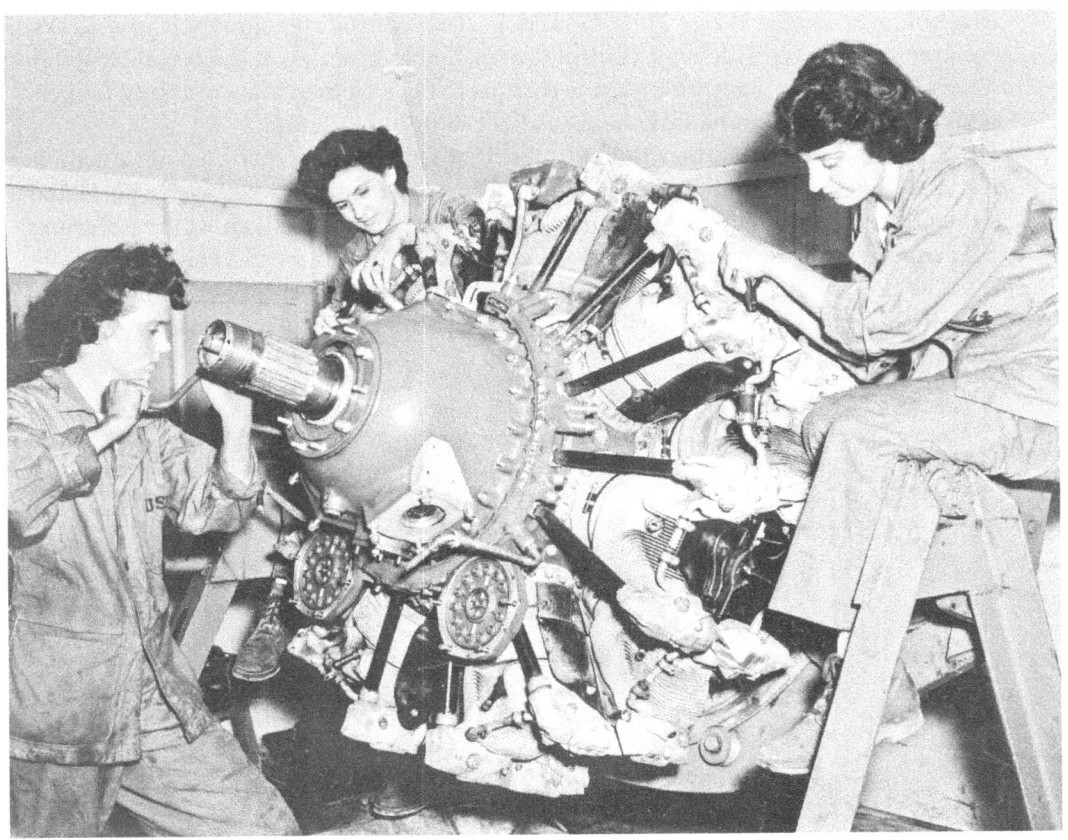

Women Marines overhaul aircraft engine (Women's Memorial Foundation Collection).

These women received regular basic Marine boot camp training and the usual "grunt" weapons training, at Camp Lejeune, North Carolina. It is a basic tenet of the Marine Corps that every Marine has a weapon and knows how to use it. They received the same pay as men and attempts were made to treat them as male Marines. Once recruit training, "boot camp," was complete, they were sent to various schools as needed to replace Marines for combat service.

The first group of women Marines commissioned as officers was based on ability and civilian backgrounds. The first Women's Marine OCS began at Mount Holyoke, South Hadley, Massachusetts. Later, when accommodations were complete, the OCS classes were moved to Camp Lejeune.

The first enlisted class of more than 700 women reported to basic training at Hunter College in New York City. Once basic or boot camp was completed, they were sent to Navy training centers for further training in specialized areas. They performed more than 200 Marine Corps assignments at a variety of Marine and Navy bases.

A contingent of women Marines was assigned to NOB Norfolk with the Marine detachment stationed there. They worked as clerk typists, stenographers, file clerks, and drivers, with WAVES in air control towers, and as orderlies at the Naval Hospital. It was surprising for many new Marine recruits to see a woman Marine asking for personal details and assigning tasks as they checked into the station.

The first women Marines to be stationed at Quantico encountered considerable resistance, but they eventually went on to serve in a variety of office ratings, in particular at the Officer Commissioning School (OCS). By the end of the war, women Marines comprised two-thirds of all base personnel in the United States and Hawaii.[8]

The most famous Marine was Annie Delp Snyder, who has been immortalized as Molly Marine. "I will allow an Associated Press news article to speak for me," she said.

> *The woman known today as Annie Snyder left a monumental mark on the Marine Corps. When the Corps dedicates a statue of "MOLLY MARINE" on the grounds of the Quantico Marine Base, in Virginia, Snyder will have a very unique opportunity. She will literally have the chance to look upon the image of her former self.*

U.S. Marines working in control tower (Women's Memorial Foundation Collection).

Snyder, then 78 and a nationally known preservationist, living in western Prince William County, was one of five women to serve as models when the statue was commissioned in 1943 to help bring more women into the ranks of the Marines.

She waited until she was 21 before enlisting in the Marines as her father would not approve. She signed up at the local Marine Recruiting Office, passed the usual physical and mental exams. She passed and was sent to Smith College OCS in Mount Holyoke, Massachusetts.

They learned to stand watches, do close order drill, when and how to salute and how to identify rates and ranks. It was all very different but yet exciting. Upon graduation, her orders were to report to New Orleans as a recruiter. She was one of five women Marines to be selected to serve as models for a "Molly Marine" statue to help bring women into the Marine Corps.

The statue was dedicated 10 November 1943, on Canal Street in downtown New Orleans. "Snyder became a symbol for women Marines," said General Carol Mutter, President-elect of the Women Marine Association. General Mutter was the first woman to gain three-star rank in the Marines.[9]

Duties of women Marines were the same as those carried out by women in other branches of the Armed Forces. The need for more and more combat personnel, especially the island-hopping Marines, required replacements at various Marine bases. Women Marines filled their role well.

SPARS

On 23 November 1942, Public Law 733 authorized the Women's Reserve of the U.S. Coast Guard. Their catchy name was derived from the Coast Guard motto, Semper Paratus, Latin for "Always Ready." Thirteen thousand women enlisted in the Coast Guard during the course of the war. These newly formed SPARS became members of America's oldest seagoing service.

Captain Dorothy C. Stratton, Dean of Women at Purdue University in Lafayette, Indiana, was appointed director of the SPARS until 1946. The SPARS were put to work in the Coast Guard service in the shortest possible time, and this was accomplished with little difficulty. Although these women would go on to serve admirably, they were not integrated into the "regular Coast Guard," but rather served as reservists. The idea was to release them when the war was finally over.

Enlisted women were eventually trained at the largest recruit training base for men, located at Manhattan Beach, New York, and at the Coast Guard Training Base, Palm Beach, Florida. Upon completion of their training the SPARS remained at the Manhattan Beach or Palm Beach bases, attending schools for specialized training as yeomen, storekeepers, cooks and bakers, and supply. All SPARS were required to be trained in the handling of all Coast Guard small arms. In some instances they were trained to handle antiaircraft weapons.

SPARS were stationed at all Coast Guard facilities, from the ice and cold of Alaska to the warmth and splendor of the tropical Hawaiian Islands, and served 26 different job ratings. SPARS maintained many jobs that men formerly held, such as: small boat coxswains, truck drivers, radio communications, motor machinists mates, and pharmacist's mates (corpsmen), as well as aviation machinists. It was not unusual to see one or more SPARS overhauling or repairing a Coast Guard PBY flying boat. Their presence relieved more shore-based men for combat duty at sea.

SPARS stationed in the Norfolk area replaced men in shore installations in some 54 ratings, sending men to sea. They worked as parachute riggers, control tower operations at Navy air stations, link trainer instructors, and aircraft radio instructors, as well as X-ray and dental technicians in the Norfolk Naval Hospital.

SPARS officers and enlisted personnel were given roles in the control of shipping through the Naval Port Director's Office at NOB Norfolk. Their duties were to ensure that port shipping of Hampton Roads and Chesapeake Bay occurred quickly, efficiently and without mishaps. These SPARS also performed many dangerous and hazardous assignments inspecting ammunition, explosives and fuel-laden ships.

The top-secret operation of the LORAN (Long Range and Navigation) Monitoring Station at Norfolk was added to the SPARS' lists of responsibilities. The work at the LORAN Station required highly trained and classified personnel.

A SPARS Officer Candidates School (OCS) was also located on the campus grounds of the Manhattan Beach and Palm Beach bases. Many of these officer candidates were schooled in supply and procurement.

Virginia women who joined and became SPARS often found themselves with orders to return to Virginia as part of the Norfolk–Hampton Roads area.[10]

WASPS and WAAFS

General "Hap" Arnold established a new aircraft ferry command. The Air Corps Ferrying Command flew aircraft of all types from their place of manufacture to airfields throughout the United States. In Virginia two airfields received planes by way of the ACFC, Richmond Army Air Field and Naval AAS Franklin. Some of these civilian pilots were women who held a commercial pilot's license. With the growing man power shortage, more and more women were sought to fill the gap.

Three flying organizations that made their marks during World War II consisted of women pilots: Women's Flying Training Detachment (WFTD), Women's Air Force Service Pilots (WASPs) and the Women's Auxiliary Ferrying Squadron (WAFS). These three flying organizations were all placed under the direction of the U.S. Army Air Force. The need for men and women to serve in the military was just as great in this branch of the service. There was a great need for pilots to ferry planes about the country, to provide planes for target towing and for flights to overseas bases. The motivation was to free military pilots for the more important roles in combat.

Women pilots were originally turned down by General Arnold, but in 1941 everything changed when Japan bombed Pearl Harbor. By 1942, Ferrying Division Commander William H. Turner decided to integrate qualified women civilian pilots into his command.

The Women's Air Force Service Plots (WASPs), Women's Auxiliary Ferrying

Squadron (WAFS), and the 319th Women's Flying Training Detachment (WFTD) were formed in 1942. Early on, the Women's Flying Training Detachment and the Women's Auxiliary Ferrying Squadron were combined to form the paramilitary WASPS.

These women were all licensed pilots, with many holding commercial licenses. The first class of orientation was held at Ellington Field, Houston, Texas. The 30-day training session graduated 23 women. Later, the pilot training center was shifted to Avenger Field at Sweetwater, Texas.

Irene Shortridge Rutherford earned her wings in May of 1940. She was the only woman to complete the first class of CPTP (Civilian Pilot Training Program) offered at Butler University, Indianapolis, where she worked as an assistant in the English Department to pay her tuition. In January 1943, Madge got a telegram inviting her to come to Chicago to be interviewed for the Women Air Force Service pilots training program in Sweetwater, Texas.

After completing her training in August, she was assigned to the 6th Ferry Division of the Air Transport Command based at Long Beach, California. In January, she earned her instrument rating in DC-3, C-46 and C-47 aircraft at Rosencrans Field, St. Joseph, Missouri. Shortly after this, she was assigned to Brownsville (Texas) Airbase for fighter aircraft training and checked out in P-40 Warhawk, P-47 Thunderbolt, P-39 Aerocobra and the P-51D Mustang. Irene Rutherford went on to qualify on four-engine aircraft such as the famed "Hollywood Bomber" and the B-17, and spent many hours flying them from production sites to Army Air Force bases.

After training, the WASPS were quickly stationed at 120 air bases throughout the United States. They would fly sixty million miles from aircraft factories to take the planes to training bases, airfields, ports of embarkation for shipment overseas, towing targets for gunnery practice and hauling cargo. Many a WASP pilot felt the shattering experience of bullets ripping through her plane while flying tow targets out of Langley Air Force Base.

Despite the carefully supervised training program, 38 women pilots were to die in the service of their country. Jane Dolores Champlin was one of these. She was born in Chicago and grew up in Richmond, Virginia. After graduating from Arcadia College, she graduated St. Louis University in 1937 with a BS. She managed to obtain a pilot's license and training by way of the Civil Air Patrol. While training at Avenger Field in Sweetwater, Texas, Jane became the first unfortunate fatality in a night exercise.

The image of a young woman at the controls of a Superfortress B-29, a Flying Fortress B-17, or a super-fast Mustang P-51 is one that, despite several good works of literature, remains little known by the public. What fewer people know is that in order for a male combat pilot to receive his aircraft, it had to be delivered to him ... and that was usually by a female WASP pilot. One thousand WASPs delivered some 12,650 aircraft of 78 different types during the duration of the war.

The WASPS were disbanded in 1944 when thousands of male military pilots returned from overseas combat tours and were available to ferry planes. But these daring women and their flying machines are important in history, for they played a vital role in a military dominated by males.[11]

Nurses

Shortly after the turn of the century, the U.S. Army Nurse Corps and the Navy Nurse Corps were formed, though they were not considered actual organizations of the Armed Forces. The Army Nurse Corps had fewer than 1,000 active duty nurses when the Japanese struck Pearl Harbor in December of 1941. Only eighty-two Army nurses were on duty at the time of the attack.

This situation quickly changed with the advent of the war. The U.S. Army Nurse Corps quickly grew from 600 on-duty nurses to nearly 20,000 by the end of the war.

Six months after the Japanese attack on Pearl Harbor, women of the nursing profession enlisted into the Army to serve as military nurses. Several of the nursing schools in Virginia were requested to increase the number of nursing students to meet the sudden demand. This action produced a shortage of hospital and Public Health Service nurses.

Unlike the training available to women entering the military services for the first time, there were no military nursing schools to train nurses. The military relied on private and state colleges to provide the needed training to their nurses. Once a woman graduated as a nurse, she was commissioned directly into the service. With the overwhelming need for qualified nurses, Congress passed the Bolton Act in 1 June 1943, establishing the Cadet Nursing Corps program. The federal government subsidized the formal education of female nursing students who would agree to serve for the duration of the war.

After graduation, the cadet nurses would spend the next six months assigned to a civilian or military hospital, helping to alleviate the civilian nursing shortage. The American Red Cross was placed in charge of recruiting women for the Cadet Nurse Corps.

The Sadie Heath Cabaniss Memorial School of Nursing Education at University of Virginia offered the first nursing baccalaureate in the South, and those cadets quickly expanded to accommodate the nursing demands of the military. The Cadet Nurse Corps was sponsored by the federal government as a means to fund the program. The School of Nursing reported that 80 percent of the enrolled students served as Nurse Officers in the U.S. Army.

Many graduates served with hospital and medical units located throughout the country, working with wounded arriving from the war in Africa and Europe. With the invasion of Europe, the need for nurses became critical. Nurses were stationed with advance hospitals located in England, France or Italy. Some were close enough to the front lines to be wounded or killed.

Several of the graduate nurses from the University of Virginia nursing program were assigned to the Army hospitals in the Philippines before World War II. The day before the U.S. and Filipino forces on Bataan surrendered, the U.S. Army evacuated the nurses to the Malinta Tunnel, on the island of Corregidor. When the decision was made to surrender the garrison, there were 55 Army nurses who remained with the many patients. Those who survived the bombing were captured by the Japanese and became POWs. Many of these nurses went on to die in the brutal Japanese concentration camps. While held as POWs, these exceptional nurses continued providing medical care for the sick and wounded.

Some Army nurses were caught in some of the harshest areas of combat. In an effort to place hospital units as close to combat as possible, some Army nurses landed on the beaches of Anzio on the actual day of the invasion. Army nurses followed the troops onto the beaches at Normandy on D-Day as well, to tend to the wounded at Advanced Hospital Units.[12]

Vivian Sheridan remembers:

Wading onto Omaha Beach, 6 June 1944, past the wreckage of burning boats, trucks and I hate to say this, we used dead bodies as a shield from German bullets. Our small unit of Army Nurses landed on Omaha Beach in the middle of the afternoon, in broad daylight because of the enormous number of wounded soldiers. We kept our helmets on, but there was a lot of exposed body under that tin hat. When we got the chance, we'd dash out and give a wounded soldier a shot of morphine to ease the pain. At the time that was all we could do. There was no place to establish a hospital under such horrendous conditions.[13]

As the war moved across the islands of the Pacific, the nurses followed, with over 5,000 women stationed in the Southwest Pacific area as well as China and India. Many served at the base hospitals on New Guinea, Guadalcanal, Saipan, Guam, Tinian and Okinawa, as well as on hospital ships.

When the Japanese began their "kamikaze" attacks on the U.S. Navy fleet off the coast of Okinawa, a suicide plane crashed into the Navy hospital ship USS *Comfort*, killing 7 patients, 5 medical officers, and 6 nurses, and wounding 5 nurses. Sixteen flight nurses died in aircraft crashes while serving in a combat area. Navy flight nurses were the first to remove Marine wounded from island combat areas while the fighting was still raging.

In Virginia, Army nurses were assigned to base hospital units, dispensaries, convalescent hospitals, and many other medical facilities. They staffed such hospitals at Langley, Fort Monroe, Norfolk Army Air Base, McGuire General Hospital, Fort Wool Hospital, and the Woodrow Wilson Hospital.

The Navy Nurse Corps followed a similar path as that of the U.S. Army Nurse Corps. There were perhaps 500 Navy nurses serving when World War II began. Their status was the same as the Army nurses. Their numbers were hurriedly increased to meet the demands of the Medical Department.

U.S. Navy nurses served at the naval hospitals in the Norfolk area. Some were ordered to follow the Marines as they went island-hopping in the Pacific. Some nurses were located at Navy base hospitals while those who served on the famed hospital ships became known to Marines as the "Angels in White." Eleven Navy nurses serving in the Philippines were captured by the Japanese on Corregidor and sent to the Los Banos Internment Camp. While they were there, they actually continued nursing the unfortunate, sick civilians.

Shortly after the bombing of Pearl Harbor, the Japanese attacked and overran the island of Guam. Five Navy nurses serving in the base hospital were captured, taken prisoner, and shipped to Japan.[14]

The most unusual Nursing service turned out to be the Nursing Air Evac Service. These Army or Navy nurses were trained to administer to wounded being evacuated from a direct combat zone. Quickly loading patients on stretchers required ten minutes, then the aircraft was airborne. While flying, the Air Evac nurse was totally responsible for the welfare of the wounded. Five hundred U.S. Army nurses were trained and served as members of 31 medical air evacuation transport squadrons; 17 of those flight nurses lost their lives.

Navy Air Evac nurses landed to evacuate wounded Marines on Iwo Jima before the island was secured. One such nurse was Lt. Kathryn Van Wagner Pribam, flight nurse, U.S. Navy:

> *While we were on the ground, at Iwo Jima, loading patients, a Jap Zero flew over. I heard a terrible noise and chatter. I was away from the tent at the time and out of the plane, possibly on a hill not far from where we landed. The plane strafed the tent holding the patients we were about to evacuate. A bullet pierced our wing tank, which did not explode because it was full and there were no fumes as such to ignite. It's also fortunate it was not a tracer round. We quickly loaded the plane after that attack and flew off.* [courtesy of Dr. Jan Herman, USN Bureau of Medicine and Surgery, Washington, D.C.].

Many Army and Navy nurses found themselves in situations where courage was a common denominator as they worked to protect and save their patients, often at the risk of their own lives.[15]

African American Nurses

Grudgingly, the Army Nurse Corps accepted a small number of black nurses: namely, 479 out of a complement of 50,000 nurses. The U.S. Army set a quota system based on the segregation of the Army. Of the 160 African American nurses accepted into the U.S. Army, none were assigned to a base or facility in Virginia. Public pressure finally forced the Army to accept more African American nurses into the Cadet Nursing Program, which boosted the total numbers to 2000 by 1945.

Thirty African American army nurses were attached to the 25th Station Hospital unit and sent to Liberia, Africa. Many of them suffered malaria, and the most serious cases had to be sent back to the United States for treatment. By the end of the war, African American nurses had served in Africa, Europe, Burma and the Southwest Pacific.[16]

Women serving with the American Military in World War II:

U.S. Army	140,000
U.S. Navy	100,000
U.S. Marines	23,000
U.S. Coast Guard	13,000
U.S. Air Force	1,000
U.S. Army and Navy Nurses	74,000

Source: U.S. National Archives

Nurses received 1,619 awards, medals, citations and commendations. A total of 201 military nurses died while serving during the war.[17]

U.S. Public Health Nursing

With the start of World War II, the Public Health Service (USPHS) provided badly needed health care to 10,000 enemy aliens interned by the Justice Department. Alien civilian health care was given to the USPHS due to a lack of civilian nurses and health care providers. During World War II, the United States confined approximately 140,000 noncombatants behind barbed wire.

Internment of foreign embassy officials and their families (in three locations in Virginia) required health services demanded by the Geneva Convention. The USPHS was assigned the task. They quickly reshuffled their staff to accommodate this; many were also sent overseas for the same reason.

Upon arrival at their new duty stations, the nurses established screening clinics to check for health problems, specifically contagious diseases. During their stay, the alien internees continued to maintain the health clinics, caring for the political prisoners until their return to the country of origin. Severe medical emergencies were immediately transferred to a local hospital along with USPHS staff to ensure the rules of confinement.

The agency was tasked with the screening of Italian and German POWs when they arrived at Camp Patrick Henry. Although the prisoners were cared for en route to the United States, many brought contagious diseases with them. Once those were detected, those prisoners were removed from the general population. The clinics were staffed throughout the duration of the war, when they were then closed down.[18]

The OSS

The Office of Strategic Services (OSS) was a spy agency during World War II that placed spies in the European and Pacific theaters of war. The OSS was the nation's secret intelligence agency. Two major training bases operated in Virginia (one in western Virginia and one at Fort Hunt, Virginia). The newly formed agency did not hesitate to enlist women within its ranks. These were often women who came from prominent families and traveled extensively in Europe before the war. Since they spoke fluent French, Italian or German, they were eagerly sought to fill the ranks as spies and couriers.

Four thousand, five hundred women served as spies, radio operators, code breakers, intelligence interpreters, guides and couriers. After completing the intensive training program in the Catochin Mountains of Maryland (today the site of Camp David), trainees were sent to small satellite camps such as West Point, Virginia, for specialized training.

One such trainee was the now famous female chef, Julia Child. She was typical of the women who volunteered to join the fledgling OSS. Too tall to be accepted in the Army as a WAC, instead she began her career with the OSS. Upon completion of her training, she was posted to a clandestine station in China.

Today, few Americans are aware of the valuable role these women played in the defense of their country.[19]

Volunteers

Men have been going off to war for centuries, leaving women to maintain the home front. During World War II, women again stepped forward and staffed millions of industrial positions, and took on many jobs and community service roles. Virginia women volunteered to support the war effort through a number of well-known organizations. They also manned civil defense programs and organized bond drives.

Maintaining the servicemen's morale was considered a priority, so the USO, which was predominantly staffed by women, was created in Arlington, Virginia, on 4 February 1941. The organization was requested by President Roosevelt and chartered by an act of Congress, but it was not a government agency. Then, as today, it has provided entertainment and support to members of the Armed Forces, but it still relies on public support to run.

One hundred and sixty USO Centers were established worldwide to care for the welfare, morale and recreation of military personnel and their families.

Under the umbrella name of the USO (United Service Organizations), six national organizations united women to offer services to the troops: the YMCA, YWCA, the National Catholic Community Service, Traveler's Aid, the Salvation Army and the Jewish Welfare Board.

Every serviceman knows and appreciates the USO. Military men think of it as their "home away from home" with its tradition of entertaining the troops. Over a million and a half Americans, mostly women, volunteered their time and financial support during the war.

The USO followed the troops wherever they went and brought live performances of famous and not-so-famous entertainers to military camps throughout the world. Hollywood was eager to show their support for the troops, and entertainers visited at bases at home and abroad. The road shows of Bob Hope and Bing Crosby are well known to many GIs. Many shows played themselves out in little-known dangerous war zones.

While at Norfolk, Private Red Skelton was known to take part in many USO shows that arrived. Many small, unknown local groups from Virginia volunteered to visit nearby Army camps and airfields to perform.

This prompted other organizations to chip in for their servicemen and women. The YMCA provided rooms, food and recreation for off-duty servicemen. The Salvation Army provided coffee and donuts to departing military at Newport News Port of

Embarkation, as well as telephone service to folks back home. The Traveler's Aid Society was available to assist servicemen and their families with travel arrangements. The Victory Book Campaign collected thousands of books from local residents and then shipped them to military bases throughout Virginia and to USO Canteens overseas. Each training camp boasted a well-stocked library and was able to meet the needs of the book-hungry servicemen because of the efforts of the various women's clubs.

These wonderful volunteers were present to see the servicemen off to the war in Europe, and they were also there when they returned when the war was over. Many wounded men remember being greeted and cared for by the Red Cross Gray Ladies.

Segregated units in Hampton and Newport News found the African American community establishing canteens and a variety of entertainments in churches and community halls. Williamsburg offered white servicemen entertainment, but not the African Americans. The Bruton Parish Church stepped in and provided facilities for the African American servicemen. Church suppers were organized and the servicemen relished the home-cooked food.

Whenever possible, many black entertainers appeared in these separate but welcomed facilities. The famed African American singer, Lena Horne, appeared at various churches for segregated troops as well as at regular USO shows. Local African American jazz bands entertained at local military bases, bringing the jitterbug music to the troops.

The Red Cross bandage rolling groups and first aid classes became a hallmark of the war. The Red Cross offered their own canteens, along with the USO canteens where servicemen would gather in numbers, especially at railroad stations. These canteens for the troops could be found in Petersburg, Portsmouth, Richmond, Roanoke and Newport News, among other areas. They were known for their coffee and donuts as well as telephone facilities so GIs could call home.

Red Cross Gray Ladies could be found at every base, supervising games, dances, parties, reading books to wounded soldiers, writing letters for those who could not. Working in the hospital wards, these wonderful ladies assisted nurses, freeing them for more important duties. Arranging telephone calls home was a greatly appreciated service. The many service organizations, such as the Rotary Club and others that offered to assist the hospitals, were coordinated by the Red Cross.

Forgotten are the many women's clubs that organized scrap drives for materials desperately needed by the ever-demanding war effort. The military needed soap, grease, lubricants and explosives. The women at home conducted drives to collect kitchen fats as a by-product from cooking. Collecting cooking fats was a way of life for most home cooks and they willingly gave to the cause. Collection points in Virginia were arranged by various local rendering companies and local supermarkets.

Children, especially those in the Girl and Boy Scouts, were organized to collect aluminum foil needed for the aircraft industry. Throughout the early stages of the war, gum was wrapped in small sheets of aluminum foil, and these were collected, made into large ½-pound balls, and delivered to collection points. Rubber bands soon became scarce, as they were also collected into balls and recycled for their natural rubber.

Schoolyards quickly became familiar sights as scrap centers. Throughout the entire war, students eagerly participated in collecting newspapers, magazines, scrap metal, rubber tires, aluminum, and for a while milkweed pods (Kapok). Recycling is a catchword these days, but it was established by women of World War II.[20]

CHAPTER EIGHT

African Americans

Before the Japanese Navy bombed Pearl Harbor on 7 December 1941, the need for industrial workers was at an all-time high. Relegated to menial work such as farming, industrial maintenance, service jobs, and servants, African Americans struggled to survive at and below poverty levels. With the war industry in full swing, 1.6 million African Americans packed their family belongings and deserted the South, heading to the big cities of the North to find war work. Many African American families moved to places such as Philadelphia, Pittsburg, and other large cities associated with heavy higher-wage industries. The lure of high wages was too good to ignore.

Transition to the North was not without its difficulties. White workers were afraid the intrusion of African Americans would produce unfair competition, causing them to work for less money.

When African Americans moved into the bustling Detroit area in 1943, a race riot erupted in which 34 people were killed and many more injured. It took the local police department three days of confrontation to ease the tension. The race riot quickly repeated itself in other Northern industrial cities.

Even in the North, mainstream Americans had grown up developing prejudicial assumptions concerning race and gender of all minorities—against Hispanics, Native Americans, Asians, Muslims and especially African Americans. This ingrained stereotyping helped to enforce the "Jim Crow" segregation that predominated in the South prior to World War II. Segregation was purposeful and designed to keep the black man in his "proper place." That proper place was at the bottom of the social scale.

Prewar military tradition and policy was little different from that of American society: it was segregated. Limited numbers of African-Americans were allowed to serve, but in units staffed by volunteer white officers. The famed Buffalo Soldiers of the 10th Cavalry was an all-black regiment kept on the American frontier, away from white towns and cities. The 9th Cavalry Regiment, 24th Infantry Regiment and 25th Infantry Regiment were segregated units that were either kept in the western United States or served foreign duty in such places as the Philippines.

African Americans who served in the Navy did so in the capacity of officers' stewards. Depending on the situation, some African Americans served as cooks and bakers at Naval Operating Bases, such as Norfolk. There were no African American pilots in any branch of the Armed Forces. They were not allowed to serve in the Coast Guard, the Marine Corps or the U.S. Army Air Force. Additionally, the National Guard, despite control by each state governor, remained segregated, as did many individual state militias.

African Americans Transportation Unit (U.S. Army Quartermaster Corps).

With the advent of World War II, pressure was placed on white American society to rethink racial and gender issues. There simply were not enough white Americans to meet the demands of the military and its war needs.

Removing years of racial segregation, physical and mental attitudes, cowardice and a lack of motivation was a difficult social problem. Both black and white women, for instance, faced severe gender stereotyping based on cultural fears that the work performance of the "weaker sex" in the line of duty would not measure up to that of a man. There were those who feared women enticing servicemen with their sex and spreading venereal diseases. However, assumptions and physical limitations did not prevent thousands from entering the booming labor force and serving their country's call to arms.

As the war progressed, there was a great need to alleviate the growing military manpower shortage, so the federal government was forced to allow African Americans to serve in the military. This lesson had already been learned during the Civil War. But despite the manpower constraints, the Armed Forces remained rigidly racially segre-

Eight. African Americans

gated. When the African American male was recruited or drafted, he was placed into a segregated unit, company, battalion, and regiment and given menial work to perform.

Late 1942 the Draft Law was amended to allow the drafting of African Americans. In Virginia as elsewhere, when called to report to his draft board, a black man was directed to stand in a separate line from the whites, medically examined in a separate line and eventually sworn in, in a separate line. Transported to a receiving camp, he was again separated, and after induction, having been issued uniforms and gear, he went on to live in segregated barracks. This African American soldier would spend his entire enlistment during the war segregated.

The officer corps considered the African American the same way as the military, but did not want to deal with them directly. So black soldiers took part in their own PT classes, field instruction, weapons instruction, and marching. The same went for their off-duty time; they had separate mess halls, barracks, theaters ... even USO tours were completely separated from white units. The white-only segregation was strictly maintained in the military.

Until African Americans were allowed to train as officers and attend OCS, they were commanded by white officers. Many of the officers were biased in their attitude and dealings with the black troops. Some 20,000 African Americans were conveniently discharged from the service as unfit for duty when there really wasn't a reason for it.

The African American units were issued a company and battalion assignment, then given a service company assignment. The companies would spend their days digging ditches or latrines, clearing stone, and/or painting anything in sight, sometimes more than once. Many were placed in the "Engineer Company," another name for menial labor. No one in authority dared to give the African American a rifle and a combat role.

Eventually, under pressure from people like A. Philip Randolph and Mrs. Eleanor Roosevelt, the situation began to change. Integrated Army units began to appear at many Northern Army bases, such as Fort Devens, Massachusetts, and Fort Dix, New Jersey. Several riots broke out when African Americans refused to serve in segregated units. Experience with African American units in the North proved their capability and helped change rigid military minds.

Despite a slow move toward desegregation in the Armed Forces, the U.S. Army and Air Force fielded several segregated units. The Navy, due to close quarters aboard ship, generally accepted the de-segregation as a way of life, but not totally. Most African Americans, when they were aboard ship, still found themselves serving as cooks and stewards to officers. This way they were aboard ship, but still segregated from the rest of the crew.

The United States Marines did not want African Americans serving in a combat role because they were considered unreliable. After the Marines were forced to accept them either as volunteers or through the draft, 20,000 were sent to Camp Lejuene, North Carolina. Utilizing an old CCC camp, they were housed and trained at nearby Montfort Point as a segregated unit commanded by white noncoms and officers. After they graduated as Marines, most of them were sent to engineering battalions as service units, serving under white officers.

When the war finally ended in 1945, over 700,000 African Americans had admirably served their country, despite the many obstacles and social hurdles. The following are but a few of the African American units associated with World War II.[1]

Tuskegee Airmen

The Tuskegee Airmen overcame many impossible political and prejudicial obstacles to become the first African American aviators in the U.S. Army Air Force. The most famous African American military unit of World War II, the airmen set an example of excellence to all black units.

The Tuskegee pilot training program officially started in June of 1941 at the Tuskegee Institute in Alabama with the 99th Pursuit Squadron. African Americans came from all over the country to be a part of this historic challenge. Thurman Sprigg,

African American Tuskegee Airmen in Italy (National Archives).

living in Virginia Beach, was one of 1000 African Americans to be selected to be trained as a combat fighter pilot. His unit, the 99th, remained segregated throughout training and continued to be so when they were shipped to North Africa to join the war in April 1943, when they joined the 33rd Fighter Group. Unwilling to allow the 99th a combat role, the officers ordered them into an aerial ground attack role.

Later, Colonel Benjamin O. Davis organized the 332nd Fighter Group, comprising the 100th, 301st, 302nd and the 99th Fighter Squadrons, located at Rimitelli Airfield, Termoli, Italy. Under Colonel Davis, the 332nd escorted the 15th Air Force heavy bombers on raids into Austria, Hungary, Poland and Germany. While flying escort for the heavy bomber fleets, the 332nd garnered an impressive combat air record. To identify themselves, they painted their aircraft tail sections crimson. Allied airmen soon recognized them as the "Red Tails." Unlike most fighter escorts, the "Red Tails" stuck close to the bombers, providing constant protection.

Meanwhile, impressed with the Tuskegee airmen, the high command placed a B-25 bomb group, the 477th, in training at Godman Field, Kentucky.[2]

The Red Ball Express

Jeremiha Stokes wrote:

When we arrived in France, African Americans weren't trusted to fight in a combat situation so we were placed in Engineering Battalions as support personnel. I was working as a truck driver in a port work battalion unloading ship cargo at the Port of LeHavre, France. 26 August 1944, many truck drivers, me included, received orders to report without vehicles to a logistics base located at Chartres, France. What a mess the Allied bombers made of the place. It was hard to believe anyone could have survived all that destruction.

I was quickly assigned, along with another driver, to a tractor trailer hauling gasoline in Jerry cans. Our job was to keep up with General Patton's tanks. We had no real idea of what was going on and where General Patton was. It did not take us long to understand what was expected of us.

A driver and a relief were assigned to each vehicle. The idea was to keep the supply column moving with no rest stops, except for fuel and hot coffee. I was matched with a driver from Alabama and he wanted to drive all the time.

With Army Military Police guiding us along the road, we did that, day and night, until it got real cold in November. Being from Hampton, Virginia, where it does not get real cold, it was a miserable situation.[3]

With the destruction of the French railway system by Allied airmen, and lacking a nearby port, the U.S. Army Quartermaster Corps assumed the burden of delivering everything the rapidly moving forward Army required. Convoys of 5,900 vehicles delivered 12,500 tons of supplies: water, ammunition, food, gasoline, and when needed, replacement tanks and artillery. These badly needed supplies were hauled by trucks over nearly impassable roads, night and day. General George Patton declared he would not have maintained his forward push had not the Red Ball Express been available. Seventy-five percent of all Red Ball drivers were African Americans. Today Ft. Eustis maintains the tradition of the famed Red Ball Express.

African American Military Police directing traffic for "Red Ball Express" in Europe (courtesy Ft. Eustis Museum).

The 95th Engineer Regiment

The building of the 1,500-mile Alaskan Highway (ALCAN) from Dawson Creek, British Columbia, north to Fairbanks, Alaska, was considered one of the great engineering feats of World War II. Four white and two African American engineering regiments gained fame as the ALCAN Engineers who built a military highway through the rugged Canadian-Alaskan wilderness.

The 95th General Service Engineer Battalion was manned by African Americans as a segregated unit. It was formed at Fort Belvoir, Virginia, as part of the U.S. Army build-up just prior to the commencement of World War II. The 95th received considerable engineering training, then took part in the large military maneuvers in the Carolinas. From there they were shipped to Camp A.P. Hill, then to Fort Bragg, North Carolina, for further specialized training.

The 95th remained a segregated unit with white officers when it was expanded to regimental size, just after the Japanese struck Pearl Harbor. The U.S. Army's black corps of engineers consisted of the 93rd, 95th, 97th and the 388th regiments. With the fear growing that the Japanese might strike mainland Alaska, the engineers were ordered to British Columbia in June of 1942 to assist in the construction of the ALCAN Highway.

Racism reared its ugly head when the four all-white regiments were issued the heavy equipment instead of the 95th, which soon found itself placed in a support role. But with a change of command, it was not long before the 95th proved themselves highly capable as Army engineers.

Despite record low temperatures, especially hard on men who were all from the warm Southern states, they persevered and performed admirably. The final construction, a road 1,522 miles long from Dawson Creek, British Columbia, north to Fairbanks, Alaska, was completed in eight months and twelve days.[4]

Notable African American Army Units

366th Infantry Regiment of the 92nd Infantry Division (Buffalo Soldiers)
369th and 371th Regiments of the 93rd Infantry Division
9th and 10th Cavalry Regiments of the 2nd Cavalry Division
27th and 28th Cavalry Regiments of the 5th Cavalry Division
332nd Fighter Group (Tuskegee Airmen)
555th Parachute Infantry Battalion
761st Tank Battalion
758th Tank Battalion
784th Tank Battalion
46th Field Artillery Brigade

U.S. Navy and Coast Guard

With few exceptions, the United States Navy maintained a segregated force throughout World War II. Several African Americans from Virginia found themselves serving aboard all types of ships, both combat and supply. They were generally assigned to menial jobs such as officers' stewards, ship's cooks and bakers, dock stevedores, warehousemen, mess cooks, and laundry services. The Navy did not think the African Americans were capable of being radio, sonar and radar operators. Eventually, they were selected to man the antiaircraft deck weapons as ammunition handlers. In Norfolk, there were several all–African American tugboat crews.

During the war, African American officers were few and far between. Unlike the U.S. Army, the Navy maintained few large combat units. Where possible, African Americans were placed into units such as the construction battalions (Seabees), serving as menial service roles. No white sailor or Marine wanted a black man tending battle wounds; therefore, they were excluded from being hospitalmen (corpsmen).

Advancement, where possible, was slow to nonexistent. Having an African American petty officer in charge of white sailors was not accepted and therefore not allowed.

Despite these unfavorable circumstances, African Americans established themselves as heroes. A mess attendant, Doris "Dorie" Miller, was awarded the Navy's second highest award, the Navy Cross, for his actions during the attack at Pearl Harbor.

Samuel L. Gravely Jr. was the first African American to command a combat ship in the U.S. Navy. Born 4 June 1922 in Richmond, Virginia, Gravely joined the Naval Reserve in 1942 and trained as a fireman. He enrolled in the Navy's V-12 college program and was accepted. He was one of thirteen African Americans to participate in the program. He received his college training at the University of California and was commissioned an ensign.

He was not allowed to serve as an officer aboard ship, so he conducted "work parties" ashore. Finally, he was assigned to the USS PC-1264, where he served as a deck officer. Later, after the war, he would rise through the ranks and be the first African American to command a major U.S. Navy combat ship. After a distinguished 38-year career, Vice Admiral Gravel retired.

One hundred and sixty-seven thousand African Americans served their country during World War II, either in the U.S. Navy or the Coast Guard.

U.S. Marine Corps

The U.S. Marine Corps was forced to give up a 167-year-old tradition in 1942 when they had to accept African Americans. Seventeen thousand African Americans served in the Marine Corps thereafter, mainly at bases in the Pacific. Upon completion of their typical Marine boot camp training, these "men of color" were not allowed to serve in combat areas as combat troops. Instead, they served in segregated units such as construction battalions, as truck drivers, as stevedores, or worked in supply units or in harbor or camp antiaircraft units.

Those few African American Marines who were allowed to fight were reported to have done well. Despite the racial handicaps, some were decorated for acts of heroism.

Merchant Marines

Despite the need for merchant marine crews to man the increasing number of cargo ships, African Americans struggled for acceptance and positions there as well. Not barred from the maritime unions that manned the ships, they were generally just ignored. Though they were unable to do so before the war, many African Americans found employment on foreign-flagged merchant ships *during* the war.

When the German U-boats began sinking more ships off the east coast of the United States, the demand for experienced seamen overcame racial problems. It was not long before African American seamen were fighting for their lives on torpedoed ships like everyone else.

However, of the 2,700 Liberty cargo ships, only 17 were named after notable African Americans. The first such ship was the *Booker T. Washington*, the famous African American chemist.

Against overwhelming racial odds, Hugh Mulzar, the ship's captain, became the first African American merchant marine officer to command an integrated merchant ship crew. Placed in command of the USS *Booker T. Washington* with a segregated crew, he demanded, and received, an integrated crew. He spent the war making 22 round trips to the Pacific war zone without losing a crew member.[5]

African American Women

In addition to the prevailing racial bias against African American women, they also had to contend with the disparity between the usual gender roles. Men considered all women to be the weaker sex and therefore unfit for the rigors of military service.

Before the direct involvement of the United States in World War II, the U.S. Army began accepting African American women in to the Army Nurse Corps, primarily to care for the African American servicemen at segregated camps. Fifty-six officer nurse positions were created. Due to war needs, in 1943, two thousand nurse officer positions were added. These nurses served overseas with distinction and honor in such places as England, France and eventually Germany.

African American women were accepted into the WAACS at its inception in 1942. Four hundred whites and 40 African Americans arrived for training at Fort Des Moines, Iowa. They were dubbed the "ten percenters" as recruitment of African American women was limited to ten percent of the white WAAC population.

The 440 women did their training in segregated units, living in separate barracks, dining at separate tables in the mess hall, and attending separate recreation facilities. All specialized schools were segregated. Officer candidates trained in integrated units, but still lived in separate quarters. African American WAC officer candidates who trained at Fort Devens, Massachusetts, did so as integrated units but also lived and ate separately.

Delphin Sleeper remembers hearing that the treatment of black servicemen was different up North. When she left Hampton, the weather was cool, but when she arrived in Massachusetts, the temperature was considerably colder ... and so was their welcome, or the lack thereof. When they arrived at the railroad station in the next town, there were buses to take them to the base. The white women rode in separate buses. They were issued uniforms in a separate line, fed at one end of the mess halls and slept in separate barracks. They trained together, learned military drills and protocols together, but lived apart. She noticed that the women were from all over the United States and learned to share a dislike of the New England cold.

She recalls: "We slowly began to adjust to each other and work together as a team, black and white. It was a novelty when we received our first pass to town. Some took off for parts unknown while several of us simply went into town. We were window shopping when some young girls came up to us and wanted to ask questions about what it was like to be in the army. We had a very nice discussion and surprisingly there were no racial remarks. It really surprised me."

Graduation placed everyone on orders, and hers was to Medical School at McGuire Army General Hospital in Richmond, Virginia, for training. Thereafter, she was placed in charge of a medical unit at an army base that was segregated.[6]

THE 6888th Central Postal Battalion

The all-black postal battalion was commanded by Major Charity Adams; it comprised 31 officers and 824 women, and it was the first segregated WAC unit to serve overseas. Comprised of all African Americans, including its officers, its chain of command was supporting. These WACS were specially selected and came from all walks of life. Some had high school educations, other less than that. Several of the WACs were from Virginia.

Receiving orders for England, the battalion shipped out of Camp Shanks on a transport ship. They were stationed in Birmingham, England, for a period of three months, then transferred to Paris. Their assignment was the redirection of mail to all U.S. personnel, a total of 7 million. These WACs worked eight-hour shifts, seven days a week to keep the mail moving at Christmas. Each shift handled on average 65,000 pieces of mail.

Despite the heavy work load, the women kept their spirits up as they realized the importance of their work and the effect on morale they were having.

In addition to affecting changes in segregation policies, these women helped to dispel racial concepts of African Americans. Many Englishmen and Frenchmen showed up just to see what they looked like ... and if, in fact, they had tails, as portrayed in many newspaper cartoons. These were the first black women they had ever seen, and many folks invited them to their homes and treated them with kindness.

Those African American women who chose to join the WAVES found themselves in a difficult position. The Navy did not want black women serving in the Navy. But

Eight. African Americans

with the need for more women in the Navy, WAVE Director Mildred McAfee urged Secretary of the Navy James Forestall to allow African American women to join.

The first African American WAVE officers were commissioned in December of 1944. Although 80,000 women served as enlisted WAVES in the war, only 72 African American women served in integrated units.

With the end of the war, racial discrimination as well as racial segregation, remained in all branches of the Armed Forces. President Harry S. Truman signed Executive Order 9921 on 26 July 1948, effectively eliminating the obvious discrimination and segregation in the military.[7]

Chapter Nine

The Civil Air Patrol

Every sailor knows the old Navy axiom, "When in doubt, run in circles, scream and shout!" While the U.S. Navy rushed about supplementing its sparse—and in some situations nonexistent—anti-submarine forces, Admiral Andrews (Commander, Eastern Sea Frontier) gave considerable thought to his woeful lack of arms and aircraft. With an undefended coastline that stretched well over a 1000 miles, he had only 100 aircraft of varying design, age and capabilities. Three-quarters of these planes were unsuited for the day-in and day-out rigors of coastal patrol and anti-submarine warfare.

One of these patrol units was stationed at the Norfolk Army Air Base in Virginia. At any one time, only half of the aircraft could be utilized for full service demands; the rest were in some state of repair and maintenance.

The solution was to somehow involve the newly formed arm of the U.S. Air Force, the Civil Air Patrol, until such time as suitable aircraft would become available.

Gill Robb Wilson, a former World War I pilot and president of the National Aeronautic Association, proposed the idea of mobilizing America's civilian pilots as a unit of "Flying Minutemen." By executive order of President Roosevelt, on 1 December 1941, the Civil Air Patrol was created. Major General John Curry was appointed National Commander, Civil Air Patrol. The Civil Air Patrol was organized a few days before the Japanese bombing of Pearl Harbor and was made up entirely of civilian pilots, many with their own planes. It was established to supplement military coastal patrols until the military could replace them with Army Air Corps pilots and aircraft.

The Army Air Corps, charged with coastal air defense, showed considerable interest and offered to utilize the CAP, as it was called, in limited over-water coastal patrols. On 8 March 1942, the CAP put a variety of private planes into the air: Cessnas, Wacos, Stinson and Pipers.

Meanwhile, Admiral Andrews was attempting to generate interest for a similar use of the CAP with the Navy. He reasoned that a "Scarecrow Patrol," if enough suitable civilian aircraft could be used, would force the German subs to remain underwater. The Navy, in its cautious wisdom, rejected the idea on grounds it posed too many "operational difficulties."

It was left for the CAP to organize its official standing with the Army. The CAP thereafter remained under the command of the Army's First Air Support, then later with the Army's Anti-Submarine Command's 25th Wing.

General Curry quickly organized the association of pilots into wings, one per state. Twenty-one bases were established in coastal states from New England to Texas, California to Washington State.

Word quickly spread throughout the flying fraternity in Virginia. Seasoned pilots gathered together and organized Virginia's wing, locating it with the U.S. Army Air Corps at Parksley, Virginia Beach. Located between Bloxom and Onley, on the Virginia eastern shore, Parksley provided access to the Chesapeake Bay; the convoys that arrived formed up and departed from Hampton Roads and the nearby shores of the Atlantic Ocean. It was an ideal hunting location for any German U-boat lying in wait for its prey.

New members of Coastal Patrol No. 4 had to clear their own airfield, cut down trees and convert a chicken farm into an operating base. After the family removed their possessions, the crews set about converting the various farm buildings into some semblance of an air base. By September pilots were winging their planes out over the nearby Atlantic Ocean, searching for the telltale signs of German U-boats.

Although a civilian organization of pilots, the CAP was established as an auxiliary of the U.S. Army Air Corps and therefore subject to military command. Volunteers wore uniforms identical to the standard Army issue, complete with the "U.S." insignia, so they would be treated as POWs if captured and not shot as spies.

Once the U.S. Army determined that Parksley was a suitable operating base, volunteers were put through a short period of organization and orientation. They studied Army Air Corps manuals, close order drill, mapping and navigation skills. Flights over open water were of particular importance because of the German U-boat scare. Eventually, pilots flew simulated search and rescue missions. All patrol aircraft were equipped with military radios and channeled to a coordinating radio center located at Langley Army Air Base.

Locating the CAP at Parksley enabled the small airfield to make use of the many nearby military facilities; such as the several Coast Guard stations, the newly formed naval outlying airfields, and NOB Norfolk. These bases were able to provide Base 4 Parksley with a variety of aviation materiel.

Not all volunteers were pilots. The newly formed CAP needed mechanics as well as radio operators and repairmen, office staff, managers and other support staff.

Many women were certified pilots before the war and were not refused volunteer CAP pilot status. However, women were not allowed to fly coastal patrols, as it was considered too hazardous. Instead, the dangerous job of towing target sleeves, for gunners to shoot at, was generally assigned to the women. The slower-flying planes gave the gunners a chance of hitting the cloth sleeve, but many a plane landed safely enough, even if peppered with the bullet holes.

The CAP did not discriminate, so both male and female African American pilots were allowed to join. Several men and women performed with such skill that they attained officer ranks.

While the CAP wing worked to establish Parksley as operating Base 4, the Japanese struck Pearl Harbor on the morning of 7 December 1941. All civilian aircraft were immediately grounded for fear of another attack.

In 1942, the order was rescinded when Germany launched its U-boat attacks along the eastern coast of the United States, sinking British and American ships. The U-boats took advantage of the lack of air patrols and remained on the surface to attack ships with their deck guns instead of torpedoes.

Meanwhile, the lack of coastal patrol aircraft and suitable patrol boats allowed the German U-boats the freedom to openly attack shipping from Mexico to Canada. With tankers burning off the coast, Sun Oil (Sunoco) and other oil companies demanded aerial patrols to locate U-boats. In response to the need of aircraft to patrol the coastal waters, the government finally sanctioned the use of the CAP until the military could provide suitable numbers and types of aircraft.

To identify these planes, a CAP insignia was designed: a red three-bladed propeller placed in the Civil Defense white triangle in a blue circle. The red markings were later removed to prevent any possible confusion with enemy markings. The new, brightly colored insignia was placed on the aircraft in military fashion, top and bottom of wings and on the fuselage.

America was poorly prepared when it came to civil defense. Many cargo ships and tankers ran at night with their running lights aglow. For several months, coastal cities did not reduce night lighting according to prescribed blackout procedures. U-boat captains had little trouble locating ships traveling at night, either by their running lights or their silhouettes against the bright nighttime coastal lights.

Photo: Owen Gassaway
Civil Air Patrol ensignia as utilized on light aircraft

Insignia of Civil Air Patrol, in black and white (photo courtesy of Owen Gassaway).

The CAP pilots at Parksley trained constantly to fly at night from the small grass airstrip and locate submarines. All pilots were volunteers and generally held full-time day jobs. They lived on base or nearby and were constantly on a one-hour call-up. Most pilots had an extremely difficult time meeting expenses on their $8-per-flying-day government money. Despite this, CAP pilots flew in all types of weather, even when military pilots were grounded.

The U.S. Weather Bureau obligingly established observation stations at the airfields and tried to provide local weather conditions as well as coastal conditions. Pilots appreciated the service as they had firsthand knowledge of the weather conditions, especially foul weather at sea.

Nine. The Civil Air Patrol

Aircraft mechanics were at first difficult to attract, as most were working for defense plants. When the call went out for aviation mechanics, many quickly responded from the eastern shore of Virginia and Maryland. It was through their unsung efforts that the diverse aircraft of the CAP kept flying. A program of full time and volunteer mechanics kept the planes in the air when needed.

Pilots' daily duties consisted of escorting merchant ships in and out of the Chesapeake Bay, always on the alert for the telltale wake of a periscope. They soon discovered that from the air a U-boat just below the surface of the water looked like an overgrown whale. Many an excited CAP pilot more than once reported a U-boat, only to find it *was* a whale.

In constant radio contact with Parksley and Langley, each plane flew with two pilots, with one acting as an observer. Generally, wherever possible, two planes flew the patrol mission to ensure safety. Despite these precautionary steps, planes and pilot crews were often lost due to engine failure, severe weather and other malfunctions. During the 18-month period the CAP flew coastal patrols, it racked up a half-million hours and recorded a loss of 90 planes. Most crews were rescued, but 26 six men lost their lives at sea. For this reason, Parksley and other coastal bases maintained either a Sikorsky S-39 or a Grumman Widgeon flying boat for air-sea rescue.

Most of these small, light, canvas-covered airplanes were owner operated, consisting mainly of Stinson AOAs, Piper Cubs and Fairchilds. Pilots flew at least one flight each day, and if circumstances warranted, 2 to 4 flights a day. A full tank of gas provided up to 4 hours of flight time.

All maintenance of the aircraft was accomplished by the CAP with no assistance from the Army Air Corps. All aviation fuel was provided at no expense to the CAP. Generally, pilots flew up to 50 miles off the coast searching for telltale signs of U-boats or survivors of a sinking. Although spotting a submarine was difficult, the CAP was credited with identifying 173 and attacking 57.

The long, irregular geographical features of the Virginia coastline offered several emergency landing facilities. NAAS Chincoteague, NAAS Creeds, NAAS Fentress, NAAS Franklin, AAB Langley and AAB Norfolk all offered radio contact and emergency facilities to disabled aircraft.

Coastal residents and commercial fishermen became accustomed to seeing the low-flying aircraft with the bright red or white triangular CAP insignia. The presence of these brightly colored aircraft soon became the nemesis of the U-boat crews. The Germans referred to them as "*die gelb Biene*," the "yellow bees."

The presence of the CAP pilots flying off the coast had an immediate effect on the morale of the German submariners, as well as the merchant marine crews. "At least we knew if we got torpedoed, the CAP would radio for help," said Ron Baptiste, who served as a crewman on a tanker.

In the beginning, once a U-boat was spotted, all the pilot could do was radio its location and call for an Army bomber. Such radio calls were generally unproductive and usually arrived too late. So once the U-boat was spotted, the CAP pilots took to diving at them, making mock attacks, hoping to force the sub to make a run for open sea, thinking a bomb was in its way.

The U-boat commanders were unaware at first that these CAP planes carried no weapons, and so would dive when caught on the surface. Soon they realized they were safe from these small, slow aircraft and would leisurely submerge to escape the search by military planes. This would eventually cost some U-boat commanders because some of these pesky yellow bees soon carried stinger-bombs or a depth charge.

CAP planes finally got bombs after arrangements were made to support them under the wing. Some of the planes were able to support a 300-pound depth charge bomb. Most planes were eventually rigged to carry two wing-attached 100-pound high-explosive bombs. Armed with these high-explosive bombs, these little planes were lethal and feared by the German U-boat captains and crews.

Most of the flying for the pilots was spent in endless hours searching an empty ocean. Some days the monotony of patrol was broken by radio calls for assistance from sinking ships. On 28 July 1942, a patrol craft called the USS *Flicker* sighted a U-boat off Buoy 2GD, Cape Henry. Navy aircraft in the vicinity arrived and were unable to verify the sighting. The slower-moving CAP planes were called in to assist in the search but they could not locate a sub. The search went on for three hours with no sign of the U-boat.

Later in the day, a CAP plane flying a routine patrol spotted a life raft and a body in the water near the entrance to Chesapeake Bay. The pilot radioed the Army at Langley and continued to hover over the site until a patrol craft arrived to pick up the body and the raft.

As more and more military aircraft became available, the Navy took over many of the CAP's duties, especially the anti-submarine patrols. The "Putt-Putt Air Force," as it was often called, remains a valuable auxiliary of the United States Air Force to this day. There possibly has never been such a noble and yet audacious service as found in the Virginia CAP during World War II.[1]

Chapter Ten

The POWs

Enemy Alien Internment Camps

Shortly after Japan bombed Pearl Harbor and Germany declared war on the United States, a number of German, Japanese and Italian diplomatic civilians were placed into a detention facility until arrangements could be made for a mutual exchange. These procedures were pursuant to Geneva Convention Article #4: "Captured combatants and civilians under authority of an adverse party are entitled to respect for their lives, dignity, personal rights and convictions. They shall be protected against all acts of violence and reprisals. They shall have the right to correspond with their families and to receive relief."

Under Article 4, in all matters relating to diplomats, every nation involved in the war was expected to make every effort to protect and house all diplomatic staff and their families. The rules of the Geneva Convention were strictly enforced.

The diplomatic corps of each of these three warring powers was stationed at embassies in Washington, D.C. Selection of the sites was based on the proximity to Washington, D.C., as much as possible.

The Camps:

Hot Springs, Bath County, Virginia.
New Market, Shenandoah County, Virginia.
Staunton, Augusta County, Virginia.
White Sulfur Springs, West Virginia

With the beginning of World War II, the Special War Problems Division of the United States State Department was tasked with dealing with the internment of alien diplomats and their families. Included with the diplomats were the Consular Corps personnel and important business executives from Japan, Germany and Italy.

Within days of the beginning of the war, the federal government leased the Homestead, a luxury hotel located at Hot Springs in Bath County, Virginia, for purposes of diplomatic detainment. The first contingent was the Japanese diplomats: 363 men, their families and their personnel belongings.

The first identification, organization and transfer of personnel was accomplished by the Federal Bureau of Investigation. Border Patrol units were assigned the duty of guarding the facility and accounting for all personnel. Great caution was used as everyone involved realized that if the accords were not handled correctly, American diplomats in any of the warring countries would be held as POWs for the entire duration of the war, and possibly mistreated in retaliation.

The Italian, German and Japanese, as well as several South American diplomats and their families, were assigned to the Greenbrier Hotel at White Sulfur Springs, West Virginia, at the Shenvalee Hotel at New Market, Virginia, or at the Ingleside Hotel located in Staunton, Virginia. With the surrender of the Italian government on 3 September 1943, American-held Italian diplomats were exchanged via the Swiss legation. The actual number remains classified.

Number of diplomats interned in the US:

363 Japanese
212 German
113 Italians
71 Hungarians
16 Bulgarians
10 Romanians
South American diplomats and businessmen: undisclosed.

These facilities were occupied by diplomats and their families from early December 1941 until early 1942, when exchanges were arranged by way of the Swiss Diplomatic Service.[1]

The Aliens

The terms "Japanese-American, German-American and Italian-American" have no legal definitions or status. The term alien or enemy alien has legal status. Chapter 3 of Title 50 of the United States Code, paragraph 21 states that persons "older than 14 years of age who are present within the United States and not naturalized of any foreign nation or government with which the United States is at war ... are liable to be apprehended, restrained, secured and removed as alien enemies...."

When Great Britain and France declared war against Germany, 3 September 1939, President Roosevelt directed the Federal Bureau of Investigation to compile a list of possible enemy aliens to be monitored in case of a national emergency. This order was directed primarily at Japanese, German and Italian aliens. In 1940 all aliens living in the United States were required to register.

After the Japanese attacked Pearl Harbor and Germany declared war, Germans and Italians in the United States, including students, workers, and temporary residents, were expelled. Those seamen who were harboring in port had their ships seized and interned. A German cargo ship in Hampton Roads was seized and impounded, and its crew interned for the war.

Thousands of Italian and German aliens working in shipyards were removed and sent further inland to detainment centers. These camps were never called concentration camps, but relocation centers. A total of 11,500 Germans and 6,800 Italians were

Ten. The POWs

interned during the war. Included were visitors, tourists, businessmen and women, as well as various temporary skilled workers.

Executive Order 9066, signed by President Roosevelt, 19 February 1942 allowed local military commanders to declare certain military areas as exclusion zones. Lt. General J.L. DeWitt, defense commander of the Pacific Coast, nervous about the large population of Japanese-Americans residing on the west coast, rife with spies, declared the area an exclusion zone.

About 110,000 Japanese-Americans lived on the west coast and 150,000 lived in Hawaii. It was the Japanese who lived in California that troubled General DeWitt. All Japanese-Americans living in California, Oregon and Washington states were to be excluded from the entire Pacific Coast and interned at inland facilities.

The Naval Intelligence unit stationed at the NOB Norfolk, along with the FBI, maintained a list of all local Japanese Americans living in Norfolk and across the Commonwealth. With the aid of the local police departments, approximately 40 Japanese-Americans were quickly rounded up and sent to Fort Lee for a short time. They were joined by small groups from other parts of the Commonwealth. After processing at Fort Lee they were sent under guard by train to an inland internment camp in the western United States.[2]

The POWs

It was the daring exploits of the German U-boats off the Virginia coast that made it inevitable that some submarines would be sunk and many of their crews rescued. Until a facility was located and equipped to handle POWs, these captured crews were held at local military bases and guarded by Military Police units.

The Prisoner of War Division of the Office of the Provost Marshal General of the U.S. Army was responsible to supervise, house and care for any and all prisoners of war held in the United States or its territories during wartime. But such a large number of prisoners was never anticipated. Two requests by the Provost Marshal were denied, and as a result there were no camps to house POWs when the war started.

The federal government decided the U.S. Army Quartermaster Corps would utilize the master plan developed for military bases to house POWs. Prisoner of war internment camps generally were located near or alongside U.S. Army training camps that had already been established. The availability of Military Police and a large number of troops provided a secure internment system, in case POWs decided to revolt or escape.

During the war, the United States abided by the Geneva Accords and incarcerated soldiers, sailors and airmen as a means of keeping them from the war. The Geneva Convention of 1929 prohibited the use of prisoners in any war-related or dangerous situations: it also prohibited mistreatment. The U.S. Army's 1942 PW Administration maintained the official U.S. policy that prisoners of war could be used to perform any type of work as long as it was neither directly nor wholly related to the war effort, nor dangerous to the health and welfare of prisoners. While enlisted men could be compelled to work, the Geneva Accords specifically excluded commissioned officers from such labors.

The number of prisoners in the early months of 1942 was small—fewer than 2,000. With the U.S. successes in Africa, the number increased. The main question quickly became where to put them until suitable camps could be constructed.

Eventually, many German POWs were sent to Camp Ashby in Virginia Beach for processing and internment, where a suitable barbed-wire compound had been constructed. Unlike the British POW system of gleaning valuable military intelligence, American-held German POWs did not undergo a rigorous interrogation ... at first. The submarine crews were considered to be some of Germany's most elite personnel, highly trained in naval warfare, and some of them should have greatly interested U.S. Naval Intelligence. When it was determined that certain specialized German POWs, such as aviation, naval, electronics and high-ranking officers, could provide valuable military information for the U.S., they were separated from their comrades and sent to specific holding areas such as Fort Hunt in Virginia.[3]

With the Allies gaining the upper hand in the North African campaign, tens of thousands of prisoners of war were taken by the British and Americans, so the POW holding compounds at Marrakesh, Oran and Casablanca were expanded. Prisoners

German POW camp under construction, 1943 (National Archives).

Ten. The POWs

were routinely put through a medical exam and then assigned a serial number, all according to the Geneva Accords.

The growing number of prisoners in the detention camps quickly became a problem for England. After lengthy discussions, the United States agreed to accept and detain a larger number of POWs for the UK.

Thousands of German and Italian prisoners were transported to American ports of embarkation, then distributed throughout the countryside. An immediate problem was to identify and separate those German prisoners who held a deep-seated Nazism from the rest of the prisoners. In the beginning, prisoners were separated by branch of service: Army, Navy and Luftwaffe. Additionally, officers were also separated from enlisted men and held in different locations.

Hampton Roads became the ideal port of embarkation and point of distribution, and eventually a location for POWs. Once the POWs landed, they were placed under the control of the U.S. Army. Military Police were responsible for guarding and controlling the POWs at all times. The Army Intelligence Agency carefully examined the rapidly growing list of incoming POWs. They detained and interrogated those POWs whom they felt were of value, usually officers and skilled enlisted men.[4]

German prisoners of war being inspected prior to shipment to POW camp in Virginia (U.S. Navy).

Camp Patrick Henry

Constructed as a large unit staging area for overseas shipment, Camp Patrick Henry would also become a staging area for the dispersal of German and Italian prisoners of war. The main camp was soon enlarged to encompass a working unit of German prisoners. These POWs lived in barracks similar to American soldiers. Except for the barbed wire, it was difficult to tell the difference between the army base and the POW facilities.

The camp was guarded by MPs, who also accompanied work groups as they moved about the camp. Most worked in the camp sanitation department, food service, camp maintenance, or laundry, or were orderlies at the base hospitals and clinics. The ardent Nazis were removed from the camp and sent to camps constructed to deal with them.

The remaining Germans were allowed to work as stevedores on the Newport News docks, handling cargo, such as loading and unloading ships. It was not uncommon to find German POWs mingling with the U.S. Army troops loading ships bound for the war in Europe.

Camp Hill

To make up for the lack of space at Camp Patrick Henry, land was taken between 58th Street, the James River Bridge, Jefferson Avenue and the nearby railroad yards to construct Camp Hill (not to be mistaken for Camp A.P. Hill near Fredericksburg, Virginia). Camp Hill had the usual two-story wooden barracks, chapels, a theater, a gym and mess halls. The facility also contained housing and facilities for a unit of Military Police.

Italian POWs were contained at Camp Hill even when they became ISU (Italian Service Units). These ISU personnel were to work on the Newport News docks as stevedores, so a training facility was erected for them. Many of the buildings were utilized for civilian purposes long after the war ceased.

At the end of 1942, only 1,881 POWs were being held in the United States. Britain, on the other hand, which had been fighting since 1939, held a staggering and growing number of German and Italian prisoners, with an estimated 150,000 from the once-vaunted Afrika Korps. Unable to house or feed the rapidly increasing numbers, Great Britain asked the United States to intern 75,000 POWs. By the end of the war, 371,683 German, 50,293 Italian and 3,915 Japanese captives were interned in the United States.

When the war came to a conclusion, there were 425,000 prisoners of war located in 700 POW main and branch camps spread throughout the U.S.

For security reasons, most POW camps were located on military installations in the southern half of the United States. These base camps normally occupied an out-of-the-way corner of an Army reservation. They were separated from the troops and facilities by a fence of barbed wire, with guard towers and searchlights. Officers and enlisted men were separated according to the standards of the Geneva Accords.

Ten. The POWs

World War Two POW Camps In Virginia

Camp Allen, Naval Operating Base, Norfolk	1,615 POWs
Camp Ashby, Virginia Beach (Branch Camp)	2,230
Camp Lee, South Petersburg (Fort Lee)	1,016
Camp Hill, Newport News	1,400
Camp Patrick Henry, Newport News	1,807
Camp Peary, Yorktown	1,706
Camp Pendleton, near Virginia Beach	723
Camp Pickett, Blackstone (Fort Pickett)	2,436
Camp Shelton, Little Creek	785
Fort John Custis, Kiptapeake	535
Fort Eustis (Fort Abraham), Newport News	800
Fort Eustis, Newport News	4,345
Fort Eustis, Special Project Center, POWs	Classified
Fort Monroe (Hospital)	580
Fort Story, Norfolk	839
Front Royal Remount Depot, Front Royal	1,590
Hampton Roads, Port of Embarkation, Newport News	1,380
Fort Hunt (Restricted, classified listing)	——
McGuire General Hospital, Richmond	465
Norfolk Army Supply Base	560
Richmond Army Air Base, Richmond	1,181
Richmond ASF Depot	1,988

Branch camps were established to house POWs in order to provide labor to the civilian contract workforce. The accords of the Geneva Convention of 1929 permitted the utilization of prisoners of war as a labor force as long as it did not involve the war industry or place them in a dangerous position. These camps were generally portable tent cities, easily installed and removed.

Once the contract with the civilian company had been completed, usually after a period of 3 months, the camps were dismantled and the prisoners returned to their main camp. It soon became a common sight for Virginians to see groups of POWs working on local and community projects, especially on the farms.

Virginians in labor-starved rural areas welcomed their additional work force. Because of the war, the Central Shenandoah Valley suffered a severe labor shortage. The 1943 harvest, which was bountiful, was salvaged with the help of the Women's Land Army, students, convicts, conscientious objectors and POWs.

Typically, the temporary camp, such as Timberville Camp, located in Rockingham County, primarily harvested hardwood timber products. These men worked under supervision of Military Police units. Additionally, the POWs provided labor to harvest the tomato, cucumber, corn, apple, pear and peach crops. Later, these same POWs would work in the production lines of Zigler Canning Cooperative.

Approximately 250 POWs worked out of the temporary camp at local farms and orchards. Nineteen temporary camps were constructed, perhaps more, in the following areas:

Catawba	Roanoke, Va.	175 POWs involved in forestry work
Cheatham Annex	York County	520 general maintenance work
Cumberland	Cumberland Co.	172 agriculture work
Danville	Pittsylvannia Co.	214 forestry
Ettinger	Northampton Co.	233 food processing/agriculture
Fairfax	Fairfax Co.	150 agriculture
Green Bay	Prince Edward Co.	225 agriculture
Leesburg	Lauden Co.	150 agriculture
Little Creek	Norfolk	142 military maintenance
Lyndhurst	Augusta Co.	228 agriculture/forestry
Naval Armed General Service, Elizabeth City (Camp Ashby)		number as needed
Radford (branch camp for Pickett)		number as needed
Salem	Roanoke Co.	172 agriculture/forestry
Sandy Level	Henry Co.	Ft. Pickett maintenance
Shelton	Ft. Pickett	
Suffolk	Nansemond	288 food handling
Timberville	Rockingham Co.	205 forestry
White Hall	Albemarle Co.	225 forestry
Winchester	Frederick Co.	236 food processing

Branch camps usually were constructed to contain prisoners for a short period of time, three to six months, near a base camp. The exact number of branch camps may never be known, despite the massive accumulation of records. More than 17,000 German prisoners were held at Virginia base camps from 1943 to 1945

These temporary camps were organized and run like the old CCC camps. Several unused CCC camps were converted into branch camps. Being involved in seasonal work, many of these temporary camps utilized U.S. Army field tents for housing, mess halls, and canteens, such as they were. When the work was completed, they were taken down and the tents stored at a nearby Army base camp. With the Military Police present at all times, these camps were erected by the POWs, lived in, then taken down when they were no longer needed.

Camp Lyndhurst, a branch camp of Camp Pickett in Blackstone, Virginia, was formerly a CCC camp known as Camp Sherando. The facility was one of the 23 unoccupied CCC camps located in Virginia. The camp buildings were single-story semi-permanent wooden constructions covered with tar paper.

Depending on the nature of the work being done, the population of a branch camp rarely exceeded several hundred. Augusta County Agriculture Extension Agent James M. Gorsline reported:

A Prisoner of War camp was secured at Camp Lyndhurst in Augusta County. 200 Germans started work 14 August 1944, under a six month contract. Contract was made by Higgs and Young, Incorporated of Staunton who then subcontracted them out in groups of 20 men to various orchardists. Whenever available these orchardists allowed farmers to use them at farm work. Their aid has been a material help to the war effort in harvesting 2,000,000 bushels of apple crop. The C.P.S. camp at Grottoes allowed us the use of 30 men for harvesting work. These men have done fairly well but not equal to the POWs.

When the apple and peach crops were harvested, the POWs were shifted to forestry labor, cutting pulpwood. The Timberville facility, known as Branch Camp #7, was located on the Herman Holler farm three miles west of town. The camp was located at Timberville solely to provide area farmers, orchardists and food processors with much needed labor.

The German laborers helped harvest the apple, peach, tomato and feed crops. They also manned the production lines of several food processing companies, such as the Rockingham Poultry Cooperative and the Zigler Canning Cooperative, employing as many as 105 prisoners.

Where possible, many companies in the Commonwealth of Virginia utilized the available prisoner of war labor force: Crumpacker Company utilized a number of POWs assigned to prune and do general orchard work; Greendale Farms used them for corn harvesting; Neuhoff Packing plant for hog preparation; and C.C. Bova for fruit harvesting and packing.

Wearing G.I. fatigues with the large white letters PW painted on the back of their shirts, they soon became a common sight on farms and forestry camps, on apple and peach orchards, and at fruit storage buildings. The general population of prisoners discovered the country they were at war with and were amazed they were accepted as human beings. It was not unusual for local communities to become socially involved with such events as dances and church functions, either at the camp or in town, under supervision of the Military Police.[5]

Camp Ashby

Originally designed to house the so-called Cape Henry Defense Force, Camp Ashby in Virginia Beach was used as a temporary holding facility for the U.S. Army. Originally designed as a tent encampment to handle a large number of American troops, Camp Ashby was changed to house Army troops guarding the nearby beaches. The camp was hurriedly erected in 1942 on land leased from the Commonwealth of Virginia. The U.S. Army stopped using the camp when the U.S. Coast Guard took over patrolling the many miles of sandy beaches.

With the growing number of German POWs embarking at Newport News, it was decided to utilize the camp as a holding facility for prisoners.

The Tidewater Victory Memorial Hospital (a tuberculosis hospital) located at Virginia Beach became the POW camp's headquarters. The military erected 20-by–100-foot barracks, each set on cement blocks. To heat the units in the winter, each barracks was equipped with a coal stove. Suitable barbed-wire fencing was constructed around the entire facility, along with the placement of several guard towers.

The area was patrolled by the Military Police, as the camp was located close to civilian dwellings. The camp soon became the largest POW base in Virginia. It was designated Prisoner of War Side-Camp 1326, a Service Unit Facility.

Late in 1942, the Army moved out, and it was then that Camp Ashby was converted to handle a large number of German POWs. The facility, as were all POW camps, was surrounded by fences of barbed wire, guard towers, searchlights and a detachment of Army Military Police.

Plain wooden single-story barracks were located about 300 yards from Virginia Beach Boulevard. A large wooden building was used to house German officers. The camp was not particularly attractive, but was plain and simple. Roads were elevated above the ground and barracks were typical army construction with tar-paper roof coverings. There was a large parade ground for roll calls and such, and POWs enjoyed their many games of "football," which Americans call soccer.

When the prisoners began to inhabit the camp, they set about dressing up the grounds as best they could, planting grass and flowers where possible. Prisoners were pleased they could attend church, had the use of a library, and were provided with movies. *Der Walbote*, a camp newspaper, was soon produced and read by many in the surrounding community.

By late 1944, the prisoner labor was needed elsewhere, and so the POWS were trucked to local farms to harvest the abundant crops. Local farmers would make arrangements through a contract to obtain the services of a number of prisoners, then pick them up at the camp and return them at the end of each work day.

Local manufacturing companies, short of workers, sought the availability of the POWs. Seven fertilizer plants in the area, such as the Weaver Fertilizer Company, utilized large numbers of prisoners.

Only lower ranking enlisted men and other volunteers were allowed to work, and then only when they were supervised by their own noncommissioned officers.

The typical military guards were not necessary, as these men had been screened, and only those who opposed the Nazis were allowed off-camp. Most POWs were just happy to be out of the war and were content with their degree of freedom. Farmers considered the prisoners to be industrious and polite, and knew they could be left without supervision.

They hand-dug acres of potatoes, picked tomatoes, cucumbers, squash and whatever fruit crops were readily available. Local farmers were pleased with the quality of the labor and paid 80 cents a day as wages, matching the 80 cents paid by the military, but the prisoners only received ten cents. The rest of the money was turned in to the U.S. Treasury to help pay for the cost of the camps. The prisoners could use their money to buy whatever the camp canteen sold. Coupons or chits were also issued to each working prisoner, which entitled him to purchase cigarettes, food and other personal items at the POW-run exchange. As with the military units stationed in Virginia, all canteen items were purchased through the PX system.

Other prisoners worked in camp laundries, bakeries, canteens, clinics, and hospitals, did KP, and did general outside yardwork, such as mowing lawns. The food at Camp Ashby was prepared by the Germans. It has been reported that they could take cabbage and ham and produce a wonderful-tasting home cooked meal.

Attempted escapes occurred but were infrequent. Eighteen POWs broke away from their guards at Camp Ashby. Within a few days they were caught roaming about nearby Princess Anne County.

Ten. The POWs

According to Earl Swift, the *Virginian Pilot*, 8 May 1995:

Danger didn't lessen with distance from camp. Three U-boat crewmen on the lam in Tennessee were drinking from a mountain cabin water pump when a tough old granny stepped out with a shotgun. The POWs waved off her orders to "git." She blasted one. Later, told that she'd killed a Nazi POW, the woman sobbed, "I thought they was Yankees."

Four hundred and seventy-seven German prisoners died in captivity, and of those, 56 were shot while attempting to escape. Many were deterred by guards with trigger itchy fingers who often taunted the POWs. One incident was reported when a guard opened fire on a group of POWs gathering in the large, open common area. No one was injured but the relationship between the guards and the prisoners became nervous. The exact number of German prisoners who attempted to escape while being held in Virginia is not known, and in many instances is still classified by the military.[6]

FORT HUNT

During the screening process of German prisoners, those whom the military felt had valuable information, such as Luftwaffe pilots and those who were on U-boat crews, were separated and sent to Fort Hunt, Virginia. It was well known that Germany had achieved technical advancements in submarine and aircraft technology and the United States military needed to understand these advances in order to combat them. These prisoners just disappeared, to be held separately from the others, then put through a vigorous interrogation process. The operation was kept secret. The holding facility was jokingly labeled "The Officer's School" and was maintained under strict guard. Submarine crews were immediately separated upon arrival and sent to Fort Hunt.

The so-called "Officer's School" contained 150 new wooden buildings, many guard towers, and several layers of electrical fence to prevent escapes. Individuals working nearby were never aware of what was happening behind the multiple layers of wire.

The strict secrecy was important, as the operations at Fort Hunt were not legal according to the Geneva Accords. The prisoners were held in great secrecy and questioned constantly. It was a difficult situation, as the officers especially would not cooperate, knowing what the interrogators wanted. The usual listening devices were planted in barracks and conversations were monitored. It appears more was learned this way than through the usual interrogation techniques.

It is known that over 3,400 German prisoners were processed through the facility. The average confinement and interrogation was three months.

FORT EUSTIS

Germany was noticeably losing the war by early 1945. Releasing prisoners of war who held the same Nazi ideology back to the homeland was a problem. Re-education of German prisoners was expressly forbidden by the Geneva Accords. Several thousand German prisoners were selected for a re-education program and sent to Fort Eustis. It was kept secret from the public, but it was not long before everyone knew what was happening.

With the arrival of German prisoners of war at Newport News, many were selected and removed from the general prisoner population because of their backgrounds. A large number had work backgrounds that included employment with manufacturing in the United States prior to the war. These "friendly POWs" were utilized to persuade the so-called hard-liners, or members of the Nazi Party, to change their minds.

The programs consisted of propaganda movies, lectures and political discussion. The movies were selected to demonstrate the inhumanity, destruction and concentration camps of the Nazi regime.

Most of these prisoners did not return to Occupied Germany until mid to late 1946.

On 8 September 1943 came a turning point for the 44,335 Italian enlisted men and their 3,278 officers: Italy surrendered to the Allies. Technically, these men were no longer prisoners of war, but what to do with them? Under the circumstances, it was almost impossible to return them to Italy, as the country was still occupied by the German and Fascist army units. It was decided to allow those who agreed to join what would be called the Italian Service Units. Most Italian POWs were hesitant and viewed the opportunity with some reluctance. When it was realized, the plan would allow them an increase of freedom of movement and a better working wage. Still, a few hesitated. Members of ISU units, as they were known, received $80 per month, of which they were given $24 per month as expenses, plus $16 in canteen coupons. Many were allowed to establish bank accounts with local banks in order to save money toward the day they were allowed to return to Italy.[7]

Diego Arnone was one such prisoner who decided to join the ISU located at Camp Patrick Henry, Hampton, Virginia. He wrote:

I was a barber for my Infantry Company, seventeen years of age when I was captured by a British soldier in 1942, Tunisia, Africa. Unable to feed us and we detested their rations of "bully beef," they handed us off to the Americans. They sent us by ship to Hampton Roads. When we arrived I was examined by a doctor, given an identification number, deloused once again with DDT, given clothes and a good pair of shoes that finally fit. We had an American who spoke very good Italian (with a northern accent) who led us around and explained how everything worked.

We were fed three times a day (no pasta), worked from 8 o'clock in the morning, had an hour for lunch, then back to work until 4 o'clock. The night was ours, within the compound, of course.

When the war ended for us, we were changed to the Service Unit. I stayed at Camp Patrick Henry and was very grateful. I worked as a barber for the ISU and the American troops passing through. These very kind soldiers tipped me for cutting their hair so much I actually made more money than I was paid.

I eventually made friends at the nearby St. Paul's Catholic Church. I now had privileges that allowed me to roam about the community, shop and visit with new found friends. With the Abruzzi family I would go to the theater, shop, attend church socials and help with their large family garden.

When the war finally ended I returned to Italy but it was not a happy place. Three years later, with help from family friends in America, I returned to live in Massachusetts. I tell everybody that I was happy to be sent to America as everyone, even the Germans, knew that prisoners were well cared for, and I was.[8]

Ten. The POWs

Four hundred and twenty-eight thousand German and Italian soldiers, sailors and airmen were imprisoned at camps throughout Virginia and the United States during the war. There were 2,202 attempts at escape and those who succeeded eventually gave up. Many former prisoners grew to like what they saw of Virginia and later returned to live or to take vacations at coastal resorts. Many became U.S. citizens.

CHAPTER ELEVEN

The '44 Hurricane

Virginians were no strangers to the violence of hurricanes that roared out of the Caribbean and danced along the eastern coast, reaping their maddening harvest of destruction. With so many military air bases, Army and Navy training facilities, and a burgeoning population located along the east coast, the fear and threat of hurricanes was ever-present. Using four-engine B-17 bombers, aircraft weather reconnaissance was established during the summer of 1943 as part of an early-warning weather system. The traditional methods of hurricane forecasting and reporting relied upon visual observations, mainly, via telegraph and radio communication of ships at sea. Radio reports from the Caribbean Islands and commercial aircraft traditionally provided the basis of forecasting, as well as the speed and direction of hurricanes. It was often a hit or miss proposition.

These were the early days of radar and it definitely had not been adapted for weather use. Nor had the use of aircraft been devised for hurricane hunting and tracking. But after the disastrous hurricane of 1943 that struck Houston, Texas, it was determined to put in place a hurricane detection and tracking system using radio, radar and military aircraft.

The first tropical storm of the season, on 19 July 1944, was detected east of the Bahamas Islands. The storm that would later be called the "Great Atlantic Hurricane" was first detected on 9 September 1944, several hundred miles northeast of the Windward Islands in the Caribbean. Until the 9th, the growing storm went virtually undetected as it swirled through the Caribbean waters.

A U.S. Army Air Force B-17 bomber was dispatched to locate and observe the storm. Observing the huge storm for an hour, the crew determined the storm was moving steadily west-northwest toward the United States.

The reconnaissance aircraft reported winds strong enough to shear rivets off the wings of the plane. When the aircraft returned to base, it was examined and found that 150 rivets had actually been sheared from one wing alone. the "Great Atlantic Hurricane" was reported to have a moving diameter of 600 miles and winds of more than 150 miles per hour. The storm had a low central pressure of 909 millibars (26.85 inches of mercury on the barometer).

Hurricane warnings were sent to all military bases along the east coast, especially the naval bases at Charleston, South Carolina, and the naval base at Norfolk, Virginia. Military and civilian airfields heeded the warning and began sending planes to airfields further inland, away from the track of the storm. Ships at sea were warned to make all preparations for heavy weather and high seas.

The U.S. Navy destroyer USS *Warrington* (DD-383) departed the Norfolk Navy Yard on 10 September for a shakedown cruise to the island of Trinidad in the Caribbean. She traveled with the naval ship USS *Hyades* (AF-28). The *Hyades* was a stores ship on its way to the Panama Canal. The *Warrington* served as an escort ship keeping a lookout for German U-boats operating in the area.

At nine p.m. on the 12th, the storm was centered near the 75th meridian and expected to begin to curve northward along the Carolina coast. Moving at 25 to 30 miles per hour over the water, it was forecast to pass east of Cape Hatteras at about 9:30 a.m. on 14 September 1944.

Immediately, the hurricane alert concerning the change was passed to all base commanders and hurricane preparations for Step Two got underway. All aircraft that remained behind were either secured inside available hangars or tied down on the field.

Troops located at Army camps such as Patrick Henry, Eustis and Little Creek were transferred by train to safer inland camps such as Pickett, Lee and A.P. Hill. All non-essential civilian personnel were removed and instructed to stay at home. German POWs located at Camp Ashby and other camps in the Virginia Beach area were transferred to POW camps inland. Patrol craft headed into port and were storm-secured to wharves at Norfolk. The CAP, with its light planes, sent them inland as far as Pennsylvania.

While preparations were being carried out along the coast, military aircraft continually tracked the massive storm, now considered to be a Category 5. All ships at sea were given constant warnings, bearings and updates of the storm.[1]

Early in the afternoon, the two ships, the *Warrington* and the *Hyades*, encountered heavy weather along the South Carolina and Florida coasts. Later in the evening, the fierce winds forced the 1800-ton *Warrington* to heave-to while the heavier cargo ship, 7,000-ton *Hyades*, maintained storm headway, continuing on her way alone.

Keeping the wind to her port, with waves towering over 70 feet, the *Warrington* rode relatively well through most of the night. The crew worked to keep the ship properly ballasted to meet the bow-on-wind and towering waves. Strong winds and heavy seas continued to build throughout the night and early hours of 13 September 1944.

The *Warrington* eventually began to lose headway and slowly, continually, shipped water through the deck vents into the engineering spaces. The water from the vents reached the engine rooms, causing a loss of electrical power, which in turn produced a chain reaction: the main engines lost power, followed by the loss of her steering engine. With the loss of steering, she could not keep her head into the towering waves and soon began wallowing in the trough of the giant swells. She continued to take on more sea water.

The radioman desperately but fruitlessly tried to radio the nearby USS *Hyades*. Unable to make contact, he resorted to a plain language distress call, attempting to reach any ship or shore station within range.

At noon on 13 September 1944, it became apparent that the *Warrington* crew could do nothing more to save their ship. Most of the crew had no sooner abandoned ship in the roiling sea than it rolled to its starboard side and sank, taking many crew members with it.

Meanwhile, the distress call had been received at Naval Base Norfolk and 8 destroyers were quickly dispatched. The USS *Frost* (DE 144), USS *Huse* (DE 145), USS *Inch* (DE 146), USS *Snowden* (DE 246), USS *Swasey* (DE 248), USS *Woodson* (USS 349) and USS *Johnnie Hutchins* (D 360) steamed south from Norfolk Operating Base to assist in the rescue of the crew.

When they arrived at the scene, they were only able to locate five officers and 68 enlisted men out of a crew of 20 officers and 301 enlisted. Only seventy-three of a crew of 321 managed to survive the storm.

In addition to the loss of the *Warrington* and her crew, the "Great Atlantic Hurricane" claimed the Coast Guard cutters *Bledsoe* (WSC-128) and *Jackson* (WSC-148).

Early in the morning of 14 September 1944, the Liberty ship *George Ade* was caught traveling alone on the surface by a German submarine. Wasting little time, the submarine fired two torpedoes and sank the ship ... but not before she managed to send an SOS radio signal for assistance. While at sea off the Virginia coast, the USCGC *Bledsoe* (WSC-128) and the USCGC *Jackson* (WSC-142) were ordered to assist in the search for survivors. Unfortunately, they were caught in the maelstrom of the hurricane and were lost at sea, taking the lives of 48 Coast Guardsmen. When the seas subsided, a Navy PBY seaplane located and rescued the survivors.

The 136-foot yard-minesweeper USS YMS-409 foundered and took all 33 crew members with her as well. Not satisfied, the "Great Atlantic Hurricane" took the Coast Guard lightship *Vineyard Sound* (LV-73), with a loss of her entire crew of 12 souls. Anchored off the New England coast at Cuttyhunk Island in the Elizabeth Island chain, the lightship served to warn mariners of the approach to Buzzard's Bay in Massachusetts. Mountainous waves built in the shallow water, pushing the lightship toward the mainland. The radio operator maintained a continuous cry for help, but due to wartime conditions and prowling submarines, it went unheeded.

Later, when the wreck was located and divers examined it, they discovered that the plates where the storm anchor hung were completely stove in. In such towering waves, the crew never stood chance of survival.[2]

The hurricane passed 75 miles to the east of Hampton Roads on 14 September 1944. Fierce hurricane-force winds swept across southeast Virginia, recorded at 73 to 75 miles per hour at the Naval Station Norfolk. Wind gusts to 90 and 95 miles per hour were recorded at the Naval Air Station Norfolk.

Cape Henry in Virginia Beach sustained winds up to 100 miles per hour, while peak 1-minute winds were recorded at 134 miles per hour, with several gusts to 150 miles per hour. Rainfall was recorded in several areas up to 4 to 4.5 inches in a period from 10:00 a.m. to 1:30 p.m. Fortunately for low-lying areas, fishermen and the Navy, the fierce storm struck the area at low tide, minimizing the damage due to flooding.

Typical of such severe storms, hundreds of old trees were brought down, blocking streets and rail lines and damaging many homes. Several small low-lying coastal communities were left ghost towns as their inhabitants were evacuated to sites further

Eleven. The '44 Hurricane

inland. Many residents of Virginia Beach, Ocean View and Willoughby (Spit) Beach boarded up their homes and sought refuge inland, on the Peninsula. Despite the hurricane's arrival at low tide, many neighborhoods in low-lying areas of Norfolk flooded during the heavy rains and remained so for several days thereafter.

With the exception of damage to some small craft, the Navy fared well, suffering little damage. Local farmers did not fare as well. Thousands of rich acres from North Carolina north to Virginia were flooded with high concentrations of disastrous salt-laden sea water, destroying thousands of acres of valuable food crops. Damage to corn, peanuts and cotton was estimated at hundreds of thousands of dollars.

Storm damage along the east coast was estimated to be $100 million with 390 lives lost. Experiments with radar located at military installations along the North Carolina and Virginia coasts and aircraft reconnaissance played valuable roles in the advance warning in saving lives and property.[3]

The lessons learned with aircraft being utilized in locating and tracking tropical disturbances were not forgotten. Today the role of the "Hurricane Hunter" aircraft and satellite imagery has grown in importance and sophistication.

CHAPTER TWELVE

War Stories

War stories are personal recollections from memory or wartime diaries. The following histories were either obtained from archives of the Women's Memorial/WIMSA, Veterans of Foreign Wars, or personal interviews. They are presented here with permission from each veteran.

Mary Edwards Wall
U.S. Army WACs

Mary Edwards Wall, like so many women who wanted to join the Armed Forces, served in the United States Army as a WAC. She was living at Manchester, New Hampshire, with her aunt the day the Japanese bombed Pearl Harbor. During the Great Depression, her parents could not afford to support she and her sister. They lived with their Aunt Celia and her husband while her parents remained in Virginia.

She worked at a nearby shoe company as a stitcher when the Japanese bombed Pearl Harbor. She wanted out of her job so badly, a year later she joined the Army as a WAC. Three weeks later she reported to the induction center at Fort Devens, Massachusetts, for recruit training.

Because she knew how to use a sewing machine she was sent to medical section SCSU Station Hospital, Fort Devens. She was promoted to private first class (PFC) after completion of schooling. She was assigned to a post surgical ward, where she became ward master.

Mid-December 1942 she was transferred to Fort Jackson, South Carolina, as part of the new Station Hospital 117th. More training followed. Finally she managed to arrange leave and visit with her mother and father in Richmond.

Shortly after returning to Ft. Jackson she received orders to go to Australia by ship. After a short stay in Brisbane, they took a ship to New Guinea. Arriving at Port Moresby, they stayed aboard while their gear was unloaded.

Their new station had been a mission for French nuns and now served as s hospital. Here they received their long overdue mail from home. They spent time getting familiar with the hospital, learning to fire a rifle in case the Japs attacked, and doing daily gas mask drills. Much of the time was spent doing combat with the voracious ants and jungle insects and caring for the continuous stream of Australian and American wounded.

On 19 November 1944 they shipped the unit to Leyte in the Philippines. They were bombed by Japanese planes the day they arrived. Later they sent her, along with another hospital man, to a forward area, a place called Palo. When they arrived, they were so close to the front line, they could hear the shooting all around them. It was jungle-wet, smelled of plant rot, and the air was filled with the smoke of war. That night she slept in her raincoat and tried to stay dry.

The makeshift hospital was made from old mess tents. Patients kept coming in, day and night. At one point they had over 800 wounded men they treated. It seemed to Mary that they were forever behind in their work, treating the wounded.

Eventually they had wooden floors put in place, tents for barracks and wooden walkways placed between tents. With the constant wind and rain it was impossible to keep dry and to control the spread of infection. They put many Korean POWs to work washing and drying clothes and hospital linens.

"It was with great relief when we heard that the United States had dropped an atomic bomb on two of Japan's cities, 6 August 1945! I can remember saying, 'Thank you, God, the war was over!'"

Harry Quinton, Sgt, USAF (Separated)

Documented Original Tuskegee Airman (DOTA)

Harry Quinton was born in Salisbury, Maryland, on 14 December 1925. Upon completion of high school, he attended the Atlantic Aviation Institute in Trenton, New Jersey, and Casey Jones School of Aeronautics in Newark, New Jersey. After completion of training and examinations, he received the Airplane Engine Mechanics License from the U.S. Civil Aeronautics Board.

Shortly thereafter in 1943, Mr. Quinton enlisted in the Army Enlisted Reserve and was assigned to the U.S. Army Air Corps. After completing basic training at Keesler Field, Mississippi, he was assigned to the 477th Bombardment Group, 602nd Air Engineering Squadron at Godman Field, Kentucky, where he served as an airplane mechanic on B-25s. While there, Private First Class (PFC) Quinton observed the racial tension and disharmony that plagued the Group. As a direct result of growing tension, which lasted from January 1944 to June 1945, the 477th never became combat ready before the end of the war. Between 15 and 20 April 1945 a battle of sorts ensued over the use of the "white only" officer's club by black officers assigned to Freeman Field, Seymour, Indiana. Although PFC Quinton was at Godman Field and did not participate in the "Battle at Freeman Field," he recognized that he did benefit from it directly.

As a result of the 101 stubborn black officers' taking a stand at Freeman Field and refusing to sign a Jim Crow–based regulation (voluntarily or under direct orders), which was punishable by death (under the 64th Article of War), their collective action was found to be justified and caused a change in the command of the 477th from a white officer to an African American officer named Colonel Benjamin O. Davis, Jr.

When World War II ended, and after having attained the rank of sergeant, Harry Quinton was honorably discharged.

Sgt. Quinton's military education included completion of the B-15 Bomber School at the North American Aircraft Plant in Pasadena, California, and ground school at Godman Field, Kentucky. He was awarded the Good Conduct Medal, American Theater Ribbon, World War II Victory Ribbon, and the Army Air Force Technical Badge with Mechanic Bar. As a Documented Original Tuskegee Airman (DOTA), Sergeant Quinton and other DOTAs were cited for the Congressional Gold Medal at the U.S. Capitol on 29 March 2007 when President George W. Bush conferred this distinct honor on all the individuals who participated in the Tuskegee Airmen Program.

Following his honorable discharge, Sgt. Quinton attended Plattsburg College and Long Island University and was awarded an associate degree in business and a bachelor of science degree in accounting. He also completed some graduate studies at Hofstra University. He retired from the United States Treasury Department after having worked as an agent for a number of years. He now resides in Williamsburg, Virginia. His wife Vera is now deceased.

Josielee V. Callahan
RN, Field Hospital Russia
(Courtesy of the Women's Memorial/WIMSA)

The following is a short history of twelve nurses who were assigned to the three base hospitals located in Russia. Captain Anna Moline, who was our Chief of Nurses, was stationed at the Eastern Command Headquarters in Poltava, Russia.

Four nurses were stationed at Pyriantin, which was a fighter base of the U.S. Army Air Forces; it was fifty miles east of the fighting front. Four more nurses were assigned to the bomber base at Mirograd, which was 100 miles east of the front lines. The remaining nurses were at Poltava, which was a bomber base and also the location of the Eastern Command. Poltava was 150 miles from the front. All three field hospitals had only tents for surgery, patient care, messing and living accommodations. The entire countryside had been ravaged by the German Army as it advanced through it, then again when it was retaken by the Russians shortly before our arrival.

Our mission in Russia was classified top-secret until the American bombing missions were underway to and from Russia. The mission code name was "Operation Frantic," and it certainly was just that!

I should tell you that all the nurses were handpicked especially for his assignment; they all had considerable experience in the care of battle casualties in our Army hospitals in England. The corpsmen were absolutely outstanding. They like all other personnel had been selected because of their proven abilities.

Stalin had been pressured into allowing American bases in his country by President Roosevelt and Churchill. Accordingly there were many frustrations in dealing with the Russian authorities. These started with an unduly long wait in Teheran while waiting for approval of our visas to enter Russia.

The assignment was hard in almost every aspect; nevertheless it was a tremendous experience that all of us who were involved will always remember. You will understand my feelings upon being faced with setting up a working surgery unit in a canvas tent without adequate supplies. I used every skill I had and some I didn't. For example, it was necessary to take hospital sheets and sew them by hand into lap-sheets and sterilization covers. Time schedules for the bases to become operational pressed both the corpsmen and myself to our limits. There was only one surgical nurse to each base, so when the rare time to relax came, we really appreciated it; often being on call for 24 hours each day was a bit difficult.

We nurses slept two to a tent and were protected by a Russian guard. He took this responsibility very seriously, but he knew neither English nor how to smile. Food was always in short supply for the first two months. The local Russians were surviving on their black bread, which we became quite fond of very soon.

The weather is very cold in the Ukraine until early summer. So bathing in one's helmet in a chilly tent leaves something to be desired. Our contact with their civilians was forbidden by Russian authorities; however, we did make some contact and found them to be very warm and kind.

We were subjected to German bombing attacks on occasion. My Bronze Star was awarded for action during one of these raids. I was flown from Mirograd, by a Russian pilot, to our base at Poltava, which had been devastated by German bombers. I was sent in answer to an urgent call for blood plasma and supplies, along with a request for a surgical nurse. About 60 American B-17 bombers had been destroyed on the ground, so naturally the flying field was practically unusable, but after many attempts we finally were able to land. I went immediately to surgery, where I was assisting with the casualties when another bombing attack commenced. My patient, who was having a leg amputated, had to be moved to a nearby slit trench because of the severity of the bombing.

Unfortunately, he did not survive. Several hours later I returned to my home base, where we were once again the recipients of German bombs. I met my husband in Russia; he commanded the air base at Mirograd. We were married in Paris in January 1945 while I was assigned to the dispensary of the USAAF Headquarters in Europe, which was located there.

Melvin H. "Jimmy" Crawford
401st Bomb Group, USAAF

Born and raised in Roanoke County, Virginia. Married Frances Wright in December 1942. Entered the Army Air Corps in April 1943, and received basic training in Atlantic City, New Jersey. Armament training took place at Lowry Air Force Base, Denver, Colorado, and Buckley Field, Colorado. I attended gunnery school at Fort Myers, Florida, and bomber crew training at Avon Park, Florida.

I shipped out to England in May 1944, as an armorer/gunner on a B-17 bomber (waist gunner). My original crew was shot down on a day that I was flying as spare gunner with another plane and crew. They were flying right beside me when it happened, so it was like losing a part of me as I watched them go down.

(I was grounded for two weeks because of this.)

I flew with other crews after that, and on my 10th mission, on September 28, 1944, we were shot down over Magdeburg, Germany. We hit our target, then we were hit and the crew was forced to bail out. I was lucky to land near some woods and hid out, tired and hungry and with an injured foot.

I was captured the following day by the Germans and taken to a Luftwaffe camp where I was kept under guard for one day. After a fashion I was put on a train for Frankfurt. Upon arrival at Frankfurt, I was taken to an interrogation center and thrown into solitary confinement with very little to eat and given no cigarettes.

After several days of continuous interrogation I was finally put into a shipping compound, then moved to Wetzlak Transient Camp for another three days. Next I was moved to Kiefheid, where I was searched, had my meager amount of food taken from me, and got kicked around.

On January 30, 1945, I was marched to a train station and put into a small, overcrowded boxcar with more than 50 other men. There was no place to sit down and little area to stand. The little amount of water they gave us was not enough for the number of men. There was no room for a toilet.

After eight miserable days of this, with many of the men sick from nausea and dysentery, we finally arrived in a place called Barte. We were then moved outside and forced to march to the camp through mud and icy slush–tired, hungry, weak and sick. I remained at this camp until the end of the war.

In March 1945, the air raids increased around our camp and the American and Russian armies were linked up and moving closer. We began to dream of going home! On May 1, 1945, the Americans took over the camp. On May 8, 1945, the war was officially over and we knew for sure that we were going home. We were finally flown home on May 13, 1945.

After getting out of the military service, I went to work for Civil Service at Langley Air Force Base and retired from there after 27 years of service.

James Downey, Jr.
Philippine Scouts

Jim was born in the Philippines, the son of a Virginia father and a Philippine mother. He enlisted in the famed Philippine Scouts at age 17, after a 1½-year waiting period. He trained at Fort Stotsenberg, and after six months of infantry training, he was assigned to the 12th Ordnance Company, Philippine Scout Division.

Jim was at Clark Field, helping load bombs onto B-17s, when the Japanese airplanes attacked. He stayed three hours in a foxhole until the attack stopped. His unit was ordered to Lubao and was one of the last units to enter the Bataan Peninsula.

Jim repaired all kinds of ordnance from pistols to howitzers, mostly at night due to the constant Japanese bombing. He witnessed the bombing of a hospital and was involved in saving many of the patients from certain death. When Bataan was surrendered on 9 April 1942, Jim tried to swim to Corregidor to continue the fight, but changed his mind when he was told of the shark-infested waters.

Jim, his brother Robert, and three friends participated in the Bataan Death March and helped each other on the road. They were witness to the Japanese brutalities en route and finally reached Camp O'Donnell. Jim's brother died in the prison camp and Jim almost followed suit, but an unknown benefactor slipped him some pills that cured his dysentery.

Being of Philippine heritage, he was released after six months. Jim joined his sister in Baguio, then joined the underground. Once again he was captured by the Japanese and again released.

Jim participated in the liberation of the Philippines and was made a member of the U.S. Army. He served in the 2nd Military Police Battalion. His unit was responsible for the security of Manila while the Japanese were still fighting block-to-block in the city.

Jim was repatriated to the United States on 27 December 1945, and arrived unassigned at Fort Bragg, North Carolina. After a short leave he was sent to Fort Meade for training and then to Aberdeen Proving Grounds for small arms training. Assigned to Fort Eustis, Jim served with the Hovercraft Company. He met his wife Frances at a USO dance. They married in 1948 and they have four children and seven grandchildren.

In 1952, Jim went to Pusan, Korea, and was assigned there for six months. He was then sent to Yokahama, Japan, as an engineer of a large tugboat. He finally retired in 1963 and worked for Hess's Department Store for 15 years. The entire family lives in the Virginia Tidewater, Gloucester, Virginia.

Dorothy Steinbis Davis

R.N., 57th Field Hospital, ETO
(Courtesy of the Women's Memorial/WIMSA)

Caring for the sick and wounded during the hostilities in the ETO during 1944–45 proved to be a demanding and exhausting task, and frequently placed the hospitals and staff in close proximity to enemy fire. There were not only the wounded from the ongoing battle situations, but there were also many casualties, such as frostbite and other cold-related injuries. During only 40 days of the Battle of the Bulge, there were 81,000 casualties, including 19,000 deaths.

I shall share with you some of the experiences of three hospitals that served in different combat areas of the ETO: the 57th Field Hospital, in which I served as an Army nurse; the 13th Field Hospital that landed on Omaha Beach on June 8, 1944, and began taking patients on June 10, thus becoming the first American hospital to open on the beaches of Normandy; and the 107th Evacuation Hospital, which received the Presidential Citation for, among other actions, evacuating 400 seriously wounded patients on December 21, 1944, from Libin, Belgium, to the less dangerous area of Carlsburg, Belgium, traveling in open trucks and ambulances just ahead of the oncoming German troops.

As some of you know, the Field Hospitals were small mobile units that included 13 physicians, 3 dental officers, 5 medical administrative officers, 18 nurses, 183 enlisted men, a chaplain and 2 Red Cross workers.

Much time was spent moving and preparing to move. Patients had to be prepared for arduous travel conditions, equipment packed and loaded, and then preparations made for the journey to a new location. On several occasions we moved into a building that was still being used by the Germans as a hospital. The German medical staff was allowed to care for their wounded and evacuate their patients as quickly as possible.

Although we were not assigned to the specific Battle of the Bulge area, we were on the "French Rim" of it and many of the wounded were cared for in the 57th Field Hospital. During the winter months we were assigned to the 3rd, 45th, 100th and 103rd Infantry Divisions, the 12th and 14th Armored Divisions, and the 2nd French Armored Division.

In January 1945, Detachment "B" of the 57th moved to Saurrebourg, France, into a building also occupied by two clearing companies and a collecting station. We were immediately overwhelmed with critically wounded. Later our Commanding Officer informed us that, at that time, our small detachment had been caring for 24 battalions of troops.

Our hospital units were bombed several times. During this period there were several times when the hospital units were in grave danger of being overrun by the Germans. Hasty retreats were necessary, requiring us to take our wounded with us. Transportation was always a problem.

During the Bulge, as hospitals we suffered from the mass confusion of the time, the continuous and never-ending need for blood, and not knowing the state of the combat situation. I distinctly remember crawling into my bedroll after one exhausting day and thinking, "My God, what if we should lose the war?"

Even though we were an Evacuation Hospital, we were constantly putting up and taking down tents. We arrived at Brest, France, in September 1944 and provided medical care to the 2nd, 8th and 29th Divisions.

William Drost
PVT., 32nd Infantry Division

Bill Drost was eighteen, living in Alexandria, Virginia, when the Japanese bombed Pearl Harbor. He had graduated from high school. His father was an Army recruiter stationed in Washington, D.C. He tried to join the U.S. Navy but was rejected because of flat feet.

He received his draft notice 1943. He was sent to Camp Livingston, Louisiana, for basic training, where he remembers seeing many Italian POWs working about the camp. After completion of basic training they were sent to the Oakland Army Terminal in California.

> After what seemed weeks we finally arrived in the Philippines, where I was assigned to a stevedore unit. I worked the night shift and so slept days, despite the noise.
> News drifted in from the front at Central Luzon and as usual it was not good. One day I found my name on the company's duty board. I was to report to Battalion HQ. Once there I found I had been assigned to the 32nd Infantry Division as a rifleman. The 32nd was somewhere in the mountains on Luzon. So I began my brief career as a combat soldier. They were stripping everyone from all kinds of work units, truck drivers, stevedores, clerks and whatnot.
> Sgt. Call came out of a hut, yelled at us to gather around. He had us issued rations and two bandoliers of ammo and told us to stay close to him."

They followed him along a jungle trail that was more like a river than a trail. He prayed to God his rifle would work.

After an hour on the trail, always straight up, they suddenly came onto two grass huts on bamboo poles. This was Battalion HQ. They were turned over to another Sergeant whose name Drost never learned. When asked, he snorted, "No one wants to know your name, kid, because they do not expect you to live out the day!"

They finally moved out, following the man ahead. "SNIPERS!" someone yelled, and they all fell to the ground. Lead rattled against the nearby rock. It started to rain heavily.

Drost was turned slightly to his left, scanning the tree line off to their right, when something hit him in the right shoulder. It was the hot lead of a bullet, but it passed through and out the other side, knocking him down.

He remembered everything going black, in slow motion, as he passed out. When he finally came to, everything was warm and dry. He could see the white ceiling and could feel the clean-smelling sheets. A beautiful angel was looking down at him and asking how he felt. He asked the angel if he would live. She informed him he would, as the surgeon had done a good job.

She was right, and so ended his brief but exciting stint as a rifleman in Luzon. "I never got to know any one and no one knew who I was."

James A. Green

Rifleman, 70th Division

James A. (Jim) Green was born on 18 August 1924, in Higginsport, Ohio. He enlisted in the Army at Fort Thomas, Kentucky, on 19 July 1943. He received basic training at Camp Haan, California (antiaircraft), and infantry training at Camp Adair,

Oregon. Following his training, he was shipped out to France in early 1944, where he was assigned to Company B, 275th Infantry Regiment, 70th Trailblazer Infantry Division.

Jim was captured by the Germans on 8 January 1944, during the Battle of the Bulge, after being surrounded for seven days and nights without food or water, and after being wounded during the battle. He spent those seven days in a foxhole, needing medical attention as well as food and water. The weather was so cold his feet were severely frostbitten.

Upon his capture, the Germans used pliers to pull off the frostbite blisters and gave him a few paper bandages to use. Despite the condition of his feet, he was then marched to the rail yard, where he was loaded onto a boxcar with many other POWs and transported to Stalag IV-B at Mulberg, Germany. After only a few days there, he was assigned to a work detail and sent to Pegau, Germany, with approximately 100 other POWs. There they were used to repair German railroads after American flyboys bombed them.

Camp conditions, food and water supply, and general treatment were all extremely poor. Medical care was limited to a doctor coming once a week.

On 12 April 1945, Jim was finally liberated by the Sixth Armored Division and returned home. He and his lovely wife, Virginia, were married on Jim's birthday, August 18. They have three children and seven grandchildren.

Jim worked for the Globe Wernicke Company and the Newport News Shipbuilding and Drydock Company, eventually retiring from the shipyard. His hobbies in retirement are sports, fishing and woodcraft.

Homer Warren Landis

6th Engineer Amphibious Brigade

Homer Warren Landis, born 23 January 1924, was inducted into the U.S. Army, 8 February 1943. Basic training was at Camp Swift, Texas, with the 6th Engineer Amphibious Special Brigade. After amphibious and beach assault training at Fort Pierce, Florida, cliff scaling and survival training began at Camp Pickett, Virginia. The brigade's training continued while they were stationed in England.

On 6 June 1944, his unit took part in the invasion of France on the Normandy beaches. Landis was wounded on 7 June and was sent back to England for three weeks' recovery from his wounds. He rejoined his unit at St. Louis.

Wounded for a second time on 23 August 1944, he was sent to a hospital. Upon recovery he was then assigned detached service to the 10th Armored Division of General Patton's 3rd Army in November to assist in the construction and repair of bridges and roads.

He was captured on December 25, Christmas Day, near Bastonge, Belgium, by German troops of the Second Panzer Division. Put in prison at Hartmansdorf, Germany, Stalag 4 for interrogation, he was transferred to the Dachau work camp two weeks later, although the camp was not listed as a military POW camp its existence was denied by the German military.

One of their group who spoke German overheard one of the guards receiving orders to shoot all prisoners rather than allow them to be liberated from the camp. Believing they had nothing to lose, three of them managed an escape on 6 February 1945. Assisted by friendly farmers, they rejoined troops of the 10th Armored Division.

They returned to the 147th Engineers on 20 February. When the war ended they remained in Europe with the occupation forces until 10 December 1945. Upon returning to the United States, Landis was processed and honorably discharged on 20 December 1945.

Landis pursued a college and seminary education and was ordained as a minister in the United Methodist Church in 1952. He then joined the U.S. Air Force serving as a chaplain in September 1955. Homer is currently serving as a chaplain with the Veterans Administration Medical Center, Hampton, Virginia.

Harvey D. Patterson
3RD Armored Division

Harvey Patterson was born on 16 February 1920 in Norfolk, Virginia, and remained in the area while growing up and attending public school. He enlisted in the Army reserve in February 1938. In view of the troubled situation in Europe, he was called to active duty in November 1940 and was sent as part of a unit with no basic training to Ft. Meade, Maryland.

He was a sergeant when called to active duty. His unit received further training while stationed at Fort Sill, Oklahoma. From Fort Sill they were transferred the desert training area in California, then to Fort Pickett, Virginia, and finally to Indiantown Gap, Pennsylvania. They were assigned to the 391st F.A. of the 3rd Armored Division and shipped out to England in September 1943.

On the date of his capture (19 September 1944) he was serving as a forward artillery observer with the infantry, trying to knock out German Tiger tanks and infantry units. While they were advancing towards Stolberg, Germany, the Germans counterattacked with several full divisions supported by Tiger tanks.

U.S. Army tanks were knocked out and all infantry officers and noncoms were either killed or wounded. Harvey was left with 200 infantrymen from three different divisions. They resisted until most of his men were severely wounded or killed. He was put out of action when a shell landed in his foxhole.

He woke up five days later in a hospital in Hanover, Germany, to find he had had the lower lobe of one lung removed. He was allowed to recover, then was moved by hospital train to a British POW camp located in Fallinghostle (Stalag XL-B), in Germany. Later two of them were transferred by train to OFLAG 64, in Poland. In January, as the Russians got closer to where they were being held, they were evacuated on foot towards Germany.

While on this forced march, two of them managed to escape but were recaptured several days later and shipped by boxcar to Stalag 111-A in Luckenwalde, Germany. They were kept in solitary confinement there until liberated by the Russians on 3 May 1945. They made their way to the Elbe River and found the American 28th Infantry Division. They were then flown to the Army base known as Camp Lucky Strike for repatriation. The next day they were on a ship heading for the United States.

His wife, Anne, and he had been married on 22 November 1942 before he was shipped overseas. They have three children and one grandchild.

After returning home from the war, Harvey worked as an insurance agent from 1946 until 1969. He served as executive vice-president of a Richmond corporation until 1982.

Robert B. Short
Pilot, 390th Bomb Group

Robert B. Short was born 21 July 1917 at Norfolk, Nebraska, a town whose only claim to fame is that it is the hometown of Johnny Carson. Robert graduated from high school in 1934, attended the University of Southern California on a one-year scholarship, then attended the University of Nebraska for one semester. In 1937, he enlisted in the army and subsequently won a competitive appointment to the United States Military Academy at West Point, New York. He graduated 29 May 1942 and married his high school sweetheart, Doris Marshall, on the same day. For a wedding present, their friends bought them a railway ticket for a bedroom suite to Ontario, California, where he began flight training.

From Ontario he went to Taft, California, for basic training, then to Luke Field, Arizona, for advanced training in the class of 42K. Next came B-17 training at Sebring, Florida, and an assignment to the 399th Bomb Group just being formed.

In July 1943, the group flew their aircraft across the Atlantic to Framlingham, England, where they joined General Curtis LeMay's wing.

On 10 October 1943, Short's plane was shot down in flames during a raid on Munster, Germany—a raid in which thirty B-17s, two P-47s, and 26 German fighters were shot down in a span of 25 minutes. Some analysts say this was one of the most intense air battles of the war, considering the number of planes lost in such a short period of time.

Three of the crew were killed; the rest parachuted safely out of the burning plane. "One German ME-109 fighter made a head-on pass at me as I descended, looked me over but did not fire his guns." He was captured immediately upon landing, and held temporarily in the burning city of Munster.

From Munster he was sent on to Frankfurt for interrogation. A few days later he

Twelve. War Stories

was sent by rail boxcar to Stalag Luft III at Sagan, Germany, located on the Polish border. Stalag Luft was famous for the "Great Escape" dramatized by Steve McQueen in his movie by the same name. In the escape, some 78 POWs from the British/Canadian sector dug their way out but were soon recaptured, except 3 who got home. Approximately half of those recaptured were executed by the Germans.

In late December 1944, all POWs were marched through the freezing snow about 35 miles and loaded onto boxcars, then shipped to Stalag 7-A located at Moosburg, Germany, near Munich. On 29 April 1945, after a sharp skirmish, Patton's Army liberated the camp.

Airlifted to Camp Lucky Strike, Short returned to the United States via a Liberty ship and resumed his career in the Army Air Force (soon to become the U.S. Air Force). After many assignments, including two as an instructor at West Point, Air Command and Staff College, and the Air War College, and flying many different airplanes, he finished by flying in Southeast Asia in 1968 and 1969, with the 8th TAC Fighter Wing, the "Wolf Pack," which was equipped with the F-4 aircraft. They were the first to be equipped with the so-called "smart bombs" in combat.

Bob retired on 1 October 1970 at Langley AFB. From 1971 to 1984 he taught mathematics at Hampton Roads Academy, then retired again. Except for occasionally teaching some math classes at Thomas Nelson Community College, he plays tennis, fishes and travels, in that order.

L. Peter Wren, LCDR (Ret)
Boat Officer, USS *Bassett* (APD 73)

L. Peter Wren entered the U.S. Navy on 28 December 1941 and completed boot camp in Norfolk, Virginia, in January 1942. He was commissioned as a line officer from Columbia University in April 1944 and assigned to the USS *Coates* (DE 685), in the Atlantic Fleet. He was transferred to the USS *Bassett* (APD 73) in April 1945. On 26 July the USS *Indianapolis* delivered the atomic bomb to Tinian Island for later dropping on Hiroshima. The USS *Indy* was sunk by a Japanese submarine on 30 July 1945, and 152 survivors were rescued by the USS *Bassett*.

Relieved of the cargo on 26 July at Tinian Island with still no knowledge what the "Black Box" contained, the *Indy* now proceeded to the southernmost island in the chain, known as Guam. Here the *Indy* was refueled and replenished. On the 28 July 1945 the *Indy* departed Guam, heading across the Philippine Sea. No escort vessel was provided.

It was on 30 July at midnight when the Japanese torpedoes punctured the *Indy*'s hull; the *Indy* sank in 12 minutes. The ship which helped introduce atomic warfare to the world took with it two-thirds of its crew.

The survivors' rescue began when a pilot on an American plane on patrol, while adjusting his aerial, saw an oil slick on the surface of the Philippine Sea and flew down to search for an enemy submarine.

On Station D, in the Philippine Sea, the USS *Bassett* on 2 August 1945 continued its search for Japanese submarines. Steaming as before, the *Bassett* received an urgent message on Wednesday 2 August 1945 to "proceed with best speed to latitude 11 degrees 34 minutes east longitude to search for survivors of an unknown origin."

The *Bassett* steamed to the scene and rescued 152 of the *Indy*'s crew.

After Ensign Wren's LCVP (boat two) was waterborne and heading in the course directed by CIC, they came upon a very large group of men, perhaps 75 to 100, of an unknown nationality. It was pitch-black with not a glimmer of a star or moon. With a battle lantern in hand he was looking at the black faces, white teeth, and round white eyes of men with black curly hair, floating together in the water. No one spoke, so he called out, "Who are you and what ship are you from?"

Back came words used only in the slang of an American sailor: "Just like a dumb officer, always asking dumb-ass questions!" There no longer was any doubt these were American sailors. Wren directed the coxswain to come about and they began hauling oil-slicked sailors into the boat.

Wren recalls, "Some of the men thought we were Japanese coming to capture them and gave us a hard time getting into the boat. Others wanted to know if we had any water onboard. At this point they did not know what ship they were from."

Although more than fifty years have passed he can still see his crew of young faces laboring with the task before them. "I can still see those oil-blackened faces in the sea and I can hear their cries of agony. When we sing the Navy Hymn I still well up when we come to the last line. 'For those in peril on the sea' will never leave me!"

(With permission from: L. Peter Wren, LCDR, USNR (Ret.), from his book, *Those in Peril on the Sea*, Wren Enterprises, Richmond, VA.)

War's End

USS *Missouri* (BB63) departed Norfolk 11 November 1944 for the Pacific, joining Task Force 58. On 6 August 1945 the first atomic bomb was dropped on the Japanese city of Hiroshima. Three days later, 9 August 1945, a second atomic bomb was dropped on the city of Nagasaki, effectively ending World War II. On 29 August 1945, while moored in Tokyo Bay, General Douglas MacArthur, along with representatives of the Allied Armed Forces, conducted a formal surrender of the Japanese government.

General MacArthur presided over the ceremonies and ended the proceedings with this famous speech:

We are gathered here, representatives of the major warring powers, to conclude a solemn agreement whereby peace may be restored. The issues, involving divergent ideals and ideologies, have been determined on the battlefields of the world and hence are not for discussion or debate. Nor is it for us here to meet, representing as we do a majority of the people of the earth, in a spirit of distrust, malice or hatred. But rather it is for us, both victors and vanquished, to rise to that higher dignity which alone befits the sacred purposes we are about to serve, committing all our people unreservedly to faithful compliance with the understanding they are formally to assume.

It is my earnest hope, and indeed the hope of all mankind, that from this solemn occasion a better world shall emerge out of the blood and carnage of the past—a world dedicated to the dignity of man and the fulfillment of his most cherished wish for freedom, tolerance and justice.

APPENDIX ONE

Military Museums in Virginia

A.A. Tank Museum
American Armored Foundation Tank and Ordnance War Memorial Museum. A nonprofit organization that educates the public as it collects, restores, preserves and displays an extraordinary display of tanks.
3401 U.S. Highway 298, Danville, VA 24540

Air Power Park
Fifteen acres of outdoor park recognizing Hampton's role in American early space exploration. Several vintage aircraft are available to view.
413 West Mercury Boulevard, Hampton, VA 23669

Alexandria Black History Museum
Focus on African American experience. Good material of life in prewar and wartime life.
902 Wythe St., Alexandria, VA 22314

Arlington Historical Museum
Good local Virginia history. Contains history and photographs of World War II.
1805 South Arlington Ridge Rd., Arlington, VA 22210

Army Quartermaster Museum
Ft. Lee portrays the history of the post from its beginning to the present. Excellent exhibits and displays.
1201 22nd Street, Ft. Lee, VA 23801

Army Women's Museum
An education museum with a comprehensive collection of documents and photos of women in the history of the U.S. Army.
A Avenue, Ft. Lee, VA 23801

Augusta Military Academy
Located in the AMA Alumni house in Fort Defiance, VA. Showcases 120 years of military history with exhibits, artifacts and memorabilia.
1640 Lee Hwy., Fort Defiance, VA 24437

Bedford City/County Museum
Museum showcases Bedford's history from early Native American through 20th century.
201 Main Street, Bedford, VA 24523

Black History Museum and Cultural Center of Virginia
Largest repository of black memorabilia with images of pre–World War II and World War II.
60 Clary Street, Richmond, VA 23219

Cape Henry Lighthouse
Located within Ft. Story military base. It has many images and displays relating to its role in World War II.
583 Atlantic Avenue, Fort Story, VA 23459

Danville Museum of Fine Arts and History
Relates history of Danville from early days to present, World War II exhibits, images and documentations based on textile presence.
975 Main Street, Danville, VA 24541

Deltavile Maritime Museum
Good references and photographic history of World War II.
287 Jackson Creek Road, Deltavile, VA 23043

Dodona Manor
Located in Leesburg, Virginia, the name was George and Katherine Marshall's residence. Excellent history of World War II.
310–312 East Market St., Leesburg, VA 20176

Fort Monroe
Museum traces the long military history of the fort, excellent exhibits and images of coastal artillery in World War II. The Casemate Museum is open to the public.
P.O. Box 51341, Ft. Monroe, VA 23651

Fort Norfolk
Last remaining of 19 harbor-front forts in Norfolk Area. Objects, records, and images of World War II.
The Norfolk Historical Society, P.O. BOX 6367, Norfolk, VA 23502

Hampton History Museum
Hampton played an important role in World War II. References and photos of activities in the Hampton Roads area.
22 Lincoln Street, Hampton, VA 23669

Hampton Roads Naval Museum
Celebrates 235 years of U.S. Navy history in the Hampton Roads area.
One Waterside Drive., Ste 242, Norfolk, VA 23510

Life-Saving Museum
The museum houses an extraordinary collection of 1,800 artifacts and more than 1,000 photographic images of the United States Life-Saving and Coast Guard Services.
24th Street and Boardwalk St., Virginia Beach, VA 23451

Lightship Museum
Fitted out with fascinating artifacts, uniforms, photographs, models and more.
London Blvd and Water St., Portsmouth, VA 23701

Macarthur Memorial Museum
Honors General Douglas MacArthur. Serves as a library and MacArthur archives. Excellent World War II history source, written and photographic.
MacArthur Sq., Norfolk, VA 23510

Marine Raiders Museum
Located at Quantico MCB, it tells the story of the Marine Raider Battalion during World War II, Pacific.
Raider Hall, Marine Corps Base, Quantico, VA 22134

Mariners' Museum
Located in Newport News, one of the largest maritime museums in the world. Great exhibits on World War II, Hampton Roads.
110 Museum Drive, Newport News, VA 23606

Military Aviation Museum
Home to one of the largest private collections of World War I and World War II aircraft.
1341 Princess Anne Road, Virginia Beach, VA 23457

Museum of Chincoteague Island
Exhibits of maritime history of the island including a good collection of World War II.
7125 Maddox Blvd., Chincoteague, VA 23336

Museum of Miltary History, Portsmouth
Exhibits and references to complete U.S. Naval history of Portsmouth. Excellent presentations of World War II.
701 Court Street, Portsmouth, VA 23704

Nasa Visitor Center, Wallops Island
Provides a visual/educational program of the history of rocket research at Wallops Island. Good World War II histories.
Wallops Island, Virginia.

National Air and Space Museum
Steven F. Udvar-Hazy Center
The large air and space exhibit is an extension of the Smithsonian National Air and Space Museum, Washington, D.C.
14390 Air and Space Parkway, Chantilly, VA 20151

Military Museums in Virginia

National Firearms Museum
Largest small arms collection and display, including military exhibits, especially World War II.
11250 Waples Mill Road, Fairfax, VA 22030

National Museum Of The Marine Corps
World class interactive exhibits tells history of the USMC. Great World War II collection.
18900 Jefferson Davis Highway, Triangle, VA 22172

Norfolk History Museum
Showcases maritime and military history, including World War II.
601 East Freemason Street, Norfolk, VA 23501

Old Guard Museum
Artifacts, exhibits and memorabilia of the 3rd U.S. Infantry Regiment.
204 Lee Avenue, Ft. Myers, VA 22211

Portsmouth Naval Shipyard Museum
Offers a unique view of U.S. Navy history at Portsmouth. Excellent World War II photographs and exhibits.
2 High Street, Portsmouth, VA 23701

U.S. Army Quartermaster Museum
Preserves the history and heritage of the U.S. Quartermaster Corps. Excellent World War II exhibits and photo references.
1201 22nd Street, Ft. Lee, VA 23801

U.S. Army Transportation Museum
U.S. Army museum of vehicles and transportation-related equipment. Located on the grounds of Ft. Eustis. Excellent World War II exhibits, especially concerning the "Red Ball Express."
300 Washington Blvd, Beeson Hall, Ft. Eustis, VA 23604

Virginia's Air And Space Center
An excellent variety of air and space craft and exhibits.
600 Settlers Landing Road, Hampton, VA 23669

Virginia Aviation Museum
Thirty-seven historic air craft, interactive exhibits, great World War II collection.
5701 Huntsman Road, Richmond International Airport, VA 23218

Virginia Holocaust Museum
Education through realistic exhibits, displays and collections, portrays actual Holocaust events.
2000 East Cary Street, Richmond, VA 23223

VMI (Virginia Military Institute)
Features over 15,000 military artifacts, including cadet uniforms, along with an outstanding 19th century antique firearms collection.
VMI Museum, 415 Letcher Avenue, Lexington, VA 24450

Virginia War Museum
Outstanding military collections of personal artifacts, weapons, vehicles, uniforms and more. Excellent photo reference collection.
9285 Warwick Blvd., Newport News, VA 23607

Women in Military Service for America Memorial (WIMSA)
The foundation presents a collection related to women's service in the Armed Forces.
Located at the National Arlington Cemetery.

APPENDIX TWO

Virginia's Military Installations, 1938–1945

Alexandria
U.S. Naval Torpedo Station
Resident Officer in Charge of Contract NOy-6943
U.S. Army, Ft. Belvoir
U.S. Army, Ft. Hunt
Beacon Army Air Field
EEBEE Army Air Field

Arlington
Naval Radio Station
Arlington Hall Station
U.S. Army, Ft. Myer
Pentagon

Blacksburg
Virginia Polytechnic Institute
U.S. Air Force Airfield

Blackstone
U.S. Army, Camp Pickett
Camp Pickett POW camp

Bowling Green
Fort A.P. Hill

Bristol
Navy Cost Inspector, National Fireworks Corp.
Shell Loading Plant

Camp Allen
U.S. Naval Advance Base Personnel

Camp Lee
U.S. Army Quartermaster School

Camp Peary
Seabee Training Camp
U.S. Navy recruit training
POW Camp

Cape Charles
Navy Degaussing Range
Fort Custis Coastal Artillery
Fisherman's Island Military Reservation Coastal Artillery

Charlottesville
School of Military Government
University of Virginia, Navy V-12 Program

Chincoteague
NAAS Chincoteague
Chincoteague Training Unit, Fleet Air Wing
USN Aviation Ordnance Test Site

Comfort
Navy Liason Officer

Creeds
NAAS Creeds
Aviation Maintenance facility

Dahlgren
Naval Proving Ground
Aviation Ordnance School
Bombsight School
USN Training Gunners Mates School
Naval Air Facility

Dam Neck
Antiaircraft Training Test Center
Fleet Rifle and Small Arms Range
Bureau of Ordnance Test Unit

Emory
Navy V-12 Unit, Emory and Henry College

Virginia's Military Installations, 1938–1945

Fentress
NAAS Fentress

Fort Belvoir
U.S. Army/Navy Engineer School
U.S. Army Quartermaster Training Schools
POW Camp

Fort Monroe
Submarine and Destroyer Mine Depot
Coast Artillery School
U.S. Army Submarine Mine School
POW Camp

Fort Story
Harbor Entrance Control Station

Franklin
NAAS Franklin

Front Royal
U.S. Army Quartermaster Depot
U.S. Army Dog Training Facility
U.S. Army Remount Service
POW Camp

Hampden-Sydney
U.S. Navy V-12 Unit

Hampton
Naval Training School: electrical, diesel, carpenter's mates, yeomen, storekeeper's and basic engineering.
Naval Ship's Store Ashore
U.S. Naval Air Center
Navy Medical Officer-in-charge, Medical Storehouse

Hampton Roads
Camp Ashby POW
U.S. Army Fort Eustis, POW Camp
Camp Wallace
Port of Embarkation, POW Camp
Camp Patrick Henry
Camp Hill, POW Camp
Fort Wool
Fort Story, POW Camp

Hot Springs
Alien Detention, The Homestead

Langley
USAAF Base Langley
National Advisory Committee of Aeronautics
Plum Tree Target Range

Lexington
VMI, ASTP Training Program
Naval Special Services School

Little Creek
Amphibious Training Base
Armed Guard Training Center
Mine Craft Training Center
CIC Group
Inshore Patrol
Naval Frontier Base
Degaussing Range

Lynchburg
Auxiliary Air Ferry Service Unit Four
Navy Ferry Service Officer

Manteo
USNAAS Manteo
Ship's Store Ashore

Marion
Resident inspector of Naval Materiel
Virginia Corp

Melfa
U.S. Naval Flight Strip Melfa

Monogram
NAAS MONGRAM

Newport News
Officer-in-charge, Ship Construction
Naval Dispensary
Naval Receiving Station
Horace N. Dodge Boat Company
U.S. Naval Inspector of Ordnance
Night Lookout Training School
Port Director

Norfolk
Naval Air Station, Norfolk
Joint Operations Center
Amphibious Training Base
Naval Operating Base

Appendix Two

Naval Net Depot
Naval Landing Force Equipment Depot
Naval Supply Depot
Branch Hydrographic Office
Marine Barracks
Naval Dry Dock Yard
Harbor Entrance Control Post
U.S. Naval Hospital
Naval Inshore Patrol
Port Director
Naval Receiving Station
Naval Training Station
Advanced Base Aviation Training Unit
Aircraft Armament Unit
Standard Landing Craft Unit #3
Ship's Store Ashore
Naval Training Schools
Base Service Unit
Destroyer Escort School
Office, Director of Harbor Tugs
U.S. Coast Guard District Office
Degaussing Range
Naval Fuel Depot
Norfolk Fighter Wing, 1st Fighter Command
District Intelligence Office
Navy V-12 Training School
Navy Barracks
Fleet Air Detachment
Base Material Office
Water Transportation Office
Naval Armed Guard School
Barrage Balloon School
Aviation Supply Depot
Atlantic Fleet Weather Central
Naval Radio Station
Fleet Post Office
Navy Disciplinary Barracks
(Plus many more; 174 Navy units total)
U.S. Army Fort Norfolk (Historic)
U.S. Army 52 Fighter Group

Oceana
NAAS Oceana
Mobile Radar Intercept Training Unit #2

Penniman
Naval Fuel Depot, Cheatham Annex

Petersburg
US Army Camp Lee, POW Camp

Pinto
Allegany Ballistic Laboratory, Naval

Portsmouth
Naval Ammunition Depot
Yard Repair Facility
Enlisted Barracks
Norfolk Navy Yard
Pre-Naval Mine Warfare School
Navy V-12 Training School, Group A
Naval Hospital
Navy Hospital Corpsman School

Pungo
NAAS Pungo

Quantico
Marine Corps Air Station
Marine Barracks
Fleet Marine Force
Naval Hospital
Marine Corps Ordnance Facility
Command and Staff School
Marine Corps School
Post Dispensary

Tappahannock
USAF Tappahanock Air Strip

Washington, D.C.
USAAF Hoover Field

West Point
USAAF Auxiliary Airfield, Richmond

Yorktown
Camp Peary, Seabee Training Facility
POW Camp
Navy Fuel Depot
Navy Mine Depot
Navy Mine Warfare School
Naval Barracks
Naval Training School, Ammunition Handling
Naval Supply Depot
Naval Ammunition Supply Depot

Appendix Three

Historical Resources

American Ex-POWs
c/o Clydie J. Morgan, Adj.
3201 East Pioneer Pkwy. #40
Arlington, TX 76010

American Ex-POWs of War
Peninsula Jimmy Hale Memorial Chapter
M.M. Turner
8041 Tarpon Place
Norfolk, VA 23518

Black History Museum and Cultural Center
  of Virginia
60 Clary Street
Richmond, VA 23219

Civil Air Patrol
Historian
1 Camp Pendleton
Virginia Beach, VA 23450

Department of the Air Force
Gustave Vinas, Historian
HQ 832 D Air Division (TAC)
Luke Air Force Base, AZ 85309

Department of the Navy
1200 Navy Pentagon, Room 48463
Washington, D.C. 20350–1200

8th Air Force Historical Society
James Allen
2638 Lakeview Drive
St. Albans, WV 25177

Fort Belvoir
Gustav J. Person, Historian
609 Abbot Road, Suite 2118
Ft Belvoir, VA 22060

Fort Monroe
David Johnson, Historian/Archivist
P.O. Box 51241
Ft Monroe, VA 23651

Fort Pickett
PIO, Capt. Matthew Nowak
Fort Pickett
Blackstone, VA 23324

449th Bomb Squadron
Jim B. Miller
125 Forest Lake Drive
Simpsonville, SC 29681

Hampton History Museum
Historian/Archivist
22 Linden Street
Hampton, VA 23609

Hampton Roads Naval Museum
Gordon Calhoun, Editor/Historian
1 Waterside Drive
Norfolk, VA 23510

Library of Congress
Customer Services Section
Washington D.C. 20541–5017

The MacArthur Memorial
James Zobel, Archivist
MacArthur Sq.
Norfolk, VA 23510

Marine Corps Historical Center
Frederick J. Graboske. Head
Archives Section
1254 Charles Morris Street, SE
Washington-Navy Yard, D.C. 20374–5040

Appendix Three

National Archives
Amy Schmidt, Archivist
Modern Military Records
8601 Adelphi Road
College Park, MD 20740-6001

National Aviation Hall of fame
P.O. Box 31096
Dayton, OH 45439

National Marine Corps Museum and Heritage Center
percent Jack Oblein, Curator
18900 Jefferson Davis Hwy
Triangle, VA 22172

National Organization of World War Nurses
10500 Rockville Pike
Rockville, MD 20853

National Park Service
Chief Historian
11th and "L" Streets, NW
Washington D.C. 20240

National Personnel Records Center
Military Personnel Records Section
9700 Page Avenue
St. Louis, MO 36132-5100

Naval Historical Center
Bldg. 44
Washington Navy Yard, Washington, D.C. 20374

9th Air Force 370
Allen Owen
629 Lafayette Blvd
Norfolk, VA 23509

Norfolk Historical Society
Historian
P.O. Box 6367
Norfolk, VA 23502

Public Information Officer
US Air Force
Langley AFB
Langley, VA 23665

Ships History Branch
Naval Historical Center
805 Kidder Breese SE, Washington Navy Yard
Washington, D.C. 20374-5060

Smithsonian Institution National Air and Space Museum
Archives Division
c/o Ralph Strong
MRC 322
Washington, D.C. 20560

Texas Women's University
Blagg-Huey Library
P.O. Box 425528
Denton, TX 76204-5528

Tuskegee Airmen
J.C. Curry, Historian
SFBAC, Tai
P.O. Box 8814
Emeryville, CA 94662-0814

U.S. Army Center of Military History
Historical Resource Branch
103 Third Avenue
Fort McNair, Washington, D.C. 20319-5058

U.S. Army Historical Foundation
2425 Wilson Blvd
Arlington, VA 20201

U.S. Army Military History Institute
22 Ashburn Drive
Carlisle Barracks
Carlisle, PA 17013-5008

U.S. Army Quartermaster Museum
Luther Hanson, Historian
ATTN: ATSM-QMG-M
Fort Lee, VA 23801-5120

U.S. Army Transportation Museum
Ms. Barbara Bower, Dir.
300 Washington Blvd.
Beeson Hall
Fort Eustis, VA 23604

Historical Resources

U.S. Department of Transportation
Coast Guard Historical Office
2100 Second Street, SW
Washington, D.C. 20593–000

U.S. Department of Transportation
Maritime Administration
400 Seventh Street, NW
Washington, D.C. 20590

West Point Historical Society
Vicki and James Dopp, Curators
West Point, VA 23181

Women In Military Service for America (WIMSA)
Britta Granrud, Curator
Arlington National Cemetery
Arlington, VA 22211

Chapter Notes

Chapter One

1. David Hinshaw, *The Home Front* (New York: G.P. Putnam and Sons, 1943), 3–10.
2. Mary Kitchner, personal correspondence.
3. Karen Anderson, "Last Hired, First Fired: Black Women Workers During World War II," *Journal of American History* 69 (June 1982): 86–97.
4. Ronald L. Heinemann, *The Depression and the New Deal* (Charlottesville: University of Virginia Press, 1983), 120–123.
5. Wayne S. Cole, *America First: The Battle Against Intervention, 1940–1941* (Madison: University of Wisconsin Press, 1953), 93–96.
6. La Vern J. Rippley and Eberhard Reichman, *The German Americans: An Ethnic Experience* (New York: Twayne Publishers, 1976), 123–125.
7. *Report on the German American Bund*, Part 1 (Washington, D.C.: Federal Bureau of Investigation, March 12, 1939), 6.
8. H.C. Allen, *Britain and the United States* (New York: St. Martin's Press, 1955), 102–105.
9. Census of 1941 (Washington, D.C.: Bureau of the Census, Department of Commerce).
10. Alan P. Dobson, *U.S. Wartime Aid to Britain, 1940–1946* (London: Croom Helm Publishers, 1986), 86–88.

Chapter Two

1. Historian, Naval History and Heritage Command, Washington, D.C.

Chapter Three

1. Historian, U.S. Army Center of Military History, Collins Hall, Fort McNair, Washington, D.C.

Chapter Four

1. Malcolm F. Willoughby, *The U.S. Coast Guard in World War II* (Annapolis, MD: Naval Institute, 1957), 68–70.
2. Alpheus J. Chewning, *The Approaching Storm: U-boats off the Virginia Coast During World War II* (Richmond, VA: Brandylane, 1994), 84–88.
3. Eleanor C. Bishop, *Prints in the Sand: The U.S. Coast Guard Beach Patrol During World War II* (Missoula, MT: Pictorial Histories, 1989), 56–59.
4. Dennis L. Noble, *The Beach Patrol and Corsair Fleet: The U.S. Coast Guard in World War II* (Washington, D.C.: U.S. Coast Guard Historian's Office, 1992), 37–39.
5. Jack Teagardten, letter to the author.
6. Theodore Taylor, *Fire on the Beaches* (New York: Norton, 1989), 81–84.
7. *The Coast Guard in World War II* (Washington, D.C.: Naval Institute Proceedings 88, September 1957), 990–1000.

Chapter Five

1. Harald Busch, *U-boats at War* (New York: Ballantine, 1955), 30–31.
2. Chewning, *The Approaching Storm*.
3. *The Submarine War*, Abstract (Washington, D.C.: Naval History and Heritage Command), 5–9.
4. James R. Powell and Alan B. Flanders, *Wolf at the Door* (Richmond, VA: Brandylane, 2004), 25–27.
5. Busch, 42–44.
6. Abstract #35 (Hampton Roads, VA: U.S. Navy Hampton Roads Museum), 5–8.
7. Noble, *The Beach Patrol and Corsair Fleet*.
8. *Submarines at War*, Abstract (Washington, D.C.: Naval History and Heritage Command), 12–14.
9. Rainer Busch and Hans-Joachim Roll, *German U-boat Commanders of World War II: A Biographical Dictionary* (Annapolis, MD: Naval Institute Press, 1999), 53.
10. Daniel V. Gallery, *We Captured a U-boat* (London: Popular Book Company, 1958), 156.
11. *U-boat 505*, Abstract (Washington, D.C.: Naval History and Heritage Command), 35.

Chapter Six

1. Hinshaw, David. *"The Home Front,"* G.P Putnam Sons, New York, 1943
2. John Whiteclay Chambers II and David Culbert, eds., *World War II: Film and History* (Oxford, UK: Oxford University Press, 1996), 124–129.
3. *Get Out the Scrap* (Washington, D.C.: Conservation Division, War Production Board, 1942), 4–14.
4. George Q. Flynn, *The Draft, 1940–1973* (Lawrence: University Press of Kansas, 1993), 36–38.
5. *Homemakers War Guide* (Washington, D.C.: Library of Congress, 1942), 1–10.
6. *Alcohol and World War II Production* (Richmond, VA: Department of Agriculture and Commerce, 1948), 52–53.
7. Beverly Gordon, letter to the author, 2007.
8. *U.S. War and War Bonds WWII*, Abstract (Parkersburg, WV: Bureau of Public Debt, 1943), 1–5.
9. Newport History Commission WW2, Newport News, Virginia, 1948, D76985, 86–88.
10. John E. Guthrie, letter to the author, 2007.
11. Phyllis Hall, "Crisis at Hampton Roads: The Problem of Wartime Congestion, 1942–1944," *Virginia Magazine of History and Biographies* 101 (1993): 45–46.
12. Anderson, "Last Hired, First Fired," 82–83.
13. Bulletin A47 (Richmond, VA: Virginia Department of Agriculture and Commerce, 1948), 34–36.
14. *History of Chesapeake and Ohio Railroad During World War II* (Clifton Forge, VA: C&O Historical Society, n.d.).
15. Marvin W. Schlegel, *Conscripted City: Norfolk in World War II* (Norfolk, VA: Norfolk War History Commission, 1951), 86–88.
16. Bulletin G37 (Richmond, VA: Virginia Department of Agriculture and Commerce, 1942), 1–35.
17. Stephanie A. Carpenter, *On the Farm Front: The Women's Land Army in World War II* (DeKalb: Northern Illinois University, 2003), 30–34.
18. *Manual of Instruction for Air Raid Wardens* (State of Virginia, Virginia Council of Defense, 1942), 5–10.

Chapter Seven

1. *WAACS* (Washington, D.C.: U.S. Army Center of Military History, Collins Hall, Ft. McNair, n.d.), 1–18.
2. Women in Military Service, Dept. 560, Washington, D.C., 1–4.
3. Mary Salm, Southern Historical Collection, University of North Carolina, Chapel Hill, NC, 1996, 1–14.
4. U.S. Army Center of Military History, Collins Hall, Ft. McNair, Washington, D.C., 5–9.
5. *The Waves*, Abstract (Washington, D.C.: Naval History and Heritage Command), 5–10.
6. Janet Marks, interview by the author, 1998.
7. *The Waves*, 15–18.
8. Colonel Mary V. Strenlow, USMCR (Ret.), *Free a Marine to Fight: Women Marines in World War II* (Washington, D.C.: Series Marine Corps Historical Center, n.d.), 25–33.
9. Annie Delp Synder, letter to the author, 1999.
10. *Women and the U.S. Coast Guard* (Washington, D.C.: Coast Guard Historian, n.d.), 5–8.
11. Historian, Texas Women's University, The Women's Collection, Denton, TX.
12. *The Army Nurse Corps* (Ft. Sam Houston, TX: U.S. Army Medical Department, n.d.), Chapter IV, 127–137.
13. Women in Military Service, Dept 560, Washington, D.C.
14. *The Army Nurse Corps*, 143–149.
15. Courtesy: Dr. Jan Herman, USN Bureau of Medicine and Surgery, Washington, D.C.
16. *The Army Nurse Corps*, 158–160.
17. *The Army Nurse Corps*, 165–169.
18. *History of the Commissioned Corps*, PHS Bulletin (Washington, D.C.: U.S. Dept. of Health and Human Services, retrieved 24 June 2008).
19. Elizabeth McIntosh, *Sisterhood of Spies: Women of the OSS* (Annapolis, MD: Naval Institute Press, 1998), 10–12.
20. Carol Harris, *Women at War, 1939–1945: The Home Front* (Stroud, UK: Sutton, 145–147.

Chapter Eight

1. Diana Simpson, *African-Americans in Military History* (Montgomery, AL: Air University Library, Maxwell Air Force Base, 1999), 3–10.
2. Ron Brewington, *Tuskegee Experience* (Tuskegee, AL: Tuskegee University, n.d.), 1–6.
3. Historian, U.S. Army Transportation Museum, Ft. Eustis, VA.
4. Heath Twitchell, *Northwest Epic: The Building of the Alaska Highway* (New York: St. Martin's Press, 1992), 46–49.
5. *African-Americans in the U.S. Navy in World War II* (Washington, D.C.: Naval History and Heritage Command, n.d.), 15.

6. *African-American Women Serving in Our Nation's Defense* (Washington, D.C.: WIMSA, n.d.).
7. Ibid.

Chapter Nine

1. *History of the Civil Air Patrol* (Montgomery, AL: Headquarters of the Civil Air Patrol, Maxwell Air Force Base, n.d.), 1–8.

Chapter Ten

1. *Political Prisoners of World War II*, Abstract (Washington, D.C.: Naval History and Heritage Command), 1–5.
2. *During the War* (Kent, OH: Kent State University, 1987).
3. John H. Moore, "Hitler's Wehrmacht in Virginia, 1943–46," *Virginia Magazine of History and Biography* 85 (July 1977): 259–273.
4. Stephen L. Rearden, *POWS in America WW2*, Synopsis (Washington, D.C.: Department of Defense, n.d.), 56–59.
5. *Station List of Main and Branch POW Camps* (Washington, D.C.: U.S. Army Center of Military History, Collins Hall, Fort McNair, September 1945), 15 pgs.
6. Judith M. Gansburg, *Stalag: U.S.A.* (New York: Crowell, 1977), 157–161.
7. Forrest B. Wall, "German Prisoner of War Camps in Virginia During World War II" (Ph.D. diss., Carnegie-Mellon University, 1987).
8. Diego Arnone, letter to the author, 2000.

Chapter Eleven

1. Charles J. Neuman, *The 1944 Hurricane* (NOAA Technical Memorandum NWS NKC-44, FL), 1–37.
2. *The Coast Guard at War: Lost Cutters* (Historical Section, U.S. Coast Guard Headquarters, May 1949), 1–4.
3. H.C. Summer, ed. "The North Atlantic Hurricane of September 8–16, 1944," *Monthly Weather Review* 72, No. 9 (September 1944): 187–189.

Bibliography

Abstract #35. Hampton Roads, VA: U.S. Navy Museum of Hampton Roads, 1999.

African-American Women Serving in our Nation's Defense. Washington, D.C.: Women in Military Service for America (WIMSA), n.d.

Alcohol and World War II Production. Richmond, VA: Virginia Department of Agriculture and Commerce Bulletins, 1948.

Allen, H.C. *Britain and the United States*. New York: St. Martin's Press, 1995.

American Merchant Marine at War. http:www.USMM.org.

Anderson, Karen T. "Last Hired, First Fired: Black Women Workers During World War Two." *Journal of American History* 69 (June 1982).

The Army Nurse Corps. Ft. Sam Houston, TX: U.S. Army Medical Department, n.d.

Bishop, Eleanor C. *Prints in the Sand: The U.S. Coast Guard Beach Patrol During World War II*. Missoula, MT: Pictorial Histories, 1989.

Brewington, Ron. *Tuskegee Experience*. Tuskegee, AL: Tuskegee University, n.d.

Bureau of the Census. *Census of 1941*. Washington, D.C.: Department of Commerce.

Burton, Harrison W. *The History of Norfolk, Virginia*. UK: Ulan Press, 2010.

Busch, Harald. *U-boats at War*. New York: Ballantine, 1955.

Busch, Rainer, and Hans-Joachim Roll. *German U-boat Commanders of World War 2: A Biographical Dictionary*. Annapolis, MD: Naval Institute Press, 1999.

Carpenter, Stephanie A. *On the Farm Front: The Women's Land Army in World War II*. DeKalb: Northern Illinois University, 2003.

Census of 1941. Washington, D.C.: Bureau of the Census, Department of Commerce.

Chambers, John Whiteclay, II, and David Culbert, eds. *World War II: Film and History*. Oxford, UK: Oxford University Press, 1996.

Chewning, Alpheus J. *The Approaching Storm: U-Boats off the Virginia Coast During World War II*. Richmond, VA: Brandylane, 1994.

The Coast Guard at War: Lost Cutters. Historical Section, U.S. Coast Guard Headquarters, May 1949.

The Coast Guard in World War II. Washington, D.C.: Naval Institute Proceedings 88, September 1957.

Cole, Wayne S. *America First: The Battle Against Intervention, 1940-1941*. Madison: University of Wisconsin Press, 1953.

Directory of Army and Navy Airfields. Washington, D.C.: Department of Commerce, December 1944.

Dobson, Alan P. *U.S. Wartime Aid to Britain, 1940-1946*. London: Croom Helm, 1986.

Dornbusch, Charles E. *Histories of American Army Units: World War II and Korean Conflict, With Some Earlier Histories*. Washington, D.C.: Department of the Army Library and Services Club Branch, 1956.

During the War. Kent, OH: Kent State University, 1987.

Flynn, George Q. *The Draft, 1940-1973*. Lawrence: University of Kansas Press, 1993.

Foss, William O. *The United States Navy in Hampton Roads*. Norfolk, VA: Dinning, 1984.

Gallery, Daniel V. *We Captured a U-boat*. London: Popular Book Co., 1958.

Gansburg, Judith M. "*Stalag: U.S.A.*" New York: Crowell, 1977.

Get Out the Scrap. Washington, D.C.: Conservation Division, War Production Board, 1942.

Hagan, Jane Gray. *The Story of Danville*. New York: Stratford House, 1950.

Hall, Phyllis. "Crisis at Hampton Roads: The Problem of Wartime Congestion, 1942-1944." *Virginia Magazine of History and Biographies* 101 (1993).

Harris, Carol. *Women at War, 1939-1945: The Home Front*. Stroud, UK: Sutton, 2003.

Heinemann, Ronald L. *Depression and New Deal in Virginia*. Charlottesville: University of Virginia Press, 1983.

Hinshaw, David. *The Home Front*. New York: G.P. Putnam's Sons, 1943.

Historian, Naval History and Heritage Command, Washington, D.C.

Bibliography

Historian, Texas Women's University, The Women's Collection, Denton, TX.

Historian, U.S. Army Center of Military History, Collins Hall, Fort McNair, Washington, D.C.

History Commission WW2: Newport News during the Second World War. Newport News, VA, 1948.

History of Chesapeake and Ohio Railroad During World War II. Clifton Forge, VA: C&O Historical Society, C&O Historical Society, n.d.

History of the Civil Air Patrol. Montgomery, AL: Headquarters of the Civil Air Patrol, Maxwell Air Force Base, n.d.

History of the Commissioned Corps. PHS Bulletin. Washington, D.C.: U.S. Dept. of Health and Human Services, retrieved 24 June 2008.

Homan, Lynn M. *Black Knights: The Story of the Tuskegee Airmen.* Gretna, LA: Pelican, 2001.

Homemakers War Guide. Washington, D.C.: Library of Congress, 1942.

Hoyt, Edwin P. *U-boats: A Pictorial History.* New York: McGraw-Hill, 1987.

Linder, Bruce. *Tidewater's Navy: An Illustrated History.* Annapolis, MD: Naval Institute Press, 2005.

Lutz, Francis Earl. *Richmond in World II.* Richmond, VA: Dietz, 1951.

McIntosh, Elizabeth. *Sisterhood of Spies: Women of the OSS.* Annapolis, MD: Naval Institute Press, 1998.

Manual for Air Raid Wardens. State of Virginia, Virginia Council of Defense, 1942.

Moore, John H. "Hitler's Wehrmacht in Virginia, 1943–46." *Virginia Magazine of History and Biography* 85 (July 1977).

Morison, Samuel Eliot, and Dudley Wright Knox. *The Battle of the Atlantic: September 1939–May 1943.* Urbana: University of Illinois Press, 2001.

National Oceanic and Atmospheric Administration. Technical Memorandum NWSTPC-1-1966.

The Naval Bases. Abstract. Washington, D.C.: Naval History and Heritage Command.

Neuman, Charles J. *The 1944 Hurricane.* NOAA Technical Memorandum NWS, NKC 44, FL.

Noble, Dennis L. *The Beach Patrol and Corsair Fleet: The U.S. Coast Guard in World War II.* Washington, D.C.: U.S. Coast Guard Historian's Office, 1992.

Political Prisoners of War. Abstract. Washington, D.C.: Naval History and Heritage Command.

Powell, James R., and Alan B. Flanders. *Wolf at the Door.* Richmond, VA: Brandylane, 2004.

Rearden, Stephen L. *POWs in America WW2.* Synopsis. Washington, D.C., Department of Defense, n.d.

Reilly, John C. *United States Navy Destroyers of World War II.* Poole, UK: Blandford Press, 1983.

Report on the German American Bund, Part 1. Washington, D.C.: Federal Bureau of Investigation, March 12, 1939.

Rippley, LaVern J., and Eberhard Reichman. *The German-Americans: An Ethnic Experience.* New York: Twayne, 1976.

Schlegel, Marvin W. *Conscripted City: Norfolk in World War II.* Norfolk, VA: Norfolk War History Commission, 1951.

Simpson, Diana. *African-Americans in Military History.* Montgomery, AL: Air University Library, Maxwell Air Force Base, 1999.

Station List of Main and Branch POW Camps. Washington, D.C.: U.S. Army Center of Military History, Collins Hall, Fort McNair, September 1945.

Strenlow, Colonel Mary V., USMCR (Ret.). *Free a Marine to Fight: Women Marines in World War II.* Washington, D.C.: Series Marine Corps Historical Center, n.d.

The Submarine War. Abstract. Washington, D.C.: Naval History and Heritage Command.

Submarines at War. Abstract. Washington, D.C.: Naval History and Heritage Command.

Summer, H.C., ed. "The North Atlantic Hurricane of September 8–16, 1944." *Monthly Weather Review* 72, No. 9 (September 1944).

Taylor, Theodore. *Fire on the Beaches.* New York: W.W. Norton, 1989.

Terkel, Studs. *Hard Times.* New York: The New Press, 2005.

Twitchell, Heath. *Northwest Epic: The Building of the Alaska Highway.* New York: St. Martin's Press, 1992.

U-boat 505. Abstract. Washington, D.C.: Naval History and Heritage Command.

U.S. War and War Bonds WWII. Abstract. Parkersburg, WV: Bureau of Public Debt, 1943.

Wall, Forrest B. "German Prisoner of War Camps in Virginia During World War II." Ph.D. diss., Carnegie-Mellon University, 1987.

Willoughby, Malcolm F. *The U.S. Coast Guard in World War II.* Annapolis, MD: Naval Institute, 1957.

Women and the U.S. Coast Guard. Washington, D.C.: Coast Guard Historian, n.d.

Newspaper Sources

Daily Press (Norfolk, VA), July 24, 2011.

Norfolk Virginian Pilot, January 20, 29, and 31, 1942; February 18 and 20, 1942; March 22, and 23, 1942; May 8, 1995.

Personal Correspondence and Interviews

Arnone, Diego. Boston, MA (1995).
Guthrie John. Seattle, WA (1999).
Kent, Beverly Gordon. Goochland County, VA. (2002)
Kitchner, Mary. Holyoke, MA (1999).
Marks Janet. Venice, FL (1995).
Salm Mary M. Chapel Hill, NC (1996).
Synder, Annie Delp. Gainesville, VA (1995).
Teagardten, Jack. Berwick, ME (1998).

Index

Accomack County 16, 58
AFFTC *see* Army Air Forces Training Command
African American nurses 122, 128–129, 141
African American Service Women 141; *see also* Armed Forces, African Americans in
Agriculture 86, 94–95, 101–102, 107–109
Air Corps Ferrying Command 124
air facility as repair site 33
Air Raid Wardens 111
Air Transport Command 65, 124
aircraft storage 20
Aircraft Warning Service 81, 11
Alexandria 12, 40
Alien Internment Camps 149
Alien POWs 56, 149
Allan Jackson 78
Always Ready 123
America First Committee 5
American Kennel Association 50–51
amphibious training base 11, 22, 37
Andrews, Admiral
Angels in White 126–127
anti-aircraft range 35
approach of war 1
Arlington 13, 42
Armed Forces, African Americans in 133–143
Armed Forces Training Command (AAFTC)
Army bases 38–66
Army Special Training Programs (ASTP) 22, 36; training at VMI 58
Arnone, Diego 160
artillery school 21, 52
artillery training site 47, 52
ASTP *see* Army Special Training Program (ASTP)
Auxiliary Flotilla #33 67, 69, 145

base hospital 45
The Basic School 31, 119
Battery Gates 52, 56
Battery Hindman 52, 56
Battery Lee 52, 56

Battery #227 and #24 49, 52, 56
beach patrol 50, 51, 67, 70; K-9s 51
Beacon Field 42
Bedford 43
HMT *Bedfordshire* 75, 83
Beery, Ruth 49
black market 93
Blackford, Dr. Staige D. 49
Blacksburg Army Airfield 44
Blackstone Army Airfield 44
USCG *Bledsoe* (WSC-128) 164
blimp K-74 75–76, 80
Bolton Act 126
Das Boot 84–85
bottom mines 82
Bowling Green 45
Bracero program 109
Bristol 14
Bristol Aircraft Corporation 14
British in 1813 56
Broad Creek housing 105–107
Bryant, William Jennings 5, 6
Buffalo Soldiers 101, 133
Byrd Field 61

C&O rail line 104
Cabaniss, Sadie Heath 126
Cadet Nursing Corps 126, 128
Callahan, Josielee V. 168
Camp Ashby (en} 46–47, 158; POW Camp 142, 155–156, 163, 185
Camp Hill 54–55; POWs 154–157, 185
Camp Lee 59; schools 60
Camp Lejeune 121
Camp Patrick Henry 8, 53; and Port of Embarkation 54
Camp Peary 37
Camp Pendleton 47
Camp Pickett, construction of 44; POW Camp 45
Camp Shanks 142
Camp Stewart site 18
Camp Wallace 153; and the world wars 53
Canning 95
CAP *see* Civil Air Patrol
Cape Charles 47, 58
Cape Charles City 15, 47, 58
Cape Charles Lighthouse 48, 58

Cape Cod, Massachusetts 75
Cargo ships, shortage of
Casablanca, Africa 50
Catochin Mountains 41, 129
Central Coca-Cola Bottling 102
Champlin, Jane Dolores 125
Charlottesville 15, 49
Cheatem Annex 36–37
Chesapeake Bay 4
Child, Julia 130
Chincoteague 16, 48, 58
CIA 37
Civil Air Patrol (CAP) 79, 144; insignia 145; pilot's daily duties 147
Civil Defense 81
Civil War harbor forts 21, 40, 52–54
civilian beach patrols 81
Civilian Pilot Training (CPT) 7
Coast Guard 67–74, 145
Coast Guard coxswains 74
Coastal Patrol No. 4 72, 145
Coastal patrol stations 72, 145
College of William and Mary 36
Combat demolition unit 22
Combat, modifying aircraft for 20
USS *Comfort* 127
Commercial fishing 4, 108
Committee to Defend America 5
Compostella Road housing 106
USS *Constellation* 27
Convoy NG-365 84
Corsair Fleet 67–68
Craney Island 27
Crawford, Melvin H. "Jimmy" 169
Creeds 16
Curry, Major General John 144

D-Day 43
Dahlgren 17
Dam Neck 18
Dan River Textile Mills 102
Darden, Governor Colgate 77
Davis, Colonel Benjamin O. 137
Davis, Dorothy Steinbis 171
Defense Supply Center 162
degaussing range 15, 22
degaussing station 22

197

Index

Delmarva Peninsula 48, 58
Department of Agriculture 94
Department of Defense 43
Depression family 3
Detroit race riots (1943) 133
Dew, Lt. CDR Irwin I. 17
Diplomats, number interned 56, 149, 150
dive bomber pilots 16
Dodge Boat site 18, 21
Donald Duck Navy 70
Dover 18
Downey, James Jr. 170
The Draft 90
Draft Law amended 1942 135
Drost, William 172
Eastern Shore 48, 58, 108
8th Evacuation Hospital 49

Elsie Project 17, 139
Emergency Farm Labor Action 109
emergency landing facilities 147
enemy aliens 129, 150–151
Engineer Officer Candidates School 40, 139
EOCS *see* Engineer Officer Candidates School
Executive Order 9066 151
Executive Order 9921 143

Fast-attack carriers 30
Federal Public Housing Authority Act 1942 29
Fentress 19–20
Fifth Naval District 21
fighter training school 19
Fisherman's Island 48, 49, 58, 102
Fisherville 50
Fleet Air Wing 5 16
USS *Flicker* 148
Flying Minutemen 79, 144
food pail 3
Fort A.P.Hill 45
Fort Belvoir 40, 139
Fort Custis 48, 58, 108
Fort Devens 114
Fort Eustis 52; Naval Hospital 22; POWs at 159; training facility 52; and World War I 52
Fort Hollywood 88
Fort Hunt 152
Fort Monroe 52, 55–56
Fort Myer 42, 45
Fort Oglethorpe 115
Fort Story 55–56
Fort Wool 55–56
Fortier, Edna Collier 113
48th Amy Air Force Base 61
Franklin 20
"Free a Man to Fight" 114
Front Royal 50, 51, 71–72

gasoline 77, 91
Geneva Accords 151

German American Bund 6, 7
German American POWs 41, 110, 149–161
German laborers 41, 157
German POWs 41; at Camp Patrick Henry 54
German U-boats 8, 75–85
Germany and Italy declare war 10
Gordon, Beverly 94
Gorsline, Agent James M. 156
Gosport Shipyard 29–30
Gravely, Samuel L., Jr. 140
Gray Ladies 131
Great Atlantic Hurricane 162
Great Depression 1, 86
Green, James A. 171
Groves, Colonel Leslie 43
USS *Guadalcanal* (CVE-60) 84
gunner's mate school 17
Guthrie, John 99

Hampton Institute 21, 52–54
Hampton naval storehouse 21
Hampton Roads 21; accident 26; during World War I 52; forts 52
Hardgen, Kapitanleutnant Reinhard 76
Hemp, supply of 107–109
Hercules Gunpowder Company 14, 61
Higgins Landing Boat 32
Hobby, Oveta Culp 112
Home Front 86
The Homestead 56, 129
Hooligan Navy 69
Hoover Field 65
Horne, Lena 131, 139
Hot Springs 56, 129, 149
Hurricane of 1943 162
USS *Hyades* (AF-28) 163

Icarus 80
Irish Americans 5

USCG *Jackson* (WSC-142) 164

K-9 dogs 70, 71–72
Kichner. Mary 2
HMT *Kingston Ceylonite* 83
Kitopeke State Park 48, 49, 58
Kuhn, Fritz Julius 6–7

labor unions 98
Lake Drummond Bombing Range 18
Landing Craft Vehicle Personnel Ramp (LCVPR) 18
Landis, Homer Warren 174
Langley 57; training schools 58
USS *Langley* 29
large unit training 46
LCPR *see* Landing Craft Vehicle Personnel Ramp
Lee Hall 22, 52
Lend-lease 9

Lewis, John L. 98
Lexington 22, 58
Liberty Ship 30
Lindbergh, Charles 5
Little Creek 22–23
Long Range Navigation (LORAN) 124
LORAN *see* Long Range Navigation
Lynchburg 22

MacArthur, General 178
MAGTF Marine Air-Ground Task Force
Marine Air-Ground Task Force (MAGTF) 33
Marine Corps 119–122
Marine Corps Schools 31
Marks, Janet 118
Marshall, George C. 112
McAfee, Mildred 117
McGuire General Hospital 62
Medical Replacement Training Center (MRTC) 59
medical training battalions 45
Melfa 48, 58
Menominee 79
Merchant Marine Armed Guard 22, 35
Merchant Marines 22, 35, 141
Merrimack Park 106
midget submarine 98
military service companies 133–145
Miller, Doris "Dorie" 140
USS *Missouri* (BB63) 178
MK-14 torpedo 13
Molly Marine 122
Mount Holyoke OCS 121–122
MRTC *see* Medical Replacement Training Center
Mulzar, Hugh 101, 123, 141

NAAS *see* Navy Auxiliary Air Station
NALF *see* Navy Auxiliary Landing Field
Nansemond Ordnance Depot 63, 116
NAS Norfolk 21, 24, 52
NAS Woodrum 34
NASA 21, 58
National Defense Act of 1932 38
National Fireworks Corporation 14, 61, 103
Naval Auxiliary Air Station (NAAS) 12, 16, 20, 23
Naval Intelligence Unit 151
Naval Observatory 14
Naval Operating Base 16, 21, 24, 52
Naval Ordnance Test Station 16
Naval Radio Station 13–14
Naval Repair Facility 30
Naval Weapons Station 36–37

Index

Navy Auxiliary Landing Field (NALF) 18
Navy bases 11–37
Navy V-12 unit 15, 34, 52
Neutrality Act of 1794 6
Neutrality Acts 4
New Deal 4
Newport News Port of Embarkation 8, 52–54
Newport News Shipbuilding 21–24, 52–54
95th Engineer Regiment 138–139
99th Pursuit Squadron 136
1943 federal census 8
Norden Bombsight 17, 40, 138
Norfolk 23; NOB support facilities 26
Norfolk Redevelopment and Housing Authority (NRHA) 106–107
Norris, Kathleen North Africa 5
NRHA see Norfolk Redevelopment and Housing Authority
Nurses 126; African American nurses 122
Nye, Senator Gerald P. 15

Ocean City, Maryland 78
Ocracoke Island 83
Office of Civilian Defense (OCD) 11
Office of Naval Intelligence 151
Office of Strategic Services (OSS) 41, 129; training camp 65
Office of War Information 94
Officer Candidates School (OCS) 31, 118, 119, 121–122, 159
OLF see Out Lying Field
192nd Fighter Wing 61
Operation Drumbeat 75–78
Operation Paperclip 41
OSS see Office of Strategic Services
Out Lying Field (OLF) 16, 29; at Buford 34

pack mules 51, 71–72
Panaminas Mines 103
Parksley 58, 145
patrol units 16, 67–71
Patterson, Harvey D. 175
Patton, General George 137
Peace organizations 6
Pearl Harbor 9
The Pentagon 42
Petersburg 59
USS *Pillsbury* (DE-133) 85
Plum Tree Target Range 60
"P.O. Box 1142" 41, 138
Port of Embarkation (POE) 8, 52–54
Portsmouth 29–30
Portsmouth Naval Shipyard 30
POW camps 37, 46, 52, 53, 6, 60, 62, 155; Prisoner of War Side Camps #1326, 157
POW staging area 37, 154
Pribam, Kathryn Van Wagner 128
Prisoners of War POWs) 146; at Defense Supply Center 62
private yachts as patrol craft 68, 75–76
propaganda 87–88
Puller, Lt. General Lewis B. 66

Quantico 31, 119
Quartermaster Depot 43
Quartermaster School (MRTC) 52–53, 59
Quinton, Harry 167

Racism 133, 139
Radford Ammunition Plant 60–61
Railroads 104
Randolph, Philip A. 135
Rathke, Kapitan Helmut 80
ration stamps 91
rationing 91
reconnaissance aircraft 162
Red Ball Express 101, 137
Red Cross 2
Remount Service 50, 70–71
Richmond 33, 61–62
Rimitelli Airfield 133, 136–137
Roanoke 34, 62
USS *Roe* (DD-418) 78
Rogers, Edith Nourse 112
USS *Roper* (DD-147) 79
Rutherford, Irene Shortridge 125

saboteurs 80
Saint Julian's reek 34
Salm, Mary M. 115
Salvation Army 3
Scarecrow Patrol 144
scrap drives 88
screening of POWs 129
Seabees 22, 37, 88, 140
Segregation 8; of the U.S. Navy and Coast Guard 139; segregated units 133
HMT *Senateur Duhamel* 83
700 series camp plan 38
79th Infantry Division 44
Shelton 35, 77, 141
Sheridan, Vivian 127
shipboard firefighters, School for 19
Short, Robert B. 178
6888th Central Postal Battalion 114
Skelton, Red 130
Sleeper, Delphin 142
Smith College 118, 121–122
Smithfield Foods 102
Snyder, Annie Delp 122
Solomon's Island 11, 22, 77
soup kitchens 2–3
SPARS 74, 123–124
Specialized Air Training Program 44
Sprowle, Andrew 29
staging area 8, 53
Stokes, Jeremiha 137
storm damage 165
Story, General John 56; *see also* Fort Story
Stratton, Captain Dorothy C. 123
Streeter, Ruth Cheney 120
submarine action 75–85
submarine war 75–85
Suffolk 63, 116
Swift, Earl 159

Tappahanock 52, 64
Tappahanock Flight Strip 64
Task Force A 52
Task Force B 52
Teagarden, Jack 71
Ten Percenters 141
Terkel, Studs 1
test station 17
Third Baptist Church 3
31st Infantry Division 39
357th Engineering Service Regiment 45
396th Bomb Squadron 84
tobacco 2, 4, 7, 103, 107, 110
Torpedo Factory Art Center 12–13
torpedo station 12–13
Touch and Go landings 19
Transportation schools 52–55
Turner, William H 125
Tuskegee Airmen 136
25th Station Hospital 128
224th Coastal Artillery Regiment 47

U-66 78
U-85 79
U-103 78–79
U-202 81
U-230 82
U-352 80
U-505 84
U-558 83
U-584 81
U-701 82
U-754 79
U-boat crews, rescued 151
United Kingdom and POWs 153
United Service Organizations USO 130
United States Rubber 102
Universal Molded Products Corporation 14
University of Richmond 33
University of Virginia 15
U.S. Army K-9 training 50
U.S. Coast Guard destroyer escorts 74; founded in 1790 67;

199

Index

officers and Navy school 76; transfer to Navy during World War II 67; during World War I 67
U.S. Marine Corps segregation *see* Marine Corps Segregation
U.S. Naval Air Station, Norfolk 27
U.S. Public Health Nursing 129
USO *see* United Service Organizations

V-12 school 34
Victory Gardens 91, 94, 101–102
Vint Hills 64
Virginia Military Institute (VMI) 22, 58
Virginian State Guard 87
Vistula River 5
VMI *see* Virginia Military Institute
volunteers 130
VRF-1 23

W.L. Steed 78
WAAC *see* Women's Army Auxiliary Corps
WAAF *see* Women's Auxiliary Air Force
WAC *see* Women's Army Corps
WAFS *see* Women's Auxiliary Ferrying Squadron

Der Walbote 158
Walker Airfield 55
Wall, Mary Edward 166
War Bonds 95–98
War of 1812 27
Warrington 64
USS *Warrington* (DD-383) 163
wartime housing 29–31, 105–106
wartime production, African American contribution to 101
Washington, George 6
Washington International Airport 65
WASPs *see* Women's Air Force Service Pilots
Waverly 35
WAVES *see* omen Accepted for Volunteer Emergency Service
weapons training 18
Weaver Fertilizer Company 158
Welding Shipyard 30
West Point 65–66
WFTD *see* Women's Flying Training Detachment
White, William 5
White Lightning 94
Williamsburg 36
Wilson, Gill Robb 144
Wise Point 48
Women Accepted for Volunteer Emergency Service (WAVES) 34, 117–119

Women Air Force Service Pilots (WASPS) 23, 64, 124–125
Women and production lines 61
Women at War 112–133
Women's Army Auxiliary Corps (WAAC) 112; at Fort Belvoir 40; officer training school 115
Women's Army Corps (WAC) 45, 50, 60
Women's Auxiliary Air Force (WAAF) 18
Women's Auxiliary Ferrying Squadron (WAFS) 124–125
Women's Flying Training Detachment (WFTD) 125
Women's Land Army 109
Women's Reserve 119
Woodrow Wilson Army General Hospital 50
World War II 5, 54, 60, 61
Wren, LCDR (ret.) Peter L. 179

Yacht members 68
Yellow bees 79, 144, 147
YMCA 130
Yorktown 36–37
Youth groups 89–90, 95–98

Zapp, Captain Richard 78
Zeiger Air Field 64

www.ingramcontent.com/pod-product-compliance
Ingram Content Group UK Ltd.
Pitfield, Milton Keynes, MK11 3LW, UK
UKHW050526150426
5217IPUK00026B/1815